C000147214

OBJECT-ORIENTED DATABASES

Setrag Khoshafian

John Wiley & Sons, Inc.

New York • Chichester • Brisbane • Toronto • Singapore

I would like to dedicate this book to my parents,
Nishan and Armenouhy Khoshafian.

In recognition of the importance of preserving what has been written, it is a policy of John Wiley & Sons, Inc. to have books of enduring value published in the United States printed on acid-free paper, and we exert our best efforts to that end.

Designations used by companies to distinguish their products are often claimed as trademarks. In all instances where John Wiley & Sons, Inc. is aware of a claim, the product names appear in Initial Capital or ALL CAPITAL Letters. Readers, however, should contact the appropriate companies for more complete information regarding trademarks and registration.

This publication is designed to provide accurate and authoritative information in regard to the subject matter covered. It is sold with the understanding that the publisher is not engaged in rendering legal, accounting, or other professional service. If legal advice or other expert assistance is required, the services of a competent professional person should be sought. FROM A DECLARATION OF PRINCIPLES JOINTLY ADOPTED BY A COMMITTEE OF THE AMERICAN BAR ASSOCIATION AND A COMMITTEE OF PUBLISHERS.

Copyright © 1993 by John Wiley & Sons, Inc.

All rights reserved. Published simultaneously in Canada.

Reproduction or translation of any part of this work beyond that permitted by Section 107 or 108 of the 1976 United States Copyright Act without the permission of the copyright owner is unlawful. Requests for permission or further information should be addressed to the Permissions Department, John Wiley & Sons, Inc.

ISBN 0471-57056-7 (cloth)
ISBN 0471-57058-3 (paper)

Printed in the United States of America
10 9 8 7 6 5 4 3 2 1

ABOUT THE AUTHOR

Dr. Setrag Khoshafian is the Vice President of Development and Chief Scientist at Portfolio Technologies, Inc., where he designs and supervises delivery of object-oriented intelligent information management products on client/server architectures. The Office.IQ product line from Portfolio Technologies is hailed as an innovative and powerful object-oriented database application in an internetworked Windows environment. Previously Dr. Khoshafian was the architect and manager of the intelligent database engine project at the Walnut Creek Advanced Development Center of Ashton-Tate. He was the principal designer of Intelligent SQL and has made significant contributions in the areas of object-oriented and intelligent database technologies. Prior to that he was the manager and architect of one of the earliest object-oriented database implementations at MCC. As an internationally recognized expert, Dr. Khoshafian has presented various seminars on client/server and object-oriented technologies. He is the author of more than 50 technical publications. He is the lead author of *Intelligent Offices* (Wiley), *A Guide to Developing Client/Server SQL Applications* (Morgan Kaufmann), and *Object Orientation* (also Wiley). He is also a coauthor of *Intelligent Databases* (Wiley). He received his M.Sc. and Ph.D. in Computer Science from the University of Wisconsin, Madison. He also holds an M.Sc. in mathematics from the American University of Beirut. His current research interests span imaging systems, intelligent offices, object-oriented systems, and intelligent user interfaces.

ACKNOWLEDGMENTS

I would like to express my appreciation to the many people and organizations that made this book possible. First and foremost I would like to thank my wife, Silva, and children, Nishan, Jonathan, Shahan, and Nareg, for their patience and support. I would also like to express my gratitude to the staff at Portfolio Technologies—special thanks to Leo Yaroslavsky, Kiane Shabazian, Jim Hess, Rae-Ann Spears, and Dr. Ted Marr. I would like to thank editors Harriet Serenkin, Terri Hudson, Diane Cerra, and her assistant Kara Raezer, and copy editor Phillip Murray, Lorraine Metcalf, Peter Feely, and others at Publication Services. I would like to thank Dr. Arvola Chan and Dr. Mohammad Ketabchi for their input, useful suggestions, and support. I would also like to thank the graphic artists Jay Nitschke and Kalen Meyer. Finally, I would like to express my gratitude to the many object-oriented database companies who gave me support and provided various materials that made this book possible.

PREFACE

The past few years have witnessed the proliferation of object-oriented technologies into every field of computer science: programming languages, simulation, graphical user interfaces, and, of course, databases. There are many pragmatic reasons for the inevitable success of this emerging technology. The application environments of the 1990s are fast-paced and complex. There is great diversity in the way information is accessed, manipulated, and presented. Object orientation is proving to be an enabling technology that makes it easy to construct and maintain complex systems from individual components. Despite any initial skepticism, object orientation has been incorporated into the mainstream of software development and is starting to provide solutions to the tremendous software engineering problems of the 1990s.

An equally important trend in the computer industry is the emergence of the *downsized* client/server architecture as *the* architecture of choice in internetworked environments. Large mainframe systems are being replaced by internetworked LANs at a much lower cost—yielding much greater efficiency. It is becoming increasingly evident that the backbone of these client/server systems is *the database server,* which serves as the repository of all concurrently shared information on the network.

Object-oriented databases *combine* and *integrate* these two trends to satisfy the computation needs of not only "advanced" database applications but general corporate computing as well. The purpose of this book is to elucidate both the object-oriented and the database capabilities of this emerging object-oriented database technology.

The database management system (DBMS) technology of the 1980s— *relational DBMSs*—fell short of providing the necessary abstraction to act as the repository for integrated, advanced, and emerging applications. Without extensions, relational technology lacks the fundamental components needed to support integrated applications that will increasingly use such multimedia data types as long text fields, raster and vector screen images, voice data, and video. Also, without object-oriented extensions relational databases cannot provide direct, natural representation of graph-structured object spaces. Advanced applications and integrated environments that will need more powerful databases include computer-aided design (CAD), computer-aided manufacturing (CAM), computer-aided software engineering (CASE), and office automation.

In the commercial world object-oriented databases started to emerge as viable products as far back as the mid-1980s. Now there are more than 10 emerging companies that characterize their products as object-oriented database systems. Equally interesting, a number of relational database vendors have started incorporating various object-oriented database features into their next-generation products. As discussed in this book, both trends are viable.

■ ADVANTAGES OF OBJECT-ORIENTED DATABASES

Object-oriented databases remove the so-called *semantic gap* between an application domain and its representation in persistent storage. Since the real world is modeled as closely as possible, the links and relationships among entities in it are *represented and manipulated* directly. Object-oriented databases achieve their modeling capability through the object-oriented concepts of abstract data typing, inheritance, and object identity.

Object-oriented databases also alleviate the *impedance mismatch* between programming languages and database management systems. In complex applications the data is retrieved from a database management system using a database query language such as SQL and is then manipulated by routines written in a conventional programming language such as C or PL/I. Conventional languages are procedural. Database query languages are higher-level and more declarative. Therefore, applications involving both languages mix (*mismatch*) these different programming paradigms. Furthermore, the data types in the different languages (SQL and C, for instance) are not the same and have to be mapped onto one another. The reason for accessing the data through a database language and then processing it through a conventional language is that the database language is limited to querying. Typically, database languages provide little support for complex computations. The computations are done in the programming language.

Object-oriented databases are more *complete* in the sense that they typically provide the necessary expressive power to perform the computations of an application through the data manipulation language of the object-oriented database management system.

■ OBJECT-ORIENTED DATABASE APPLICATIONS

The main target of object-oriented databases has been engineering—computer-aided design (CAD), computer-aided manufacturing (CAM), computer-aided software engineering (CASE), and intelligent offices (office automation). These applications have characteristics that are different than the traditional business or accounting applications. In the CAD/CAM/CASE and intelligent office applications the amount of information stored in the database is much larger, and the connections among this information are more complex. The size and complexity of the data make it nearly impossible to cluster related data. Thus, a considerable amount of navigation is necessary to access and update objects in the database. Accessing the subparts of an automobile transmission, for example, can take a very long time. Associative and ad hoc queries are also common, with queries such as "retrieve all subparts heavier than 2 pounds." The structures of databases in these applications are heterogeneous and complex; there are many object types corresponding to each individual component and composite object. Imagine all the different parts of a Boeing 747! A database for the airplane would need a different object type for each different type of part. Furthermore, in typical design applications each design object will undergo refinements and have multiple versions or alternatives. Many of the features of object-oriented databases are attempts to satisfy these requirements.

■ THIS BOOK

This book is a comprehensive overview of the *concepts, capabilities,* and *alternatives* for these next-generation database management systems and applications. It shows how the *object-oriented* concepts of abstract data typing, inheritance, and object identity can be integrated with *database capabilities* (persistence, transactions, integrity, etc.) to produce these powerful object-oriented database management systems.

This book is intended for a wide variety of audiences. At small and large corporations MIS managers and database administrators can use the book to understand the impact of object orientation on next-generation database management systems. This book will serve the needs of software engineers and computer scientists who are interested in object-oriented database technologies. At universities it could be a supplementary text for database management systems and design engineering courses or for a graduate course dedicated to object-oriented systems and databases. The book is also suitable for short courses, continuing education, and professional self-teaching. Prerequisites in data structures, compilers, databases, and operating systems will be useful.

This book describes various alternative strategies for object-oriented databases. Although there are some attempts to introduce novel environments and languages for object-oriented databases, there are more pragmatic *evolutionary* approaches that introduce object-oriented features to existing relational systems. All approaches will be illustrated with examples, with special emphasis on some of the predominant strategies. Extending existing relational systems (especially SQL-based systems) with object-oriented capabilities is one of the important emerging alternatives to object-oriented databases.

■ OVERVIEW OF THE CHAPTERS

Chapter 1 gives a brief introduction to object-oriented concepts. It examines the evolution and provides an overview of object-oriented directions and database concepts. It surveys alternative approaches to object-oriented databases, commenting on the relative merits of each. It also provides a brief overview of object-oriented database applications, with a special emphasis on intelligent offices.

Chapter 2 provides a more detailed coverage of object-oriented concepts. The key object-oriented concepts covered in this book are

> *Abstract data typing:* Abstract data typing allows the implementation of an object's interface routines to be hidden. Abstract data typing allows the construction of complex software systems through reusable components—the classes.
>
> *Inheritance:* Through inheritance new classes or software modules can be built on top of an existing, less specialized hierarchy of classes instead of redesigning everything from scratch. This is accomplished through specialization. The complement of specialization is generalization. Through generalization the common components of existing modules can be abstracted. Specialization and generalization enhance software extendibility, reusability, and code sharing.
>
> *Object identity:* Object identity allows the objects in an application to be organized in arbitrary graph-structured object spaces. This chapter shows the superiority and generality of the strong notion of object identity when compared to the conventional techniques of referencing objects in programming languages and databases.

Chapter 2 provides a detailed and self-contained introduction to all of the aspects of these fundamental object-oriented concepts.

Chapter 3 provides an overview of various data-modeling and object-oriented database design strategies for object-oriented databases. It discussed strategies for constructing object-oriented database object spaces using *values* and *identities*. It surveys the traditional hierarchical and network data models, as well as relational and postrelational complex object models. The chapter also discusses entity-relationship and semantic data models. The chapter explains various approaches and methodologies of *object-oriented design* for developing object-oriented database applications. It illustrates the major steps for building top-down an object-oriented database application. Algebraic operations for complex object models and complex object modeling features in Intelligent SQL are discussed. Also, integrity constraints in object-oriented databases are presented and explained.

The first three chapters are dedicated to surveys, explanations of fundamental concepts, and overviews. Chapters 4 through 6 provide a more detailed exposure to the object-oriented and database capabilities of object-oriented databases.

Chapter 4 illustrates how persistence is integrated into object-oriented database data models. It also provides a comprehensive treatment of the data definition and data manipulation alternatives in object-oriented databases, including novel approaches and extensions of existing database languages (most notably SQL). It discusses various techniques for implementing persistent object identities. Other topics covered in the chapter include object-oriented application development steps for C++ environments and persistent complex object storage strategies.

Chapter 5 is dedicated to concurrent transaction management in object-oriented databases. In addition to "conventional" transaction mechanisms object-oriented database applications typically involve long-duration transactions and nested transactions. The chapter surveys alternative locking schemes used in a number of object-oriented databases. In object-oriented databases, locking can be associated with various granules that are manipulated by users, including classes, instances, and complex objects. To support durability of transactions object-oriented databases provide recovery managers to bring the database back to a consistent state, making sure that all of the effects of failed transactions are undone and that those for committed transactions are consistently reflected in the database. The chapter also covers recovery in object-oriented databases. Finally, reflecting the need for various versions of an object as it undergoes modifications in the database, the chapter discusses versions and alternatives in object-oriented databases.

Chapter 6 discusses the client/server architectures in object-oriented databases. It provides an explanation of local area networks. In database servers there are different types of functionalities that could be provided by the database server, ranging from high-level database programming language processing (such as the processing of SQL or object-oriented extensions of SQL) to database servers that provide concurrent accesses to I/O blocks or objects. Various alternatives and partitionings of the client and server functionalities supported by different OODB database systems are discussed. Since databases can be large and accessed frequently at various locations, in enterprises this raises the need for *distributed databases* and various distributed database concurrency control strategies to keep transaction semantics consistent when transactions involve multiple databases. The distributed database characteristics and strategies, as well as the two-phase commit protocol for coordinating distributed databases, are discussed.

Chapter 7 provides a summary of the book.

CONTENTS

1

INTRODUCTION

1

2
OBJECT-ORIENTED CONCEPTS   41

3

MODELING AND DESIGN FOR OBJECT-ORIENTED DATABASES 109

4

PERSISTENCE

175

5
TRANSACTIONS, CONCURRENCY, RECOVERY, AND VERSIONING IN OBJECT-ORIENTED DATABASES 241

6
CLIENT/SERVER ARCHITECTURES
AND OBJECT-ORIENTED DATABASES   281

7

SUMMARY

319

1

INTRODUCTION

The September 30, 1991, issue of *BusinessWeek* had on its cover a picture of a baby typing happily on the keyboard of a workstation. The cover caption read, "It's called object-oriented programming: a way to make computers a lot easier to use." Object orientation has come a long way. Despite earlier skepticism, object orientation has emerged from the realm of "hype" and the obscure to become a viable software development discipline. Object-oriented programming is now widely accepted for use in most large-scale projects.

Besides the emergence of object-oriented systems, an equally important trend has been the evolution of database management systems and the propagation of client/server architectures. Perhaps the term that best captures the spirit of the 1990s is *downsizing*. From government to large corporations to small businesses and even households, dire economic conditions are forcing everyone to replace more powerful but expensive systems with simpler, downsized alternatives. In computer applications, the need to share information in networked environments and the downsizing trend away from mainframe systems are contributing to the emergence of the database server as the backbone of downsized client/server computing. This brings us to object-oriented databases, the focus of this book.

The use of object-oriented database management systems is an emerging trend that integrates databases and object-oriented technologies. On one hand, the need to perform complex manipulations for existing databases and a new generation of database applications is generating requirements that are satisfied more directly by object-oriented databases. On the other hand, applications of object-oriented languages and systems are requesting database capabilities such as persistence, concurrency, and transactions from their environments. These needs are leading to the creation of powerful systems called *object-oriented databases*, illustrated in Figure 1.1. The larger arrows represent "inheritance." Object-oriented databases combine (inherit from) the object-oriented features and database capabilities.

Object-oriented databases started primarily as research projects in universities and research centers; in the mid-1980s they began to become viable commercial products. Today there are more than 25 products on the market that can be characterized as emerging "object-oriented database" products. In addition, relational database vendors are starting to incorporate object-oriented features into their next-generation SQL-based products. Even the upcoming ANSI SQL3 standard includes a number of powerful object-oriented concepts such as user-defined abstract data typing and inheritance (ANSI, 1991; Melton

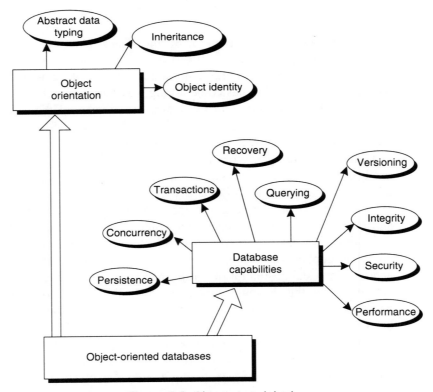

Figure 1.1 Object-oriented database.

and Simon, 1992; Khoshafian et al., 1992a). All of these exciting developments are stimulating the construction of a number of exciting products that utilize underlying object-oriented databases.

▪ 1.1 WHAT IS AN OBJECT-ORIENTED DATABASE?

Although a consensus is starting to form as to what object orientation and object-oriented databases are, there is still some confusion. Some of the critics of object-oriented programming have brushed it aside as a "high-flying fad" (Guthrey, 1989). Nevertheless, there are some very specific object-oriented concepts that provide practical benefits for the prototyping, modeling, and programming of advanced applications. Furthermore, the object-oriented software market (which includes object-oriented databases) is expected to boom to $3.5 billion by the mid-1990s (from a $200 million market in 1990).

As mentioned earlier, object-oriented databases integrate object orientation with database capabilities. Object orientation allows a more direct representation and modeling of real-world problems. Through object-oriented constructs users can hide the details of implementation of their modules, share objects referentially, and extend their systems by specializing existing modules. Database functionality is needed to ensure persistence and concurrent sharing of information in applications. Through databases users can have the state of objects persist and be updated between various program invocations, and various users can concurrently share the same information. Object-oriented databases combine the benefits and concepts of object orientation with database functionality.

In this book, therefore, the following definitions will be used as a framework to characterize object-oriented databases:

Object orientation is defined as follows:

Object Orientation = Abstract data typing
+ Inheritance
+ Object identity

Database capabilities are defined as follows:

Database capabilities = Persistence
+ Concurrency
+ Transactions
+ Recovery
+ Querying
+ Versioning
+ Integrity
+ Security
+ Performance

Object-oriented databases are thus defined as follows:

Object-oriented databases = Object orientation + Database capabilities

Therefore object-oriented databases are an extension of two concepts: *object orientation* and *databases*. The potential of object-oriented databases lies in the tight integration of these two technologies.

There have been many definitions of object orientation and object-oriented databases (Atkinson et al., 1992; Khoshafian, 1990; Stonebraker et al., 1990a; Brown, 1991; Cattell, 1991; Hughes, 1991; Kim, 1991). The taxonomy presented here is by no means the only one. Nevertheless, it does attempt to elucidate the most important concepts in these two disciplines and how the combination of the two provides ideal repositories for advanced database applications.

Object-oriented databases consititute an important step in the evolution of database technologies, illustrated in Figure 1.2. In the 1950s and 1960s, *data definition* products were developed by large companies. This laid the foundation for *network* and *hierarchical* database management systems. Both the hierarchical and network data models were primarily *navigational*. These

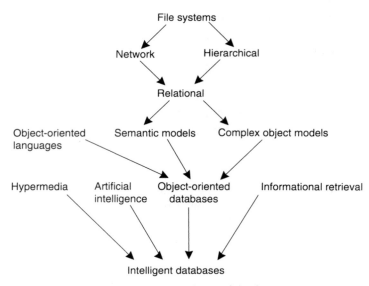

Figure 1.2 The evolution of databases.

earlier models did not have a strong theoretical foundation and did not support the notion of physical and logical data independence. In order to provide more flexibility in organizing large databases and to alleviate some of the problems of the earlier models, Dr. E. F. Codd of IBM introduced the *relational data model* in the early 1970s. Relational database management systems became increasingly popular in the 1980s, and their use and popularity are steadily increasing in the 1990s.

One of the earliest alternative database data modeling proposals was the *semantic data model*. The forerunner of the semantic model was the famous entity-relationship model, introduced by Chen (1976). Like the semantic models, *complex object* models also attempted to relax the restrictions of the relational model, but they also retained the strong theoretical foundation of the relational model. The complex object models and the semantic data models laid a strong foundation for the development of a number of object-oriented databases, both in research and in industry. In addition to inheritance and object identity, object-oriented databases also incorporated abstract data typing, another fundamental concept of object orientation.

As mentioned earlier, object-oriented database systems and products started to appear in the mid-1980s. Today many companies market powerful object-oriented database products. In addition, relational database management systems from ASK, Oracle, Microsoft, Borland, Informix, and others are incorporating object-oriented features into their relational systems. The list of companies marketing products characterized as object-oriented database products includes Servio, Ontos, Object Design, Objectivity, Versant, O2 Technology, Hewlett-Packard, UNISYS, Itasca, Raima, and others. Section 1.4 provides a detailed account of the evolution of databases toward object orientation.

■ 1.2. ORGANIZATION OF THE CHAPTER

This chapter is organized as follows: Section 1.3 provides a brief introduction to object-oriented trends in the software industry. It then discusses the history and evolution of programming languages toward object-oriented database systems and presents an overview of the basic object-oriented concepts. Section 1.4 summarizes the recent trends in databases, describes the database concepts in object-oriented databases, and gives an overview of the history and evolution of database data models. Section 1.5 discusses approaches to object-oriented databases. Section 1.6 presents some applications of object-oriented databases, including CAD, CAM, CASE, and intelligent offices. Section 1.7 summarizes the chapter.

■ 1.3 OBJECT ORIENTATION

Object orientation is an all-encompassing discipline that has permeated many areas in computing, including:

Languages
User interfaces
Artificial intelligence
Operating systems
Databases

In terms of languages, user interfaces, and artificial intelligence (AI), object-oriented concepts and techniques are being used very successfully to model and implement prototypes and/or large projects. C++ (which extends the powerful high-level language C with object-oriented constructs) is turning out to be the object-oriented language of choice for power developers. The standardization effort of the C++ language; the support of C++ compilers by major vendors such as Microsoft, SUN Microsystems, and Borland; as well as the development of a number of C++ libraries for graphical user interfaces, mathematical libraries, and object databases are contributing to the popularity of the language.

When it comes to applying object-oriented concepts to databases, things are not as clear. Part of the confusion stems from the fact that there is no single agreed-upon definition of object orientation. As mentioned earlier, proposals and descriptions of object-oriented database managements systems have been made to clarify the confusion and define the important features and characteristics of object-oriented databases (Atkinson et al., 1992; Khoshafian, 1990; Stonebraker et al., 1990a; Brown, 1991; Cattell, 1991; Hughes, 1991; Kim, 1991).

In this book object-oriented databases are presented as combining object-oriented concepts with database capabilities. Nevertheless, all of the proposals and explanations have merit and can help us better understand the main features of object-oriented databases.

1.3.1 What Is Object Orientation?

Object orientation can be loosely defined as *the software modeling and development disciplines that make it easy to construct complex systems out of individual components.*

The intuitive appeal of object orientation is that it provides concepts and tools with which to model and represent the real world. The advantages of object orientation in programming and data modeling are many. As pointed out by Ledbetter and Cox (1985),

> . . . object (oriented) programming allows a more direct representation of the real-world model in the code. The result is that the normal radical transformation from system requirements (defined in user's terms) to system specification (defined in computer terms) is greatly reduced.

The previously mentioned *BusinessWeek* cover article (September 30, 1991) describes it this way:

> The key breakthrough in object technology is the ability to build large programs from lots of small, prefabricated ones. That's possible because objects completely change the traditional relationship between programs and data, which have been strictly segregated for 40 years.

Figure 1.3 illustrates the advantage of object-orientation. Using conventional programming techniques, the code generated for a real-world problem consists of first encoding the problem, then transforming the problem into the terms of a von Neumann computer language. Object-oriented disciplines and techniques handle the transformation automatically, so the bulk of the code encodes the problem and the transformation is minimized. In fact, when compared to conventional styles of programming, code reductions ranging from 40 percent to an order of magnitude have been reported.

Who benefits from object-oriented programming? It is interesting to note that the beneficiaries of this emerging paradigm are not only the "production" programmers but also the end users as well. Through real-world modeling constructs, object orientation brings specific benefits to end users and thus becomes a market opportunity.

More specifically, the object-oriented programming discipline promises (and has delivered) significant benefits to each of the following groups of computer users:

1. *End users*, including engineers, office workers, managers, secretaries, and executives. For this largest group of users, object orientation promises friendlier user interfaces. Object orientation provides direct representation of the "physical" objects manipulated by end users and a more natural "object-message" paradigm for interacting with objects. In addition, it helps integrate multimedia data types into the computing environment. Thus voice, image, and animation sequences as well as text data will be part of the computer's repertoire of stored and manipulated objects.

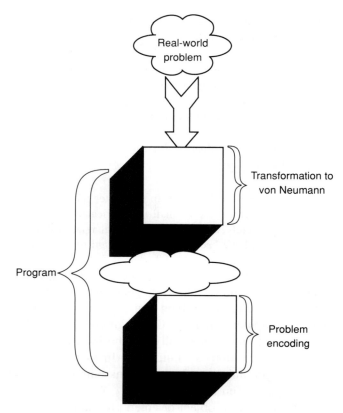

Figure 1.3 Conventional programming.

2. *Application developers*, including database designers and administrators, vertical application developers, and custom software developers. Object orientation will help application developers by providing tools that are easier to use. Object-oriented hypermedia tools will help organize and link the multimedia nodes of an application. Object-oriented database design tools will help create the most natural abstractions of the end user's object space.

3. *System programmers*, including developers of spreadsheets, word processors, operating systems, and databases--the power users of computing systems. For these expert programmers, object orientation enhances the engineering and configuration management tools. Through specialization of existing software components, programmers will be able to build complex systems more quickly.

1.3.2 The Evolution of Object-Oriented Languages

Assemblers were the earliest computer "languages" that introduced symbolic representation of the underlying machine instructions. Some of the earliest assemblers include Soap for the IBM 650 (mid-1950s) and Sap for the IBM 704 (late 1950s). But the first milestone of "high-level" programming was undoubtedly the development of FORTRAN. FORTRAN (mid-1950s) introduced several important programming language concepts including variables, arrays, and control structures (e.g.,iteration and conditional branching) (Backus, 1978).

FORTRAN is still one of the most popular programming languages. The language has an active ANSI standardization committee that periodically releases substantive enhancements and extensions to the language. High-level programming languages that followed FORTRAN and found wide acceptance include PL/I, Algol, and COBOL (still a very popular language). Algol (and many of these earlier structural languages in office environments—especially for financial applications) had barriers to using separate variable names within program segments. This gave birth to *Begin . . . End* blocks in Algol 60 (Randell et al., 1964). Since the variable names appearing within a block are known only to that block, their use will not conflict with the use of the same variable name in other blocks of the program. This was a first attempt at providing protection, or *encapsulation*, within a programming language. Encapsulation is an important object-orientation concept. Block structures are now widely used in a variety of languages including C, Pascal, and Ada.

In the early 1960s, the designers of the language Simula-67 (Dahl and Nygaard, 1966; Dahl, Myhrhaug, and Nygaard, 1970) took the block concept of Algol one step further and introduced the concept of an *object*. Although Simula's roots were in Algol, Simula was mainly intended as a simulation language. Thus, Simula objects had an existence of their own and could, in some sense, communicate with each other during a simulation. Conceptually, an object contained both data and the operations that manipulate its data. The operations were called *methods*. Simula also incorporated the notion of *classes*, which are used to describe the structure and behavior of a set of objects. Class inheritance was also supported by Simula. Inheritance organizes the classes in hierarchies, allowing implementation and structure to be shared. Simula also distinguished between two types of equality, identical and shallow equal, reflecting the distinction between *reference* (identity)-based versus *value* (content)-based interpretations of objects. Therefore, Simula laid the foundation of object-oriented languages and some of the object-orientated terminology. In addition to the object-oriented concepts, Simula was a *strongly typed* language. This means the type of each variable is known at compile time. With strong typing, type errors *will not* be generated at run time but will be discovered when the program is compiled. In retrospect, if Simula implementations had been marketed more effectively, Simula could have become a much more widespread lanuage.

Another important milestone in the development of programming languages was the Lisp (McCarthy et al., 1965) functional programming language, introduced in the late 1950s and early 1960s. Lisp was and still is one of the most elegant languages, using a few simple programming constructs (lists and function applications) to perform complex computations. Lisp is the language of choice for many artificial intelligence applications, and a number of companies actively support Lisp versions. Some companies, such as Symbolics, have built Lisp machines.

In the early 1970s, the concept of *data abstraction* was pursued by language designers in order to manage large programs (Parnas, 1972). There are two fundamental aspects of abstract data typing. One is clustering the structure of the type with the operations defined on the type. For instance, with Algol or Pascal the language does not encourage the grouping of all of the operations on a record type in the same module as the definition of the record type. Simula achieved clustering, or grouping, of structure and operations through classes.

The other aspect of abstract data typing is *information hiding*, for which the details of implementation and representation of the objects are hidden and cannot be directly accessed by the users of the object. Languages such as Alphard (Wulf, London, & Shaw, 1976) and CLU (Liskov et al., 1977) introduced data abstraction. In CLU, for instance, abstract data types were implemented through *clusters* (an appropriate name). As these languages were developed, a good deal of the foundation and mathematical theory for abstract data types began to evolve. This helped the development of a rigorous mathematical basis for using object orientation (Goguen, Thatcher, Wegner, and Wright, 1975; Burstall and Goguen, 1977; Guttag, 1977).

One of the most important programming languages to support abstract data typing was *Ada* (Booch, 1986). The U.S. Department of Defense (DoD) commissioned the design of Ada to reduce and control the cost of software development. The DoD intended Ada to be the language of choice for the development of new embedded systems. The language contains the usual control flow constructs (*if . . . then . . . else, while*, etc.) and the ability to define types, functions, and subroutines. The DoD defined the design requirements in a document called STEELMAN. Based on the requirements stated in STEELMAN, several language proposals were submitted, all based on the Pascal language. A large collection of people contributed to the design of the Ada language. Most of the language designers were from European nations: Jean Ichbiah from France was the primary language designer, and several other authors were from France, the United Kingdom, Germany, and the United States. It has been debated for a long time whether or not Ada is an object-oriented language. Ada supports several object-oriented concepts such as abstract data types, overloading of functions and operators, parametric polymorphism, and even specialization of user-defined types.

During the 1970s and 1980s, the object-oriented concepts from Simula and other earlier prototypes were embodied in one of the most influential object-oriented languages: Smalltalk. Smalltalk (Goldberg and Robson, 1983) was initially a research project at the Xerox Palo Alto Research Center. During the 1970s, a group of researchers at XEROX PARC were revolutionizing the future of the computer industry. XEROX PARC researchers invented or solidified many technologies now recognized as object-oriented, in the realms of languages (Smalltalk) and user interfaces (the Star workstation and its predecessor prototype, the Alto, which influenced the design and look and feel of Apple's Macintosh, Aldus' PageMaker desktop publishing software, Microsoft's Windows, and Metaphor's DIS software environment).

In fact, Smalltalk is not just a language. It also incorporates a whole programming environment and a menu-based interactive user interface. The Smalltalk environment includes an extensive initial class hierarchy. Programming in Smalltalk entails opening a working window, browsing and extending the class hierarchy through another window, and so on. The programmer interacts with the system through dialogs and pop-up or pull-down windows, depending on the particular implementation of the environment.

Learning how to use the initial Smalltalk class hierarchy is a substantial but important investment in time. Programming in Smalltalk can be viewed as extending this class hierarchy.

There were several versions and dialects of Smalltalk: Smalltalk-72, Smalltalk-74, Smalltalk-76, Smalltalk-78, Smalltalk-80, and, more recently, Smalltalk/V from Digitalk. The most important and stable version remains Smalltalk-80. The computer scientists who were most influential in the development of the Smalltalk language include Alan Kay, Adele Goldberg, and Daniel Ingalls. The book by Goldberg and Robson on Smalltalk-80 (1983) remains one of the most important and frequently referenced pieces of literature in object orientation.

The Smalltalk language incorporates many of the object-oriented features of Simula, including classes, inheritance, and support of object identity. However, information hiding is enforced more rigorously in Smalltalk than in Simula. Furthermore, Smalltalk is *not* a typed language. The types of the variables in Smalltalk *are not specified* at variable declaration time. The same variable can assume different types at different times in the same program. The type of a variable is the class of the object referenced by the variable. Classes are like factories that create *instances* from templates. Methods can be defined for class instances or can apply to the class itself.

Smalltalk is extremely rich in object-oriented concepts. In Smalltalk everything is an object, including classes and base types (integers, floating point numbers, etc.) This means that throughout the entire Smalltalk environment, programming consists of sending messages to objects. A message can add a number to another number, or it can create a new instance of a class, or it can introduce a new method in a given class.

Smalltalk will remain a powerful influence on object-oriented programming. Variations and dialects of Smalltalk, implemented on a host of different hardware platforms, are continually being designed and developed.

Besides Smalltalk, other influences and concepts swayed the world of object orientation. Object orientation attempts to model the real world as closely as possible, and another aspect of the real world is *concurrency*. For example, in an office environment, secretaries, managers, and other employees function simultaneously and independently. They communicate with each other through conversations, memos, electronic mail messages, and so on.

Although some object-oriented languages (most notably Smalltalk) introduced terms such as *messages* to describe the *activation* or *invocation* of a method by an object (thereby giving the illusion that objects are acting independently and concurrently), the underlying semantics and execution model of the language are purely sequential; the semantics of messages is nearly identical to the semantics of procedure calls. In order to support concurrency, Smalltalk uses another construct, namely, a *process*. Thus there are two concepts to concentrate on: objects and processes (Yokote and Tokoro, 1987).

To alleviate this problem, there have been some attempts to incorporate parallelism and design concurrent object-oriented languages. The most notable and influential of these was Hewitt's actor model (Hewitt, 1977; Agha and Hewitt, 1987). Other concurrent object-oriented languages include Lieberman's Act 1 (Lieberman, 1981) and ABCL/1 (Shibayama and Yonezawa, 1987). The model represented by concurrent object-oriented languages captures the intuitive notion of objects sending and responding to messages more directly. For example, one of the most important applications of concurrent object-oriented languages is intelligent office. In this environment, office objects such as FAX servers, printers, and scanners can be modeled as independent concurrent objects (or "agents") providing services to various office workers or applications.

Throughout the 1980s, object-oriented concepts (abstract data types, inheritance, object identity, and concurrency), Smalltalk, Simula, and other languages began to merge and give birth to a number of object-oriented languages, extensions, and dialects. The strategic direction of object-oriented programming language development is categorized below:

1. *Extensions, dialects, and versions of Smalltalk:* There have been several proposals (and prototypes) to extend Smalltalk with typing (as was mentioned earlier, variables in Smalltalk are not typed), multiple inheritance (original dialects of Smalltalk allowed a class to inherit from only *one* parent or superclass), or *concurrent programming* constructs (Yokote and Tokoro, 1987). These are primarily research projects or prototypes.

   In terms of actual products, Xerox offers Smalltalk-80 on some of its machines; so does Tektronix. Another notable vendor of Smalltalk is ParcPlace systems, which supports Smalltalk-80 versions on a number of platforms. Digitalk offers Smalltalk implementations for IBM-compatible personal computers and Macintoshes.

2. *Object-oriented extensions of conventional languages.* One of the most popular object-oriented languages is C++. This language was designed by Bjarne Stroustrup at AT&T in the early 1980s (Stroustrup, 1986). The first implementation of the C++ language was released as a preprocessor to C compilers. C++ provides two constructs for class definitions. The first is an extension of the *struct* construct, and the other is through the new *class* construct. C++ allows hierarchies of classes and allows subclasses to access methods and instance variables from other classes in their hierarchy. The language permits ad hoc polymorphism by allowing overloading of function names and operators. But, unlike Smalltalk, C++ does not come with a large collection of predefined classes. This task has been left to vendors that supply C++ libraries.

   Another popular dialect of C is Objective-C (Cox, 1986). This language is a superset of C that incorporates object-oriented features from Smalltalk. It uses a modified version of Smalltalk syntax to add these features. Just like Smalltalk, it comes with a large collection of predefined classes to ease the software development process. Objective-C supports abstract data types, inheritance, and operator overloading. Unlike C++, however, Objective-C does not extend the definition of any existing C language constructs. It relies totally on the introduction of new constructs and operators to perform tasks such as class definition or message passing. Objective-C was chosen as the primary development language of the earlier releases of the NeXT computer.

   For Pascal, popular object-oriented extensions include Object Pascal for the Macintosh and Turbo Pascal from Borland for IBM personal computers.

Object Pascal (Schmucker, 1986) was designed by Niklaus Wirth and a group of Apple Computer, Inc., engineers. It extends the Pascal language to support the notions of abstract data type, methods, and single inheritance. It extends the Pascal *type* and variable declaration statement to support the notion of object and class definition. MacApp is a large collection of class definitions developed mostly in this language.

3. *Strongly typed object-oriented languages.* Simula, the "father" of object-oriented languages, has already been mentioned. Simula was standardized in 1986, and a number of companies (mostly in Sweden—Lund Software and Simprog AB) offer Simula implementations on a host of platforms.

There have been some novel strongly typed object-oriented languages. A very interesting and commercially available language is Eiffel (Meyer, 1988) from Interactive Software Engineering, Inc. In addition to encapsulation and inheritance, Eiffel integrates a number of powerful object-oriented capabilities such as *parametric types* and *pre-* and *post-conditions for methods*. Other strongly typed object-oriented languages include Trellis/Owl (Schaffert et al., 1986) from DEC and Ada.

4. *Object-oriented extensions of Lisp.* There have been several extensions of LISP. The most notable object-oriented extensions include Flavors (Moon, 1986), which is supported by Symbolics, CommonLoops from Xerox, Common Objects (Snyder, 1985), and the Common List Object System (CLOS). Common Objects is interesting because it attempts to resolve an apparent conflict between encapsulation and inheritance. CLOS is significant because an ANSI X3J13 committee is standardizing the language (Bobrow et al., 1988). Both Xerox and Symbolics are involved in its development. CLOS introduces novel and interesting approaches to some of the object-oriented concepts, such as method combination for resolving method conflicts in multiple inheritance.

1.3.3 Overview of Object-Oriented Concepts

The three most fundamental aspects of the object-oriented paradigm are *abstract data types, inheritance*, and *object identity*. Each of these concepts contributes to the software engineering *and* modeling properties of object-oriented systems. Many object-oriented notions are associated with all three concepts. In addition, each specific object-oriented language, system, or database emphasizes one or two of these concepts without supporting the others directly. For example, Ada does not support inheritance; C++ and Eiffel support object identity in a limited way; and Smalltalk has a problem in how it supports inheritance and encapsulation.

Abstract Data Types

Data types are used to describe a set of objects with the same representation. Several operations are associated with each data type. Abstract data types extend the notion of a data type by "hiding" the implementation of the user-defined operations ("messages") associated with the data type. Languages that support abstract data types provide constructs to define data structures *and* the operations used to manipulate occurrences ("instances") of the data structures directly. In addition, *all* manipulations of instances of the data type are done exclusively through operations associated with the data type.

As an example, consider a salesperson as represented in Figure 1.4. The class `SalesPerson` has an interface or protocol: `AddNewAccount` adds new accounts for a salesperson, `GiveRaise` gives a raise to a salesperson, `ChangeQuota` changes the quota of a salesperson, and so on. The essential

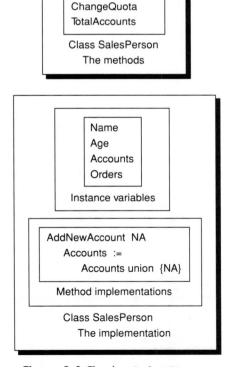

Figure 1.4 The class `SalesPerson`.

thing to remember is that in order to interact with an instance of `SalesPerson`, these operations are sufficient. In the implementation of an automated office supporting salespeople, we do not need to worry about *how* each of these operations is implemented. All we need to do is use these operations to extract information or update the state of salespeople. This basically captures the notion of abstract data typing or encapsulation. A language that supports abstract data typing will allow the instances of the data type to be manipulated only through a prescribed collection of operations associated with the type.

Inheritance

The second powerful object-oriented concept is *inheritance*. Through inheritance new software modules (e.g., classes) can be built on top of an existing hierarchy of modules. Inheriting behavior enables *code sharing* (and hence reusability) among software modules. Inheriting representation enables *structure sharing* among data objects. As will be shown later, the combination of these two types of inheritance provides a powerful modeling and software development strategy.

Consider the hierarchy of people illustrated in Figure 1.5. Here each office worker is a `Person`. Similarly, each student is a `Person`. Sales people, engineers, and secretaries are sales people and (by transitivity) persons. The "inheritance" relationship indicates that in addition to attributes or operations particular to a subclass (such as `Salary`, `Bonus`, or `GiveRaise` of

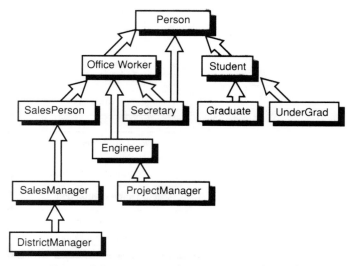

Figure 1.5 More comprehensive `Person` hierarchy.

OfficeWorkers), all of the operations and attributes of the superclass (such as Name, Social Security Number, Date of Birth, Address of Person) are *inherited* by the subclasses. This is the essence of inheritance hierarchies: Object types inherit most of their attributes from generic or less specialized types.

Object Identity

The third powerful object-oriented concept is *object identity*. Identity is that property of an object that distinguishes each object from all others. With object identity objects can contain or refer to other objects. Object identity organizes the *objects* of the object space manipulated by an object-oriented program. Abstract data types and inheritance are used to model and organize the *types*, or classes, of objects.

The benefits of object identity may be illustrated through an example involving relationships between people. Consider the relationships among people illustrated in Figure 1.6. The arrows indicate the *references* from one object to another. Object identity allows the *same* object to be referenced through

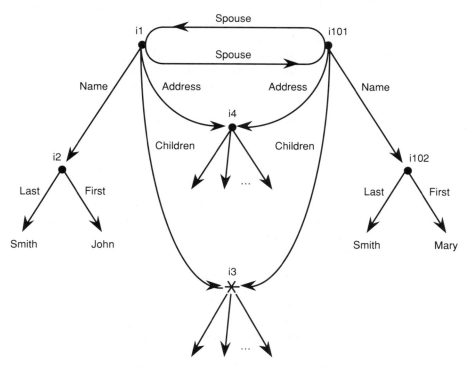

Figure 1.6 Object references with cycles.

attributes of many other objects. This is called *referential sharing*. Note that *any* object can be shared: sets (the set of Children in the example), tuples (the spouses and addresses in the example), and so on. As the figure illustrates, there can be graph structures with cycles in them. In object-oriented languages, this graph-structured representation is made possible through the notion of *object identity*.

■ 1.4 DATABASE MANAGEMENT SYSTEMS

Database management systems (DBMSs) allow *persistent* databases to be concurrently shared by many users and applications. To achieve this with efficiency, DBMSs use underlying concurrency control, storage management, and optimization strategies.

Object-oriented concepts are being integrated into database management systems in a variety of ways. One trend in database management system technologies is the incorporation of powerful object-oriented capabilities. The object-oriented features provide powerful modeling and application development alternatives for a number of advanced database applications.

The other trend in databases is the downsizing of the environment in which database management systems operate. In many corporations the internetworked LANs with file, database, and other servers are replacing mainframe environments for sharing information concurrently. Since departmental and corporate information needs to be accessed and shared concurrently, database management systems and database servers are becoming the backbone of client/server computing.

Therefore the ensuing discussion of the evolution of databases will focus on two trends:

1. More powerful database data models that incorporate advanced features such as complex objects; as illustrated in Figure 1.2, the trend is toward more powerful data models that incorporate both declarative and navigational features. The declarative features have a foundation in the complex object models. The navigational aspects come from traversing collections in object-oriented languages.

2. Powerful distributed database management systems that operate in an internetworked environment; the downsizing trend of the computer industry is to move away from large mainframe databases and to downsize to client/server architectures that incorporate database servers. Also, smaller corporations that utilize workstations are upgrading to LAN (local area network) environments because they also feel the need for sharing information concurrently.

1.4.1 Evolution of Database Data Models and Object Orientation

The forerunners of database management systems were file management systems that performed common routines on files independent of their data. Examples of these routines include sorting, filing maintenance, and report generation.

In the 1950s and 1960s, *data definition* products were developed by large companies such as IBM, General Electric, and Honeywell. These products led to databases that were accessed by many users. These early data definition products eventually evolved into COBOL, developed by CODASYL (Conference On DAta SYstems and Languages) in 1960. The COBOL language had a DATA DIVISION construct that separated the description of the data or the database from the routines that accessed and updated the data.

The CODASYL Language Committee eventually proposed an extension of COBOL for databases. The group commissioned for this task was the Data Base Task Group (DBTG). In 1969, DBTG defined the Data Description Language (DDL) and the Data Manipulation Language (DML) for databases. This laid the foundation for *network* database management systems. The DBTG specification was actually influenced by General Electric's IDS (Integrated Data Store), which was sold in the early 1960s. Other early network database products were IDMS from Cullinet (1970), DMS 1100 from Sperry (1971), and IDS-2 from Honeywell Information Systems (1975).

The underlying data model of all network database management systems provides the user with a network view of databases. This network view consists of record types and one-to-many relationships (sets) among the record types. For example, an organization can have an employee record type, in which each employee has a name, address, social security number, and salary. It can also have a department record type, which has department name and department budget. The network view includes a one-to-many relationship (set) between department and employee record types, indicating that each department contains many employees who work in that department.

The network model allows a record type to be involved in more than one relationship. A less general model is a tree-structured hierarchical relationship among record types, which is the basis of the *hierarchical data model*. The hierarchical data model allows a record type to be involved in *only one* relationship as a child. The earliest hierarchical database management systems were the IMS (Information Management System) family of products developed by IBM. IMS was the result of a project that began in the 1960s in response to the massive information-handling needs generated by the Apollo moon program. Another hierarchical database management system product was the Time-Shared Database Management System developed by the System Development Corporation. Both hierarchical and network databases are still in use today.

Both the hierarchical and network data models were primarily *navigational*: A user would start from a *parent* or *owner* record and navigate through the members of a relationship through *get next*, *get first*, or *get last* constructs. The owner-member relationship (for the network model) or parent-child relationship (for the hierarchical model) were explicitly stored in the database records. More specifically, the network and hierarchical database implementations did not have *physical data independence*. This meant that the user's view of the navigational and hierarchical databases reflected the way the data was organized, stored, and accessed from the underlying physical storage media. In some cases, the user or the database management system administrator (DBA) needed to specify details of record placement, storage areas, record ordering, record locations, and so on. Besides the specification hassle, this approach severely limited the extensibility, maintainability, reusability, and portability of the database management system applications that were developed from these models.

In order to provide more flexibility in organizing large databases and to alleviate some of the problems of the earlier models, Dr. E. F. Codd (1970) in the early 1970s introduced the *relational data model*. Relational database management systems continue to be popular, especially in downsized client/database server environments.

Relational query languages such as SQL (Structure Query Language) are more declarative than navigational languages. With SQL the user specifies what is wanted from the database in a high-level declarative style of programming, specifying *what* is to be accessed from the databases rather than *how* to access it. The relational model is simple and elegant. The underlying theory is based on the mathematically well-founded and well-understood concepts of relational algebra and first-order predicate calculus. Relational algebra consists of only a few operations: set operations (union, intersection, difference, Cartesian product) and the relational operations (selection, projection, join).

Commercial relational systems and the propagation of relational databases stem from the ambitious System/R (Astrahan et al., 1976) and INGRES (Stonebreaker et al., 1976) relational database inplementation efforts. The System/R and INGRES papers were crucial in understanding and implementing transactions, concurrency control, relational query optimization, and access methods for relations.

In the early 1980s IBM developed a line of commercial relational database products called SQL/DS. In 1983, IBM marketed the DB2 relational database products for the MVS platforms. DB2 is significant because many relational database vendors attempt to provide compatibility with its dialect of SQL.

(The American National Standards Institute SQL proposal, ratified in 1986, is based on DB2's dialect.)

Semantic Data Models

In the late 1980s, almost all of the commercial database management systems were based either on the hierarchical, network, or relational model. There were, however several alternative database modeling proposals. Most of these post-relational data models were prototyped in research labs and were never commercialized. One of the earliest alternative database modeling proposals was the *semantic data model*. The motivation behind the development of semantic data models (and most data models, for that matter) is similar to that of object orientation: *to model the real world as closely as possible*.

The forerunner of the semantic models was the famous entity-relationship model introduced by Chen (1976). In the entity-relationship (ER) model, an entity is an object or a thing that exists and can be distinguished from other objects. An entity might be a person, an institution, a flight, and so on. Entities are described through attributes, or properties. In terms of regular database constructs, entities generally conform to records, and their attributes are represented as the fields of those records.

Semantic data models, especially the ER data model, are used primarily as database design tools for network and relational databases. Often a *schema* (structure) of a database is designed using an ER model. The semantic schema is then mapped onto a relational schema using a relational database language data definition language (e.g., DDL of SQL). The user then retrieves and updates the data stored via the schema using a relational data manipulation language (e.g., DML of SQL). This is somewhat inconvenient and unnatural. There were some attempts to incorporate data manipulation capabilities into a semantic data model using functional relationships. This resulted in number of "functional" data models (Kerschberg and Pacheco, 1976). Perhaps the most often referenced functional model is DAPLEX (Shipman, 1981). In this model, attributes are treated as functions. Values are retrieved by applying functions to entities.

Complex Object Models

The semantic data modeling approach was not the only one that tried to add more semantics to traditional data models. Some data models attempted to *incrementally* extend the relational data model to allow more flexibility while maintaining a solid theoretical foundation. Examples of such models are given below.

The object space in the relational model consists of a collection of flat tables. Each table is a set of rows (or tuples). The column values in each row (attributes of tuples) can only be instances of base atomic types such as integers, floats, or character strings. The flat-table representation is known as the *first normal form*. *Complex object* models attempt to relax the first normal form restrictions while maintaining a solid mathematical foundation like the relational model.

With a nested relational model, the user is able to have a *relation* (set of tuples)-valued attribute and thus is able to represent, store, and retrieve a set of tuples directly. Early nested relational models include VERSO (Bancilhon et al., 1983) and the nested relational model of Schek and Scholl (1986).

More general complex object models (i.e., not only nested relations but nesting of *arbitrary objects*) can be constructed by building object spaces on top of a collection of base atomic types using two object constructors, *sets* and *tuples*. Bancilhon and Khoshafian (1989) and Khoshafian (1989) present more general complex objects using set and tuple objects constructors.

The post-relational complex object models mentioned so far only allow *tree-structured* object spaces. Although conceptually well-founded, these models do not allow the same object to be a subobject of multiple parents. They do not support *graph-structured* object spaces. To have this ability, object models need to support the object-oriented concept of *object identity* (Khoshafian and Copeland, 1986).

One of the earlier object-oriented models that fully supported object identity was FAD (Bancilhon et al., 1987), which was implemented at the MCC research consortium in Austin, Texas. Objects in FAD were constructs from sets, tuples, and atomic objects. Each object has an identity independent of its type (set, tuple, or atomic) or value. Other object models that allow the construction of general graph-structured object spaces included GEM (Zaniolo, 1983) and LDM (Kuper and Vardi, 1984). More recently algebras for object-oriented databases have started to appear. Important ones include those of Shaw and Zdonik (1989) and Straube and Ozsu (1990).

As stated earlier, the semantic data models and the complex object models were mostly research prototypes. As such, they laid a strong foundation for the development of object-oriented databases. Thus, the object-oriented database was influenced by the complex and semantic data-modeling alternatives. Perhaps through an eagerness to explore, developers of novel and emerging technologies took quick notice of the opportunities and potential of the integration of object-oriented concepts with database capabilities such as concurrency, persistence, access methods, and querying.

In 1986 and 1987, with the introduction of object-oriented database systems such as GemStone from Servio Corporation, Gbase from Grapahel, and Vbase from Ontologic (currently Ontos Inc.), object-oriented databases became commercially available. During the summer of 1986, the first object-oriented database workshop in Asilomar, California, demonstrated that there was a great deal of enthusiasm in the database community, similar to that in the object-oriented programming community. The following years witnessed the development of several commercial object-oriented databases. A number of companies, including Servio, Itasca Systems, Objectivity, Object Design, Ontos, Versant, O2 Technology, Symbolics, Hewlett-Packard, Unisys, Persistent Data Systems, Raima, and others market products that are characterized as "object-oriented databases" or "object managers" or "persistent object managers." Of course, several relational database vendors are also incorporating object-oriented features in their next-generation products.

From Dumb Terminals to Distributed Databases

In tracing the history and evaluation of databases, it is necessary to include the evolution of *client/server architectures,* especially with regard to database technologies. Figure 1.7 shows the evolution from environments involving

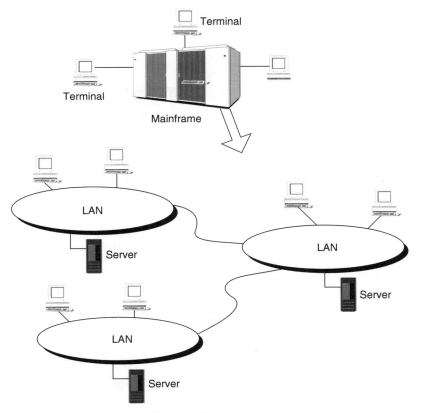

Figure 1.7 Downsizing.

dumb terminals to distributed databases involving internetwork LANs. Each of the LANs can contain one or more servers. These can be file servers, database servers, or other "application" (or peripheral) servers such as optical disk servers, printer servers, FAX servers, or scanner servers. The servers allow the various clients on the network to share information and resources.

In the 1960s almost all computers were mainframes, and interaction with computers took place through either input/output devices such as card readers and printers or dumb terminals. In the 1970s minicomputers were introduced, but interaction still took place through dumb terminals. In the early 1980s, soon after the introduction of the personal computer, *file servers* on local area networks enabled the sharing of files and some resources such as printers. Figure 1.8 illustrates a file server and its functionalities on a LAN. File servers allow the concurrent sharing of files and physical I/O blocks. When it comes to database management system functionality, with the file server architecture the DBMS code executes on the client nodes. One of the most popular file servers and network operating systems is Novell's Netware.

The late 1980s and early 1990s saw the emergence of *database servers* such as the SQL Server from Microsoft and Oracle's OS/2 Server. Figure 1.9

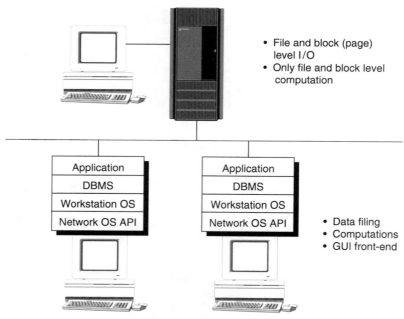

Figure 1.8 File server.

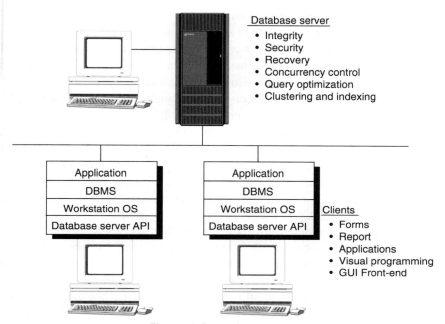

Figure 1.9 Database server.

illustrates the functionalities provided by a database server. By contrast to the file server, the database server executes the main database engine functionality. This could include integrity, security, concurrency control, and query optimization. This means that the partitioning of the functionality between clients and servers is much more robust; client software concentrates on the front-end components, and server software encapsulates of all the database engine functionality.

In the early stages these servers were *single-database servers*, with no way to execute transactions involving multiple servers and multiple databases. Next came a number of distributed database trends. The earlier distributed databases allowed the execution of transactions spanning various databases and servers involving DBMSs from the *same vendor*. These are sometimes called *homogeneous* distributed databases.

The next step is to support distributed databases involving DBMSs from *various* vendors involving *various* database models (relational *and* object-oriented). In other words, the next step is to support *heterogeneous distributed databases*.

Object-Oriented Databases in the 1990s

Besides downsizing trends the 1990s will also probably be known as the decade that launched the object-oriented era of computation. This applies to object-oriented languages, systems, databases, and interfaces. For languages and user interfaces, we are already witnessing the emergence of standards: C++, Smalltalk, CLOS, and Ada for object-oriented languages and Microsoft's Windows, IBM's OS/2 Presentation Manager, and Apple's System Seven for user interfaces and environments. Also, a new generation of object-oriented products for LANs is starting to appear. Like Office.IQ from Portfolio Technologies, these products attempt to organize information in an office environment through objects.

For databases, things are not so clear. Despite the efforts by ANSI (SQL2/SQL3 standardization), object-oriented database management system vendors, and the Object Management Group, standards of the same scope and extent as SQL are *not* emerging. Currently, the market share of object-oriented databases in the near future is negligible when compared to the relational, network, and hierarchical market shares. However, this market is expected to grow from less than $15 million in 1992 to more than $400 million by the mid-1990s. Object-oriented databases are still concentrating on niche markets (CAD, CAM, CASE, and intelligent offices). In fact, relational databases will continue to dominate in the 1990s. However, relational database management systems are starting to incorporate object-oriented features. Many companies involved in the development of relational systems are incorporating object-oriented features into their products.

When discussing databases it is necessary to take a broader perspective and remember that another trend in databases is *intelligent databases* (Parsaye, et al., 1989; Khoshafian et al., 1990b). These are databases that integrate artificial intelligence, information retrieval, object orientation, and multimedia technologies with traditional databases. Therefore, databases with additional capabilities are not limited to object orientation. Support of inferencing (artificial intelligence), full-text retrieval (information retrieval), and multimedia data types (voice, text, graphics) is equally important. These capabilities are also expected to be incorporated in next-generation database management systems.

1.4.2 Overview of DBMS Concepts

As stated earlier, database management systems support the concurrent sharing of information under transaction control. As such, they have features and functions that, when combined with object-oriented concepts, provide the foundation of powerful systems called object-oriented databases.

The capabilities of object-oriented databases include the following:

1. *Persistence:* The ability of objects to *persist* through different program invocations. Data manipulated by an object-oriented database can be either *transient* or *persistent.* Transient data are only valid inside a program or transaction; they are lost once the program or transaction terminates. Persistent data are stored outside of a transaction and survive updates. In other words, they persist across transactions, system crashes, and even media crashes (e.g., magnetic disk head crashes). These data are the *recoverable* objects of the database.

2. *Transactions:* Units executed either entirely or not at all. Transactions are *atomic.* If the user performs updates to the persistent database within a transaction, either *all* of the updates must be visible to the outside world, or *none* of the updates must be seen. In the former case, the transaction has *committed.* In the latter case, the transaction was *aborted.* Transactions in databases take the DBMS from one consistent state to another.

3. *Concurrency control:* In the typical execution environment of a database management system, transactions run concurrently. To guarantee database and transaction consistency, database management systems impose a *serializable* order of execution. That is, the results of the transactions are the same as if the transactions were executed one after another (in a series) instead of at the same time. To guarantee serializability of transactions, database management systems use concurrency control strategies.

4. *Recovery:* The database management system must guarantee that *partial* results or partial updates of transactions that fail are not propagated to the persistent database. There are three types of failures from which a system must recover: transaction, system, or media errors. Reliability and the graceful recovery from these types of failures are important features of a database management system.

5. *Querying:* Queries are used to select subsets and subobjects from database collection objects or sets. Queries are expressed in terms of high-level declarative constructs that allow users to qualify *what* they want to retrieve from the persistent databases. Some query languages have solid theoretical foundations (e.g., relational calculus). Other database management systems use more ad hoc query facilities. Query languages of object-oriented databases often fall in the second category.

6. *Versioning:* In database management systems the *same* persistent object undergoes many changes, or state transitions, and it is desirable to access or investigate previous states of the object. Versioning in an object-oriented database consists of tools and constructs to automate or simplify the construction and organization of versions or configurations.

7. *Integrity:* Through transactions, database management systems map one *consistent* database state onto another. The consistency of the database can be typically expressed through predicates or conditions on the current state of the database. Predicates can also apply to objects or attribute values in the database. The conditions that capture the consistency of a database are called *integrity constraints*.

8. *Security:* Database management systems incorporate security primitives for accessing or updating persistent objects. A security mechanism (for example, through a *grant* and *revoke* of privileges) and the protection of persistent databases from adverse access are integral parts of any database management system, including object-oriented databases.

9. *Performance issues:* Object-oriented databases have developed the reputation of being rich in functionality but poor in performance. So, for object-oriented databases, the need to excel in performance is even more critical than for other applications. Database management systems use a number of strategies to enhance the overall performance of the system: indexes and accelerators, storage management techniques, query optimization, and caching of frequently accessed objects.

■ 1.5 APPROACHES TO OBJECT-ORIENTED DATABASES

Currently there are at least six approaches for the incorporation of object-oriented capabilities into databases.

1. *Novel database data model/data language approach.* The most aggressive approach for incorporating object-oriented capabilities into databases is to develop an entirely new database language and database management system with object-oriented capabilities. Most of the research projects in object-oriented databases have pursued this approach. For example, SIM from Unysis Corporation is a commercial database management system based on the semantic data model. SIM introduces novel DML (Data Manipulation Language) and DDL (Data Definition Language) constructs for a data model based on semantic and functional data models.

2. *Extending an existing database language with object-oriented capabilities.* Languages such as C++, Flavors, and Object Pascal have incorporated object-oriented constructs into conventional languages. It is conceivable to follow a similar strategy with database languages. Since SQL is a standard and is by far the most popular database language, the most reasonable solution is to extend this language with object-oriented constructs, reflecting the object-oriented capabilities of the underlying database management system. This approach is being pursued by vendors of relational systems as they develop their next generation of products. SQL is being extended with object-oriented features by both relational vendors and object-oriented database vendors. Relational vendors typically provide powerful support of SQL and comply to the SQL standard. The Data Definition Language and the Data Manipulation Language of SQL are supported as the main interface of the DBMS functionality. (For a detailed discussion as to how applications are developed using SQL in client/server architectures, see Khoshafian et al., 1992a.) Relational database management system vendors such as Ask, Oracle, Informix, and Borland are incorporating object-oriented features into their products. In order to provide more declarative high-level querying capabilities to the object-oriented DBMSs, however, some object-oriented DBMS vendors such as HP, Versant, and Ontos have their own object-oriented dialects of SQL. These dialects of SQL are typically much weaker in their relational capabilities and in full DDL, DML, and DCL features than the SQL dialects supported by the relational DBMS vendors.

3. *Extending an existing object-oriented programming language with database capabilities.* Another approach is to introduce database capabilities into an existing object-oriented language. The object-oriented features (abstract data typing, inheritance, object identity) will already be supported by the object-oriented language, and the extensions will incorporate database features (querying, transaction support, persistence, etc.). Object-oriented database extensions have been incorporated into C++ and Smalltalk as *language extensions.* For instance, Servio's OPAL language extended Smalltalk with database management classes and primitives. OPAL introduced constrained collections of objects to store bulk data of the same structure as well as selection blocks to allow quantified queries on the constrained collection objects. Similarly Object Design's ObjectStore incorporated language extensions to C++ that are specifically for persistent database manipulations.

4. *Providing extendable object-oriented database management system libraries.* Whereas some object-oriented database companies introduced new language

constructs to an existing object-oriented language, Ontos, Versant, and others introduced a C++ client library for database management. In fact, especially in the case of C++, the distinction between a language extension, which needs to be preprocessed, and a library is often blurred; *both* mechanisms could be used to "embed," or incorporate, database capabilities within the object-oriented language (C++). These libraries provide persistence to C++ objects. The libraries include classes for persistent aggregates (sets, lists, arrays) and types. There are methods for start/commit/abort transactions, exception handling, object clustering, and other object-oriented database features.

5. *Embedding object-oriented database language constructs in a host (conventional) language.* Database languages can be embedded into host programming languages. For example, SQL statements can be embedded into PL/I, C, FORTRAN, and Ada. The types of SQL (i.e., relations and rows in relations) are different from the types of systems of these host languages. Some object-oriented databases take a similar approach with a host language and an object-oriented database language. For example, O2 (Bancilhon et al., 1988) provides embedded extensions for C (called CO2!) and Basic. The extensions include special types of constructors and different embedded escapes to the object-oriented database environment of O2.

6. *Application-specific products with an underlying object-oriented database management system.* Another interesting approach is the development of application/domain-specific tools and environments that either use object-oriented database technologies or provide an object-oriented database view for the application domain. The intention in application/domain-specific solutions is not to provide a general-purpose object-oriented environment. Rather, only useful or application-specific constructs, possibly with some object-oriented features, are made visible to the user. This book concentrates on one exciting application-specific area, namely *intelligent offices*.

▪ 1.6 OBJECT-ORIENTED DATABASE APPLICATIONS

Most descriptions of object-oriented databases characterize them as "next-generation" database management systems for *advanced* applications. Traditionally, these advanced applications have included *computer-aided design (CAD)*, *computer-aided manufacturing (CAM)*, *computer-aided software engineering (CASE)*, and *intelligent offices*, which includes office automation and document imaging.

Most of the examples in this book involve intelligent offices (office automation and document imaging). For a detailed description of the environment, objects, and work flow that automate the office, refer to Khoshafian et al. (1992b).

1.6.1   Computer-Aided Design

As its name suggests, computer-aided design denotes the use of computerized systems and tools for designing products. Any product development (computerized or otherwise) has a design life cycle. The steps include requirement specification, analysis and design, implementation, testing, manufacturing, and so on. With CAD, computerized tools are used specifically in the design phase of product development

There are at least two variations of CAD: *electronic CAD* (ECAD), for the design and implementation of VLSI circuits, and *mechanical CAD*, for the design and implementation of physical machines and their parts. Figure 1.10 provides an overview of the computer-aided design cycle for ECAD. First, there is a specification of the functionality and desired performance for the VLSI chip. Then there are *design steps* involved in the implementation and testing of the circuit. These include *behavioral design, functional design,*

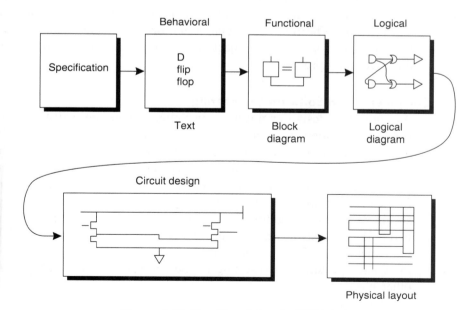

Figure 1.10 The different steps for ECAD design.

logical design, and *circuit design.* The output of these is represented in a *physical layout,* which contains all of the details of the implementation of the VLSI chip.

CAD tools are software systems that offer assistance in the complex design process of electronic circuits. Through a direct representation of the hierarchical structures of complex VLSI design objects, the support of *versioning* when designs are iterated upon, and the control of concurrent accesses and updates in projects, object-oriented databases provide ideal persistent repositories for CAD objects.

1.6.2   Computer-Aided Manufacturing

CAM refers to a software system that offers assistance in the manufacturing or production of components or machines. The output of an ECAD physical design layout, for instance, is the input to the manufacturing process of the VLSI chip. Depending on the complexity or the type of unit being produced, CAM involves different stages, including *control of the manufacturing process* (e.g., sequencing of events or tasks) for the plant or production process as a whole and *robot function control* for the production.

With CAM, computer systems are involved in monitoring and controlling the production cycle. This means that computer networks operate the manufacturing floor. The status of various machines and monitors is continually processed and communicated by the system. This might involve the monitoring of temperature and pressure. The role of the underlying object-oriented database system is the storage of the objects, the object states, and the history of object states in the manufacturing process.

1.6.3   Computer-Aided Software Engineering

As with most design engineering disciplines, there are well-known steps in the software development cycle. These are illustrated in Figure 1.11. The *requirement specification* is a high-level description of the problem or the product. *Requirement analysis* is a detailed specification of the problem, identifying the *entities* or *classes* and the *relationships* between the entities and operations performed for the *application* or the *product.* The *design specification* is a detailed specification that, in addition to the entities, relationships, and operations identified in the analysis phase, specifies the *algorithms* and *supporting classes* for the implementation. The *implementation* deals with the coding. *Testing* deals with the quality assurance and testing of the software. *Release* and *maintenance* are other phases.

Object-oriented databases can be used to store and retrieve the code base of complex software engineering projects. The various libraries that are used

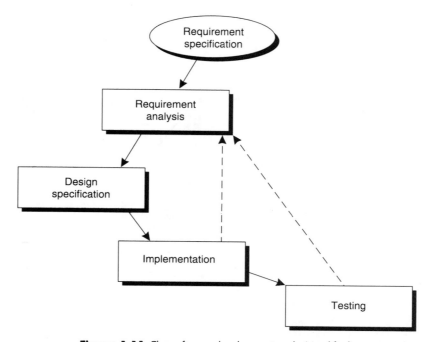

Figure 1.11 The software development cycle (simplified).

to construct the system can be modeled as complex objects. Also, the object-oriented database can be used to keep track of the various versions and "builds" of the system. It can also provide a check-out/check-in mechanism for controlling the concurrent updates of software modules.

1.6.4 Intelligent Offices

Intelligent offices (Khoshafian et al., 1992b) incorporate both office automation and document imaging. These concepts encompass two issues of paramount importance in office automation today:

1. How to model and organize information
2. How to communicate and transport information

The issues are illustrated in Figure 1.12 and discussed in detail below.

Modeling and Organizing Information

The underlying conceptual model of the intelligent office is *object-oriented*. Objects that are manipulated by the intelligent office user are *persistent*. The

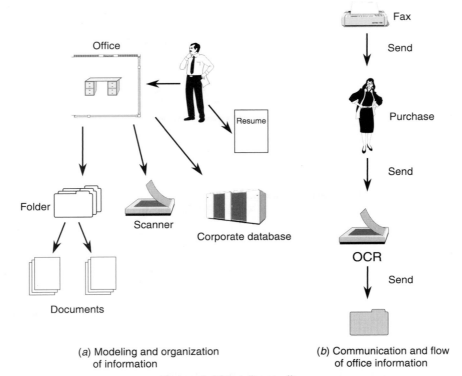

(a) Modeling and organization
of information

(b) Communication and flow
of office information

Figure 1.12 Intelligent offices.

interaction between these objects occurs when they send messages to and request services from one another.

Each object in the intelligent office (whether a cabinet, fax machine, or person) pertains to a *class*. Classes are organized in inheritance hierarchies, and office workers can *specialize* or *generalize* the classes of their office objects. Thus, they can categorize container objects as folders or cabinets, office workers as managers or salespeople, and office peripherals as printers or scanners. The application of object orientation to the intelligent office allows objects to *referentially* share other objects; for instance, the intelligent office model can represent the fact that a particular document is contained in many folders by allowing the folders to reference the *same* object. This referential sharing is supported by the concept of *object identity*.

All of the objects of an intelligent office (the images, folders, workers, peripherals, etc.) must be *concurrently accessed* by the office workers in the LAN environment in which the intelligent office system operates. Thus the end users (office workers) check out concurrently shared data, manipulate (and

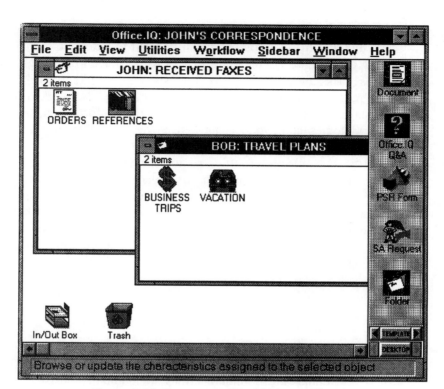

Figure 1.13 Concurrently shared folders in Office.IQ.

possibly update) them, and subsequently check their updates into the database. The underlying object-oriented database management system thus acts as the server (repository) of the intelligent office object; it manages the concurrent accesses, the searches, and the transactions of office object updates.

Figure 1.13 illustrates how Portfolio Technology's Office.IQ intelligent office product organizes persistent and concurrently shareable information in folders, documents, and desktops. As illustrated there are two folders on John's correspondence desktop. One folder contains the faxes recieved by John. This folder belongs to John. However, because he has permission to do so, John has also opened another folder, namely the folder that contains Bob's travel plans. Note that these folders are *concurrently* shared and accessed by all the users on the network.

Communicating Information

The communication and flow of information through an office can take many forms: electronic mail messages, conference calls, meetings for project management, document routing in the office, and so on. An inverse relationship exists between the percentages of work dedicated to communication and computer usage. In other words, the more communication involved in an office task, the less likely a computer will be used to automate the task.

Of course, we could argue that office managers and high-level executives (whose tasks are communication intensive) do not like to work with a computer, but a more fundamental and serious problem exists. Networked computer systems in today's offices concentrate on the *sharing* of information, but no agreed-upon methodologies and products have been developed to help office workers and executives communicate that information.

To be sure, electronic office solutions that enhance and automate communication and information flow *will not* replace human interaction. However, these solutions can help the process of communicating information among workers, especially with respect to searching for and navigating through information, performing project management, and handling task (work) assignments.

The following are some needs that can be successfully addressed by implementing electronic office solutions:

> Communicating and coordinating the tasks involved in building a complex system
>
> Creating folders and documents from existing documents based on specific quantifications, such as creating a folder of all invoices generated by selected office workers
>
> Enhancing communications to maintain consistency among several information sources

In all of these examples, "automation" could successfully meet the needs for enhancing both the communication of information and the flow of information through the system. Like all other intelligent office objects, the classes that implement workflow templates as well as the classes that implement the instantiation and status of workflow instances are managed by the object-oriented database system.

Figure 1.14 illustrates how Portfolio Technology's Office.IQ intelligent office represents workflow. The figure illustrates a resume-tracking workflow. Each node and link in the figure is an object. Nodes can be users or groups. The entire workflow is an object, and each instance of the workflow (or each "instantiation") is also an object. This workflow illustrates the corporation's hiring policy. The resume is received by an administrator and is sent to a hiring manager and a department manager. After the department processes the candidate, the recommendation is sent to the hiring manager.

Multimedia Data Types and Peripherals

Another fundamental aspect of the *intelligence* of intelligent offices is the ability to scan, store, and retrieve *image* and *voice* data objects.

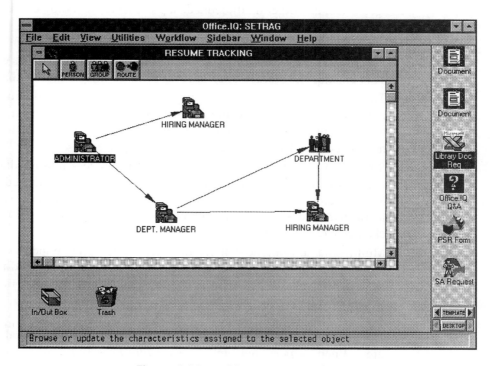

Figure 1.14 Workflow template in Office.IQ.

Compared to text, images are easier to understand and interact with because they provide a more natural interface for the user. In the intelligent office environment, images represent the physical metaphors of the office environment: the office objects (files, folders, cabinets, etc.), the objects of the particular business (construction sites in an engineering office), scanned images of forms, and so on.

Voice data is also a natural and effective communication medium in office environments and can be used to send messages or to create voice annotations to documents. Other increasingly popular multimedia technologies used in the intelligent office model are animation and videos. Office workers can incorporate video and animation in their documents, so a multimedia document may have some text-based components, other components that are images, and yet others that are voice annotations. Multimedia documents generated by intelligent offices can even be animation strips or full-blown motion video excerpts.

Image, voice, and other multimedia data processing technologies are becoming viable because of several significant technological advances:

1. Storage (magnetic, optical, and magneto-optic) has become less expensive. This enables the storage and retrieval of large image/multimedia bases.

2. The hardware components for the I/O (input/output) and processing of multimedia data have become less expensive; devices such as scanners, high-resolution display monitors, laser printers, and high-resolution printers have become affordable and more commonplace.

3. Software to display, link, store, model, and process multimedia data has matured and become more common. When Microsoft launched Windows 3.0, the company released studies that showed that end users were able to learn, use, and adapt much more easily to graphical user interfaces than to character-based interfaces.

4. Multimedia development tools for such systems as Windows 3.1, System Seven from Apple, or NextStep from NeXT have enabled third-party developers to build powerful software systems and products that support multimedia data types and peripherals.

In the environment of the intelligent office, multimedia peripherals and data types are defined as *persistent and concurrently accessed objects* stored in (or managed through) underlying database management systems.

■ 1.7 SUMMARY

Object-oriented database management systems combine object-oriented concepts with database capabilities and thus have the potential to provide powerful repositories for advanced database applications such as intelligent offices. There have been several proposals for defining *what* an object-oriented database system is. Although these proposals emphasize different aspects, certain features and capabilities are generally desirable in any object-oriented database system. The fundamental object-oriented concepts are abstract data typing, inheritance, and object identity. The fundamental database concepts are persistence, transactions, recovery, security, querying (and a query data model), and performance constructs.

Several approaches for object-oriented databases have been identified in this chapter. The two most popular (and perhaps most promising) are the extension of object-oriented languages such as C++ with database capabilities and the extension to the most popular database language, SQL, with object-oriented constructs.

The advanced applications particularly suited to object-oriented database applications are CAD, CAM, CASE, and intelligent offices. Most of the examples of this book are intelligent office examples (Khoshafian et al., 1992b) that include imaging and office automation. Intelligent offices allow the organization of the heterogeneous information in an office. They also help organize the flow of information in internetworked environments.

2

OBJECT-ORIENTED CONCEPTS

Object-oriented languages and tools allow real-world technological problems, such as complex office environments or various engineering problems, to be expressed more easily and naturally by using modularized components. Object-oriented systems attempt to make programming more direct and straightforward.

In many programming projects much time is spent dealing with peripheral issues such as compiler limitations, operating system limitations, path and environment parameters, and compatibilities. In fact, in some hostile programming environments, object orientation attempts to enable the programmer to concentrate on solving problems and getting the desired results rather than dealing with the restrictions of the environment.

The term *programming* is intentionally used rather loosely here. A program is basically *any procedure that is used to solve a problem and get results from a computing environment*. Thus, interacting with a word processor, navigating a file manager, creating spreadsheet macros, writing 4GL database code, designing dialogs through a GUI tool, and writing C++ programs are all examples of programming. Object orientation and object-oriented concepts could manifest themselves in each of these tasks.

This chapter provides an overview of the three most fundamental concepts of the object-oriented paradigm: *abstract data typing, inheritance,* and *object identity*. These are the underlying concepts that make programming in object-oriented systems more natural, direct, and immediate. As stated in Chapter 1, besides supporting these concepts, object-oriented databases incorporate *database management* features such as persistence, transactions, and querying of large bulk databases.

■ 2.1 CHAPTER ORGANIZATION

Section 2.2 discusses abstract data typing, explaining the *object-message* paradigm and the notion of *classes* to encapsulate object types. Section 2.3 discusses inheritance and shows how it can be used to organize the classes of intelligent office objects. Section 2.4 concentrates on *object identity*, discussing how it can be used to support the *referential sharing* of objects and to organize the *instances* of intelligent office object spaces. Section 2.5 discusses operations with identity. Section 2.6 summarizes the chapter.

Throughout the chapter, examples are based on various intelligent office objects. In order to illustrate various features more clearly, there will be slight variations in the examples representing similar classes or object types.

■ 2.2 ABSTRACT DATA TYPES AND THE OBJECT-MESSAGE PARADIGM

In conventional "procedural" programming, a program written in a high-level language such as C or Pascal consists of a series of procedures that call one another. The procedural model of computation is illustrated in Figure 2.1. The *procedure* (also known as a *subroutine* or *function*) is the central unit of

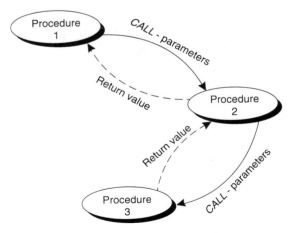

Figure 2.1 Procedural model.

computation in these models. By contrast, object orientation is often described by the *object-message* paradigm, in which objects make up the computational universe. Each object responds to a prescribed collection of messages that form that object's interface.

In procedural models of computation, routines or functions call each other to return data values or update input data parameters. In the object-message model, every datum is an object capable of processing requests known as *messages*. These messages may do one of two things: ask the object to perform a computation and return a value or modify the object's content, changing the state, or the value, of the object. The *data* are therefore the active computational entities in the object-message model of computation. An interaction within an object-oriented environment entails a number of objects sending messages to one another.

Figure 2.2 illustrates three objects sending messages to each other. Here, object 1 received message 1 and then sent message 2 to object 2. In turn, object 2 sent message 3 to object 3. For example, object 1 could be a FAX server that received a fax (message 1). It could then send the FAX (message 2) to an OCR (optical character recognition) processor (object 2) to determine the destination of the FAX. The OCR processor (object 2) determines the recipient and sends message 3 to the destination object (object 3).

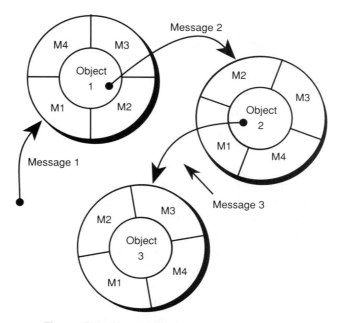

Figure 2.2 Objects sending messages to each other.

2.2.1 Data Types and Abstract Data Types

All programming languages provide some support of data types. For example, Pascal supports base types such as integers, reals, and characters and type constructors such as arrays and records. Abstract data types hide the implementation of the user-defined operations associated with the data type. This information-hiding capability allows the development of reusable and extensible software components.

Data Types

A data type describes how a set of objects is represented. For example, an item can consist of the following:

Name: the name of the item
Number: the identifying number of the item
Description: the item's characteristic features
Cost: the cost of the item

Name, Number, Cost, and so on are the attributes (also called fields, slots, or instance variables) of the Items data type. Every item will have specific values for each of these attributes.

Here are some specific Items:

Name: Wrench
Number: 1
Cost: $20.00

Name: Hammer
Number: 2
Cost: $10.00

Notice that the name of an item is a string of characters; the number of an item is an integer; the cost of an item is expressed in dollars. Characters, Integers, and Dollars are themselves data types. Every programming language comes with a collection of base data types, which usually includes characters, integers, and reals, such as dollars. Programming languages also support a number of built-in type constructors to generate more complex types; for example, Pascal supports records and arrays.

So far the term *data types* has been used to describe a set of objects with the same representation. In addition, data types have operations associated with them. We can, for example, perform arithmetic operations on integer and float data types, concatenate character strings, and retrieve or modify the cost of an item.

Thus, an informal definition of a data type is

Representation + operations

In conventional languages such as Pascal or C, the operations of a data type consist of type constructors and base type operations; thus,

Operations = constructor operations + base operations

For example, suppose we want to increase the cost of an item by 10%. To do so, we access and update the Cost attribute of the item. If ITM is the item record, the Pascal implementation of the operation will be

```
ITM.Cost := ITM.Cost * 1.1;
```

Type constructor operators typically are generic extraction operations. For example, the selection operation for retrieving a field from a record needs two arguments:

1. The name of the object (ITM in the previous example)
2. The name of the record's field (Cost in the previous example)

Field selection is generic in the sense that the same mechanism is used for all record types. Some common type constructors are records, arrays, lists, sets, and sequences.

From Data Types to Abstract Data Types

Abstract data types (ADTs) provide an additional mechanism to data types whereby a clear separation is made between the interface and the implementation of the data type. Abstract data types define encapsulated sets of similar objects with an associated collection of operations. Therefore, abstract data types specify both an object's structure (appearance) and behavior (which messages are applicable to the object). Abstract data typing "hides" the internal representation of objects from the outside world and protects the internal algorithms that implement the objects' behavior from external meddling.

Languages that support abstract data types provide constructs to directly define both data structures *and* the operations used to manipulate occurrences ("instances") of those data structures. In addition, *all* manipulations of instances of a data type are performed exclusively by operations associated with that data type.

Abstract data typing and the object/message computational model provide a more "delegatory" mode of computation: An object sends a message to another object, which determines how to respond to the message. In effect, the objects say to one another, "Tell me what you want me to accomplish. I'll do it in my own way."

Consider the abstract data type definition for `SalesPerson` in an intelligent office example:

> Representation:
>
>> `Name`
>> `Age`
>> `TelephoneNumber`
>> `OfficeLocation`
>> `Salary`
>> `Commission`
>> `Accounts`
>> `Quota`
>> `Orders`
>
> Operations:
>
>> `AddNewAccount`
>> `RemoveOrder`
>> `GiveRaise`
>> `ChangeQuota`
>> `ChangeCommission`
>> `TotalAccounts`

and so on.

The actual data structures chosen to store the representation of an abstract data type are invisible to its users or clients. The algorithms used to implement each of an ADT's operations are also encapsulated within the ADT.

The information-hiding feature of abstract data typing means that objects have *public* interfaces. However, the representations and implementations of these interfaces are *private*. This is illustrated in Figure 2.3. Figure 2.3a illustrates the distinction between the public interface, or *protocol*, of a class

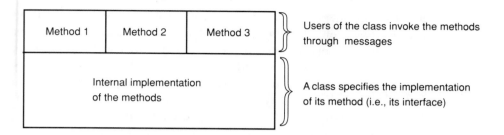

(a) Methods and implementation

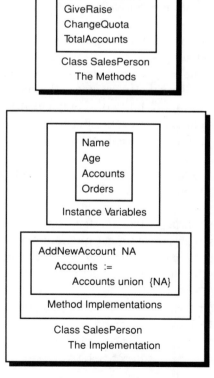

(b) The class SalesPerson

Figure 2.3 Methods and implementation of class SalesPerson.

and its implementation. Users or clients of a class deal only with the interface (the *methods*, or *operations*) and not the implementation of the class. Figure 2.3b illustrates this for class `SalesPerson`. As stated earlier, users only need "invoke" methods such as `AddNewAccount`, `GiveRaise`, and so on. They do not need to know or interact with any of the implementation details of these operations (methods). They also do not need to know how the *state* of a `Sales-Person` (`Name`, `Age`, etc.) is presented internally.

To understand the basic idea behind this type of abstraction, consider a base type such as integer in a conventional programming language such as C or Pascal. The language provides a finite number of operations such as +, *, and − that represent the addition, multiplication, and subtraction operators of integers. Other operations are *remainder* and *quotient*, which, respectively, evaluate the remainder and quotient of integer division. (For example, 15 remainder 4 is 3, and 15 quotient 7 is 1.) These operators have well-defined associative, commutative, and distributive properties that fully define the behavior of integer objects.

Most users invoke these operators to manipulate integers (although some lower-level languages like C allow the bitwise manipulation of base types). Indeed, in some languages *only* these operations are permitted on objects of type integer. In Pascal, for instance, the internal bit-string representation of an integer (e.g., using 32-bit two's complement) is completely hidden. Pascal programs that manipulate integers can easily be ported and compiled on systems that use entirely different internal representations for integers. This is illustrated in Figure 2.4.

A language that incorporates abstract data types extends these benefits to every object or datum in a program. The abstraction mechanism that enforces the access and update of objects with user-defined types is encapsulated. Hence, it can only be performed through the interface operations defined for the particular type. Contrast this with conventional programming languages such as C or Pascal for which the set of integers defined below can be manipulated by any function or procedure within the scope of the record's type:

```
type SetOfIntegers = ^ ListElem;
     ListElem = record
                    IntegerElement: Integer;
                    Next: ListElem
               end;
```

In other words, we can traverse an object that is a `SetOfIntegers` as a list. We can directly retrieve or update any particular `Integer` (i.e., any

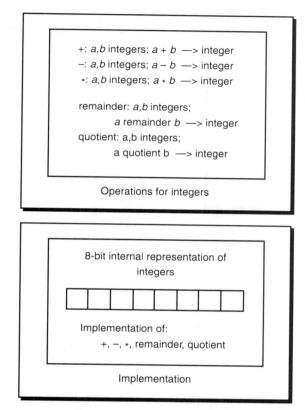

Figure 2.4 The integer data type.

one of the object's elements). Figure 2.5a shows alternative implementations of a collection. Using the linked list representation alternative, Figure 2.5b illustrates how the function `Find` traverses the linked list to see if a given element is in the linked list. Now suppose that the representation of a set of integers is changed, perhaps implemented through an array of integers. The `Find` function and all other functions that depend on the data structures used to manipulate the object type must be modified.

If instead we use abstract data typing, a number of set operations can be defined for sets. Manipulations of sets will be done only through these "external" operations. These operations should completely capture the behavior of sets of integers. Internally, a set of integers can be stored and implemented as a linked list of records, as an array of integers, or by any other representation.

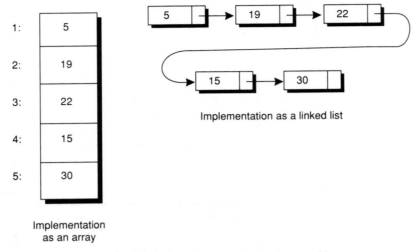

Implementation
as an array

Implementation as a linked list

(a) Alternative implementations of a set of integers

```
Procedure Find:          (X: integer, L: SetOfIntegers)

        /* returns true if and only if X is in L*/




begin
            while L is not Nil do
            begin
                if X = L^.Element
                        return True
                else L ;= L^.Next
            end /* while */
        end
```

(b) The function *Find*

Figure 2.5 Repeating and finding elements in a set of integers.

It will make absolutely no difference as far as the users of these sets of integers are concerned. However, when the representation is modified, the function Find and all other functions and operations of the abstract data type have to be modified.

In the intelligent office example, sets are used to store the accounts, active orders, salespersons managed by a district manager, districts, and so on. To perform set operations such as insert element, delete element, union, and intersection, you use the abstract data type interface operations AddNewAccount, GiveRaise, ChangeQuota, TotalAccounts, RemoveOrder, and AddNewOrder. The internal representation and implementation of these operations could be modified any time without affecting the interface of the abstract data type SalesPerson. For instance, the sets that store accounts for salespeople could use an array or a list representation without affecting the public interface of salespeople. Or we could have an entirely different representation for sets that store the salespeople who report to a sales manager. Changes in attribute implementation do not result in changes to the ADT interface.

2.2.2 Classes

A *class* is the language construct most commonly used to define abstract data types in object-oriented programming languages. A class incorporates the definition of the structure as well as the operations of the abstract data type. Elements that belong to the collection of objects described by a class are called *instances* of the class. A class definition (minimally) includes the following:

1. The name of the class.
2. The external operations for manipulating the instances of the class. These operators typically have a target object and a number of arguments. The interface operations are called the *methods* of the class.
3. The internal representation, which captures the values of various states of the class instances. Examples of internal *instance variables* for the corresponding objects are the set of documents contained in a folder or the salary of an office worker.

The interface operators (methods) of class SalesPerson include the following:

1. Name: AddNewAccount
   Argument: The account to be allocated to the salesperson.
   Effect: Add and allocate a new account to the salesperson.

2. Name: `RemoveOrder`
Argument: The order that is no longer active
Effect: Remove the order from the set of pending orders allocated to the salesperson

3. Name: `Total Accounts`
Effect: Return the total number of accounts allocated to the salesperson

A class definition must also include the code that implements the class's interface operators plus descriptions of the internal representation of objects (object states) in that class.

The values of the variables in the internal representation of the instances of the class pertain to individual objects. For instance, John's internal representation consists of his description (name, address, etc.) and the accounts and active orders he has handled. (Some of the values that describe John might also describe other objects; for example, John shares his office with his coworker Jim, so the office is a shared value.) The aggregation of the full set of these values captures the state of John as an instance of `SalesPerson`.

Although the values of the variables in the internal representation vary for each instance of a class, all of the instances share the codes that implement the interface operators. Interface operators have a purpose similar to procedure calls in conventional programming languages.

Thus, a single code base implements such operators as `AddNewAccount`, `RemoveOrder`, and `TotalAccounts`. These operators are always invoked with a target object as an argument. The object-oriented system knows how to apply the appropriate operations to the target objects without violating their internal states.

2.2.3 Containers and Class Extensions

Conceptually, a type or an abstract data type represents the set of all possible objects with the prescribed structure and behavior. Thus `Integer` represents the infinite set of integers, `Float` represents the infinite set of floating point real numbers, `String of Character` represents the infinite set of strings of characters, and so on.

By contrast, the *extension*, or extent, of a class corresponds to the actual instances of a class that have been created but not destroyed. It consists of the existing instances of a class. Thus, the extent of class `SalesPerson` corresponds to all existing instances of `SalesPerson`: `John`, `Mary`, `Susan`, `Jim`, and so on.

In object-oriented programming languages such Smalltalk or C++, the user defines a class explicitly as a template to generate objects. Although these object-oriented languages provide the primitives to create and (implicitly or explicitly) destroy objects, they do not support class extensions.

Why do we ever need to know or access the extension of a class? Actually, for some types such as `Integer` or `Float`, the notion of an extent does not make sense. Indeed, in Smalltalk/V the class method `new` (which is used to create new instances of objects) generates an error for classes `Integer` and `Float`.

The most important use of class extensions is for the type of bulk information processing traditionally performed by database management systems. One of the main functions of a database management system is to process large numbers of objects of the same type. This leads to an interesting contrast between database management systems and programming languages with respect to use of types and classes.

To see how the notion of extension of a type is incorporated into database management systems, consider SQL (structured query language), which is the most popular relational database language. The SQL Data Definition Language could be used to create *tables*. Actually, a table definition in SQL creates both a type and a handle to an extension. Thus, the statement

```
CREATE TABLE WORKER
     (Name              CHAR(32),
      Address           CHAR(100),
      TelephoneNumber   CHAR(14),
      Salary            FLOAT)
```

creates the "type" of an office worker (i.e., the attributes and the type of each attributes) as well as a handle to the set of all existing office workers. This is precisely the *extension* of the `WORKER`. When users of the class `INSERT` and `DELETE` rows in this table, they are inserting and deleting into the extension of the `WORKER` type.

None of the most popular object-oriented languages (Smalltalk, C++, Ada, etc.) support the notion of a type or class extent explicitly. However, through *collection* objects we can achieve the same goal. As with class extents, we can create a collection (set, bag, array) that includes all instances of objects of the same class.

Most object-oriented languages support several constructors that are containers of other objects. The instances of these classes are actually collections of objects. In most cases, a collection object can be used instead of an extent to achieve the same function. Collection objects can be sets, arrays, or *bags* (sets that can have duplicate values). Users can employ them in place of class extents as handles to collections of objects that are all instances of the same class. Hence, there are two strategies to access and traverse the existing instances of a class:

1. Through the class extensions (*if* the language supports extents)
2. Through a collection object that contains the existing instances of the class (almost all object-oriented languages support collection objects)

For different applications one of these strategies will be preferable. If, for example, the application incorporates only one interesting collection of objects, say salespeople, the extent approach is preferable. If, on the other hand, object collections are naturally partitioned and accessed in different subsets, the collection object approach is better. For example, suppose each library in a department contains a set of objects: folders, documents, and so on. The application traverses and manipulates the set of objects in a library but rarely or never the set of all objects in all libraries. In this case the `Folder` (or `Document`) class extension is less interesting, although a collection could be used to implement it.

2.2.4 Overloading and Dynamic Binding

One of the most powerful concepts of object orientation is operation, or method, *overloading*. Overloading allows operations with the *same name* but different semantics and implementations to be invoked for objects of different types. Overloading is neither new nor particular to object orientation. In conventional languages such as C or Pascal, programmers frequently use overloaded operations.

In object orientation, overloading includes arithmetic operators, I/O operations, object creation functions, and value assignment operators. In the GUI environments of intelligent offices, for instance, the following operations will be overloaded:

```
CREATE
CUT
COPY
PASTE
```

A `CREATE` in an opened folder window creates a new document, and a `CREATE` in an opened cabinet window creates a drawer. Similarly, a `CREATE` method can be used to create new office workers, procedures, or policies.

A concept closely associated with overloading is *dynamic binding*. Dynamic binding (also called *late binding*) is one of the most frequently cited advantages of the object-oriented style of programming. With dynamic binding the system binds message selectors to the methods that implement them at run time, instead of at compile time. The methods used in binding depend upon the recipient object's class.

Run-time binding capability is needed for two reasons:

1. Because object-oriented languages support operator overloading, determination of the method to be executed for a message is performed dynamically at run time. For instance, consider the message "*C1* + *C2*." To determine which method needs to be executed for the message "+ *C2*," the system sends the message to the target object *C1*. The target object checks whether the selector is in its protocol. If it is, the target object executes the appropriate method.

2. A variable's object class or type may not be known until run time. This situation is true for languages such as Smalltalk that do not type the variable. In these languages it is difficult or even impossible to determine at compile time the type of the object referenced by a variable.

To illustrate the advantages of overloading and dynamic binding, imagine a *Print* message applied to every element of a heterogeneous collection of office objects. Assume that we have a stack that can contain any kind of object and that we want to print every entry in the stack. Further assume that a different print method is associated with each class. Each print method relies on a different implementation and is totally unrelated. The Smalltalk/V code for printing every element of the stack is represented by

```
for i:= 1 to Top St[i] Print
```

Here the stack is St, and it is implemented as an array 1 to Top of objects. Each object St[i] executes its appropriate print method, depending on the class to which it belongs. The object itself decides what piece of code to execute for the print message. Unlike procedure names in more conventional programming languages, the selector Print does not identify a unique piece of code. Instead, the code is determined by the class of the target object to which the print message is sent. The object responds to the Print selector by using the printing method appropriate for its class.

If the language did not support overloading and dynamic binding, a large *case* statement would be needed. The appropriate print routine would then be invoked based on the selected object's type. Using a case construct, each entry in the stack would be a pair:

```
<object-type-class> <object>
```

A collection of print operators such as `PrintDocument`, `PrintImage`, and `PrintFolder`, correspond to the number of types. The process of printing a cabinet or a folder entails printing all of the documents in the cabinet and/or folder. Printing each element of the stack involves checking the type of the stack and calling the appropriate routine. Using a Pascal-like syntax, the pseudocode would be

```
for i := 1 to Top do
    case St[i].type
        Folder:       PrintFolder (St[i].Object)
        Cabinet:      PrintCabinet (St[i].Object)
        Document:     PrintDocument (St[i].Object)
```

Note that if a new type X were added, the case statement would have to be extended with `PrintX`. This addition would force the recompilation of the entire routine that prints the elements of a stack.

In contrast, for system that uses overloading and dynamic binding, any number of new classes may be added. These extensions will never affect the method that prints all of the elements of a stack, nor will they force modification of any other previously defined method that uses generic selectors such as `Print`.

The ability to manipulate collections of objects of different types (heterogeneous collections) implies that the language allows this flexibility. Some object-oriented languages such as Smalltalk do not require the types of variables be declared explicitly. Smalltalk is a *typeless* language whose programmers benefit tremendously from the power of overloading and dynamic binding.

2.2.5 Constraints

Ideally, full support of abstract data typing requires the operations associated with an abstract data type to be *complete* and *correct*. An abstract data type represents a "type" of objects, be it an information container such as a folder, a peripheral such as a scanner, or a data structure such as a stack. The full semantics of this abstract data type exist only in the mind of its creator. Therefore, the completeness or correctness of the ADT is only as good as the completeness or correctness of the code that captures its behavior.

To help programmers better express the behavior of abstract data types, object-oriented programming languages need to provide constructs to indicate the *constraints* that test the correctness or completeness of the abstract data type.

There are two approaches to providing such language constructs:

1. The first approach is to place constraints on objects and instance variables. Access and update constraint routines are executed when manipulating instances of the abstract data type. These constraint routines are incorporated into the definition of the class. They may be associated with either the object instance as a whole or particular instance variables of the object. This is similar to the notion of integrity constraints in databases. The integrity constraint might specify, for example, that an office worker's salary should not exceed that of his or her manager. Every time the salary of an office worker is updated, the system checks the constraint. When this constraint is violated, an error results, and the system will reject the update. With object-oriented databases the system can support some integrity constraints for object states directly through, for instance, key constraints, existential constraints, or *NOT NULL* constraints. However, there are other more general mechanisms of integrity constraints that can be used to enforce the integrity of the persistent databases. These latter strategies are more general and allow the user to specify particular actions when an integrity rule is violated.

2. The second approach associates preconditions and postconditions with the operations (methods) of the abstract data type rather than with the objects. Preconditions allow us to introduce certain constraints on the instance variables that must be satisfied before a particular method is executed. Postconditions allow us to articulate other constraints that must be satisfied upon terminating the execution of the method. This is the approach taken in Eiffel (Meyer, 1988), in which, for example, we can attach pre- and postconditions to the *Push* and *Pop* operations to guarantee the semantics of a stack. A precondition for *Push* is the requirement that the stack instance must not be full. A precondition for *Pop* is the requirement that the stack instance must not be empty. Similarly, a postcondition for *Pop* is the requirement that the stack instance must no longer be empty and its total number of elements must be increased by one.

The choice between object constraints and conditions on methods is mainly a matter of convenience and taste. The two approaches attempt to achieve the same effect. Both help the programmer express the semantics of the abstract data type as directly as possible. However, there is no magic in constraints and conditions on either objects or operators. The completeness or correctness of the abstract data type is still only as good as the completeness or correctness of the code used to capture its behavior. It remains the programmer's responsibility to use these constructs to express the semantics of the abstract data type explicitly.

2.2.6 Advantages of Abstract Data Typing

The advantages of abstract data typing can be summarized as follows:

1. It allows better conceptualization and modeling of the real world by enhancing representation and understandability and by categorizing objects based on common structure and behavior.

2. It enhances the robustness of the system. If the underlying language allows the specification of the types for each variable, abstract data typing allows type checking to avoid run-time type errors. In addition, integrity checks on data and operations greatly enhance the correctness of programs.

3. It enhances performance. For typed systems, knowing the types of objects allows compile-time optimization. It also permits better clustering strategies for the persistent objects.

4. It more successfully captures the semantics of the type. Abstract data typing clusters, or localizes, the operations and the representation of attributes.

5. It separates the implementation from the specification and allows the modification/enhancement of the implementation without affecting the public interface of the abstract data type.

6. It allows extensibility of the system in that reusable software components are easier to create and maintain.

■ 2.3 INHERITANCE

In addition to modeling real-world applications as closely as possible, object orientation attempts to achieve software reusability and software extensibility. Another powerful object-oriented concept that provides these capabilities is *inheritance*. Inheritance, which has its roots in common-sense knowledge-representation paradigms used in artificial intelligence, enables the construction of new object types and software modules (e.g., classes) on top of an existing hierarchy of modules. This avoids the need to redesign and recode from scratch.

New classes can *inherit* both the behavior (operations, methods, etc.) and the representation (instance variables, attributes, etc.) from existing classes. Inheriting behavior enables *code sharing* (and hence reusability) among software modules. Inheriting representation enables *structure sharing* among data objects. The combination of these two types of inheritance provides a powerful modeling and software development strategy. Inheritance also provides a natural mechanism for organizing information. It "taxonomizes" objects into well-defined inheritance hierarchies.

An example of inheritance is Ross Quillian's (1968) psychological model of associative memory. The "node-and-link" model introduced by Quillian is one of the earliest *semantic network* knowledge-representation models. Semantic networks consist of *nodes* that represent *concepts* (objects) and *links* that represent relationships. In semantic network representations, nodes and links have labels. The most powerful label representing inheritance relationships is the IS-A ("is a") link. Figure 2.6 illustrates a semantic network for salespeople, in which a salesperson IS-A office worker. Similarly, a sales manager IS-A salesperson, and a district manager IS-A sales manager. A salesperson has Account and Order attributes, and a salesperson works in a department.

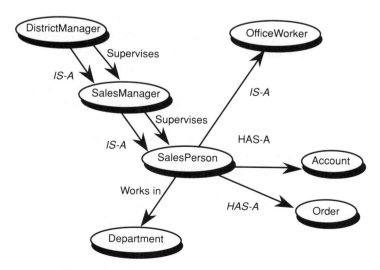

Figure 2.6 A semantic network for SalesPerson.

2.3.1 Facets of Inheritance

Inheritance introduces some complexities, especially when it is integrated with other object-oriented concepts such as encapsulation, typing, visibility, and object states. The six facets of inheritance that characterize most of the approaches used by object-oriented languages are given below.

1. **Inheritance and subtyping:** In most object-oriented languages inheritance and subtyping are used interchangeably. However, it is useful to distinguish between these two notions. A few languages even provide different constructs to support each concept. Section 2.3.2 illustrates the differences between inheritance and subtyping.

2. **Visibility of inherited variables and methods:** Some object-oriented languages allow the direct manipulation of instance variables. Other languages distinguish between public and private instance variables. With inheritance there is yet a third alternative called subclass-visible.

3. **Inheritance and encapsulation:** The visibility of instance variables violates information hiding (i.e., class encapsulation). In fact, if the instance variables of superclasses are accessed directly, there is a conflict between inheritance and encapsulation. Furthermore, encapsulation and overloading could be used to support some of the functionality of inheritance. However, inheritance is a much more direct and natural mechanism to share code and structure.

4. **Specializing:** Inheritance is achieved by specializing existing classes. Classes can be specialized by extending their representation (instance variables) or behavior (operations). Classes can also be specialized by *restricting* the representation or operations of existing classes.

5. **Object inheritance:** Most object-oriented languages support *class* inheritance (i.e., the ability of one class to inherit representation and methods from another class). An alternative approach is to allow *objects* to inherit from one another. Object inheritance allows an object to inherit the *state* of another object. Some models of computation also incorporate operations with objects and use *only* object inheritance for organizing object spaces. These are called *prototype* systems. In these models objects *delegate* messages to one another, thereby "inheriting" methods or values stored in other objects.

6. **Multiple inheritance:** In many situations it is desirable to inherit from more than one class. This is called multiple inheritance. When a class inherits from more than one parent there is the possibility of *conflicts* created by methods or instance variables with the same name but different or unrelated semantics inherited from different super-classes.

2.3.2 Inheritance and Subtyping

A type is a set of objects and a set of operations on the objects. The common elements of different types can be abstracted to form *subtype* hierarchies. In general, inheritance deals with implementation, and subtyping is therefore a semantic relationship among types of objects.

Keep in mind that the concepts of subtyping and inheritance are often confused. As Moss and Wolf (1988) point out,

> ... the two concepts (inheritance and subtyping) are merged into one mechanism in many programming languages.... As language designers have switched from the term *class* ... to the term *type* ..., it is natural for some that they also switch from the term *subclass* to refer to inheritors. The term *subtype*, therefore, can have different meanings in different languages. In sum, there has yet to arise any widely accepted set of definitions and terminology for inheritance and subtyping.

With inheritance, programmers can construct more specialized systems from existing class hierarchies. It is a mechanism that allows software modules to refer to and reuse existing modules.

Subtyping

A type T_1 is a subtype of a type T_2 if every instance of T_1 is also an instance of T_2 (Cardelli and Wegner, 1985; Bruce and Wegner, 1986). For example, every prime number is also an integer. Therefore, the set of prime numbers is a subtype of the set of integers. The definition of subtype implies that we can use an instance of T_1 whenever an operation or a construct expects an instance of type T_2. For example, we can use prime numbers in integer addition, multiplication, or division. The ability to use an instance of a subtype in a context in which an instance of its supertype is expected is called the *principle of substitutability*.

Subtyping is a reflexive (every type is a subtype of itself) and transitive (if T_1 is a subtype of T_2 and T_2 is a subtype of T_3, then T_1 is a subtype of T_3) relation. Subtyping is also antisymmetric: If T_1 is a subtype of T_2 and T_2 is a subtype of T_1, then (for all practical purposes) T_1 and T_2 are the same. Thus, the subtyping relation imposes a partial order on the types of a system.

In object-oriented languages this partial order expresses itself in the inheritance hierarchy. The hierarchy is a *tree* if the language supports single inheritance (e.g., Smalltalk). The hierarchy is a directly acyclic graph (DAG) if the object-oriented language supports multiple inheritance.

The subtyping relationship can be established through subsets, subtyping of structured types (e.g., tuples), and subtyping of functions. The following sections concentrate on subsets and subtyping of structured types. Subtyping of functions, or methods, is crucial when a subclass (subtype) overrides or re-defines an inherited method in a superclass (supertype). Function subtyping is not discussed here. The reader is referred to Section 3.3.2.3 of Khoshafian and Abnous (1990).

Subsets as Subtypes

Since types are *sets of objects*, the most obvious candidates for subtypes of a type are its subsets. For example, consider the type *Integer*. Each of the following are subsets of the set of integers:

$$R = \text{the integers in the range } 1\text{--}100$$

$$P = \text{the prime numbers}$$

$$E = \text{the set of even integers}$$

Each set satisfies the principal of substitutability: we can use an element of R, P, or E in any context in which an *Integer* can be used. However, there is a fundamental difference between set E and sets R and P (besides the contents of the sets). R and P do not have the property of closure, which is explained below.

Remember that a type is a set of objects *and a set of operations on these objects*. Thus, for the set of integers, we have the usual arithmetic operations (addition, multiplication, subtraction, integer division, etc.). These operations have algebraic properties with respect to one another (associativity, distributivity, etc.). With a formal algebraic specification, the data type will be described through

1. The *signatures* of its operators (i.e., the types of the input and output parameters to the operators).
2. The *axioms* that define the semantics of the operations (and hence the semantics of the type). These axioms are also called *reduction rules, rewrite rules,* or *equations*.

For example, the associativity of addition and multiplication and the distributivity of multiplication with respect to addition can be expressed by the following equations:

$$X + (Y + Z) = (X + Y) + Z$$
$$X^*(Y^*Z) = (X^*Y)^*Z$$
$$X^*(Y + Z) = X^*Y + X^*Z$$

Besides these algebraic properties, the operations + and * have the important *closure* property: Their signature maps pairs of integers onto integers. In other words, the sum or product of two integers is also an integer.

For the sets R and P this important property is violated. For R there are cases in which the sum or product of two integers in R is greater than 100 (and hence *not* in R). For P it is worse, since the sum or product of two primes (other than 1) is *never* a prime!

The set of even integers E, however, satisfies the closure property for addition, subtraction, and multiplication. Thus, these three operators on E behave the same way as their corresponding operations do on integers. For a type T_1 to be a *complete subtype* of T_2 the operators of T_2 should behave compatibly with arguments from T_1. The closure of inherited operations is the most important area in which behavioral compatibility can be found.

Strict closure is not always necessary for subtyping relationships, though. We can maintain the subtyping relationship of subsets in two other ways:

1. By defining a set of constraints that will indicate on which pairs of values the operations (such as + or *) are well behaved (i.e., satisfy the closure property). This is possible with the integers in R, but it is awkward with P, since the result of the + operation is never a prime and the result of the * operation is a prime if and only if one of the arguments is 1.

2. By "inheriting" the operators of the supertype but abandoning the closure requirement and refining/restricting the signature of the operators. This is a more reasonable approach. For example, for P we can define + to be an operator from a pair of primes to integers. The problem with this alternative is that inherited operators on the subtype do not act quite the same way as the corresponding operators on the supertype.

Subtyping of Structured Types

When the semantics of a type is defined properly, the *inclusion* semantics of subtypes can be extended to more complex types such as *tuples* (records) or arrays.

Assume $t_1, \ldots, t_n$ are types and $a_1, \ldots, a_n$ are attribute names. Furthermore, assume that each type has an interpretation that we indicate by $\text{dom}(t_i)$ (i.e., the *domain* of t_i). Then we define

$$[a_1 : t_1, a_2 : t_2, \ldots, a_n : t_n]$$

to be a tuple type whose interpretation is the set of all tuples that have *at least* attributes $a_1, \ldots, a_n$ whose values are in $\text{dom}(t_1), \ldots, \text{dom}(t_n)$. Note that a tuple can have other attributes in addition to $a_1, \ldots, a_n$ and still be a member of this type.

For example consider the following type:

```
Type Person
        [ Name: Character String
          Age: Integer
          Address: Character String ]
```

The domain of Character String is the set of all strings of characters. The domain of Integer is the set of integers. The domain of Person is the set of all tuples that have at least the attributes (fields) Name, Age, and Address such that the value of Name is a string of characters, the value of Age is an integer, and the value of Address is a string of characters. Thus,

```
[ Name: "Mary Beth"
  Age: 21
  Address: "202 Spring St., Madison, WI, 76503" ]
```

is of type Person. But so is

```
[ Name: "John Smith"
  Age: 20
  Address: "101 Spring St, San Pedro, CA, 94563"
  Social Security Number: 111-222-333
  Salary: $25,000
  Major: "Music" ]
```

With this semantics any instance of a tuple type that includes the attributes Name of type Character String, Age of type Integer, and Address of type Character String is automatically an instance of the type Person. Actually, Person is just a shorthand for indicating the (conceptual) type.

In general, the subtyping relationship ($\leq$) for tuples is defined as follows: If $t_i \leq u_i$ for $i = 1, \ldots, n$, then

$$[a_1 : t_1, a_2 : t_2, \ldots, a_n : t_n, \ldots, a_m : t_m]$$

$$\leq$$

$$[a_1 : u_1, a_2 : u_2, \ldots, a_n : u_n]$$

where $m \geq n$. For example, we could have

```
[ Name: Character String
  Age: 1..21
  Address: Character String
  Salary: Dollar ]
```

$$\leq$$

```
[ Name: Character String
  Age: Integer
  Address: Character String ]
```

This subtyping relationship is close to the inheritance relationship in object-oriented programming languages. In Smalltalk, for example, the set of instance variables of a subclass is a subset of the set of instance variables of its superclass. Thus, the subclass is a subtype of the superclass.

Similar subtyping relationships hold for collections and parametric types. For example, if $S = \{t\}$ indicates a "set" type whose instances are sets with elements of type t, then

$$S_1 = \{t_1\} \quad \leq \quad S_2 = \{t_2\}$$

if and only if $t_1 \leq t_2$. For example, {SalesPerson} $\leq$ {OfficeWorker}; the set whose instances are salespeople is a subtype of the set whose instances are office workers. The reason is that the SalesPerson type is a subtype of OfficeWorker. The same subtyping relationship holds for other container types such as arrays, stacks, and tables.

Contrasting Inheritance with Subtyping

As indicated earlier, the concepts of subtyping and inheritance are often confused and used interchangeably. Therefore, it is not uncommon to find languages that claim to support subtyping yet provide only a form of class inheritance that is more constrained than subtyping.

The discussion of subtyping in the previous sections presents subtyping as an ordering relationship among type structures. In an object-oriented framework subtyping needs to be analyzed in conjunction with *abstract data typing*. Thus, for an *ADT1* to be a "subtype" of an *ADT2*,

1. The structure of *ADT1* as captured in its instance variables must be a subtype of the structure of *ADT2*.
2. The behavior of *ADT1* as captured in the signature and specification of its methods must conform to the behavior of *ADT2*.

Since an ADT is fully defined through its interface (i.e., its methods), the more important requirement is the behavioral relationship. In fact, if we strictly follow the encapsulation paradigm, it should be possible to establish subtyping relationships among data types or abstract data types without worrying about the representation (structure) at all; each type could have an entirely different implementation of representation but maintain the behavioral subtype compatibility.

For the second requirement above, it follows that *ADT1* is a subtype of *ADT2* if for each method *M* of *ADT2* there is a corresponding method *M* of *ADT1* that conforms to it. When does a method in a subtype conform to a method in a supertype? Unfortunately, the conformance rules are not the same across all strongly typed object-oriented languages.

It is conceivable for one abstract data type *ADT1* to be a subtype of another abstract data type *ADT2* and yet have an entirely different implementation for each of its methods (even for the methods that have the same signature as the corresponding methods in the supertype).

For example, Set is a subtype of Bag (bags are collections that can have duplicates; in sets an object can occur only once). The operations (methods) on Set (union, intersection, difference, insert, delete, etc.) have signatures that are subtypes of the corresponding operations for Bag. Nevertheless, we can have entirely different internal representations for Set and Bag. Instances of Set could be implemented as arrays, and instances of Bag could be implemented as linked lists. Figure 2.5a illustrates the same collection as an instance of an array (a set) and a linked list (a bag). With these different representations, the implementations of the same operators for Bag and Set are completely different. With respect to its behavior, however, Set is a constrained Bag and thus a subtype of Bag.

This behavioral definition of subtyping is independent of implementation, and subtyping can be viewed as a *behavioral hierarchy*. Inheritance, on the other hand, is an *implementation hierarchy*.

Subtyping Relationship: Explicit Inheritance versus Implicit Subtyping

The subtyping relationship can be established in one of three ways:

1. Explicitly, by naming a type to be a subtype of another type, which actually indicates that the subtype is inheriting from the supertype. Inheritance is typically indicated explicitly through a "superclass"/"supertype" clause. The superclass(es) are indicated by name. In Smalltalk, for example, we can indicate that OfficeWorker is a subclass of Person and SalesPerson is a subclass of OfficeWorker through the declarations

```
Object subclass: #Person
    instanceVariableNames: 'name address age'


Person subclass: #OfficeWorker
    instanceVariableNames: 'salary rank
        department manager
        telephone officeLocation'


SalesPerson subclass: #OfficeWorker
    instanceVariableNames: 'accounts orders
        commission  quota'
```

2. Implicitly, by inferring the subtype relationship from the properties of the types (using the definitions of the previous sections). The subtyping relationship uses *structural* equivalence. Although it is very rare to find a language in which the subtyping relationship is not explicitly expressed in the type (class) definitions, some languages such as Emerald use implicit subtyping (Black et al., 1987).

3. Through hybrid schemes, in which the subtype relationship is sometimes inferred and sometimes stated explicitly. The most frequently used scheme is inheritance of parameterized or generic types. Thus,

```
Set[OfficeWorker] ≤  Set[Person]
```

because OfficeWorker is explicitly declared to be a subtype of Person, and the set construct preserves the subtype relationship.

Most conventional programming languages use explicit type name equivalence to establish type relationships. For example, two variables x and y in Pascal are of the same type if and only if their types have the same name, that is,

```
x: T;
y: T;
```

Semantically, structural equivalence is really all that matters; names of types are nothing but convenient *abbreviations* for the types. However, even in strongly typed object-oriented languages, the type relationships are established explicitly through naming.

2.3.3 Subtyping and Dynamic Binding

Earlier the advantages of overloading and the need for dynamic binding in object-oriented languages were presented. Binding messages to methods at run time for languages that do not specify object or argument types makes a lot of sense. In Smalltalk, for example, the same variable X in the same program block can reference to (or represent) an instance of a `Person` and later an instance of a `Fish`. Therefore, messages sent to X are bound to particular methods dynamically (i.e., at run time, not at compile time).

Can we support some sort of dynamic binding with strongly typed languages such as Eiffel, Trellis/Owl, or C++? In these languages, the types of variables are declared statically. For example, if variable `John` is of type `Person`, I is an `Integer`, `Mary` is an `OfficeWorker`, and `Jim` is a `SalesPerson` in the same program module, we must have the following declarations:

```
John: Person;
I: Integer;
Mary: OfficeWorker;
Jill: SalesPerson;
```

It would seem to be a clear violation of strong typing (and even typing in general) to be able to assign objects of a different type to any of these variables. Furthermore, in conventional languages such as Pascal the assignments

```
Jim := I;
Mary := Jill;
I := John;
```

won't even be executed since the *compiler* will detect a type error long before the program could be run.

Nevertheless, within the confines of subtyping it is indeed possible to assign an object reference Y of type T', that is,

```
Y : T';
```

to a variable X,

```
X := Y;
```

that was statically defined to be of type T,

```
X : T;
```

as long as T' *is a subtype of* T. Note that the assignment X := Y is dynamically *binding* X to an object of a different type (i.e., different from its static type). Therefore, if OfficeWorker is a subtype of Person and SalesPerson is a subtype of OfficeWorker the following assignments are all valid:

```
John := Mary;
John := Jill;
Mary := Jill;
```

Dynamic binding can also apply to methods. Assume that the method EvaluateBonus is defined in class OfficeWorker and is redefined with an entirely different implementation in class SalesPerson. Then if we invoke EvaluateBonus on Mary (using syntax as in C++), that is,

```
Mary.EvaluateBonus(...);
Mary := Jill;
Mary.EvaluateBonus(...);
```

before and after the assignment Mary := Jill, we will end up executing the code defined in OfficeWorker *before* the assignment and the code defined in SalesPerson *after* the assignment!

As long as the overridden methods and instance variable redefinitions are confined to the subtyping constraints, there will be *no* type errors generated at run time (strong typing). The implications of these dynamic bindings are tremendous: We can have the flexibility of dynamic binding in addition to the advantages of strong typing.

2.3.4 Class Inheritance

In most object-oriented languages inheritance is incorporated in object-oriented languages through *class inheritance*. As discussed earlier, classes can implement encapsulated sets of objects that exhibit the same behavior (i.e., abstract data types). The earliest object-oriented programming language, SIMULA, allowed classes to inherit from one another. In the most common object-oriented languages such as SIMULA, Smalltalk, Eiffel, and C++, classes can inherit both methods (behavior) and instance variables (structure) from superclasses. Besides providing a powerful tool for organizing information, the most important contribution of inheritance is *code sharing* or *code reusability*. Figure 2.7 illustrates a class hierarchy involving single and multiple inheritance. All of the classes inherit from the root class *C1*. For a more concrete example to illustrate code reusability and the appropriateness of class inheritance in object-oriented systems, the classes rooted at OfficeWorker can be further

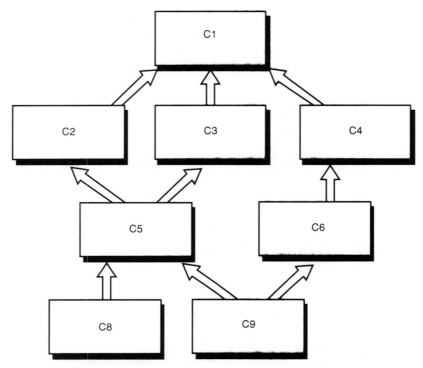

Figure 2.7 Class hierarchy with single and multiple inheritance.

"specialized." Figure 2.8 shows the additional classes and the inheritance hierarchy: Secretaries and sales persons are office workers, sales managers further specialize salespeople, and district managers specialize sales managers.

The classes `Developer`, `Secretary`, and `SalesPerson` are *subclasses* of `OfficeWorker`. The class `OfficeWorker` is a *superclass* of `Developer`, `Secretary`, and `SalesPerson`. The subclass and superclass relations are transitive. Thus, if X is a subclass of Y and Y is a subclass of Z, then X is also a subclass of Z. For example, since `DistrictManager` is a subclass of `SalesManager`, it is also by transitivity a subclass of `SalesPerson` and `OfficeWorker`. Incidentally, office workers are very appreciative of inheritance since their superiors are just instances of one of their *subclasses*. If the class `OfficeWorker` implements the following methods, then subclasses of `OfficeWorker` such as `SalesPerson`, `SalesManager`, and `District-Manager` can *inherit* these methods without having to reimplement them:

```
EvaluateBonus
GiveRaise
ChangeDepartment
```

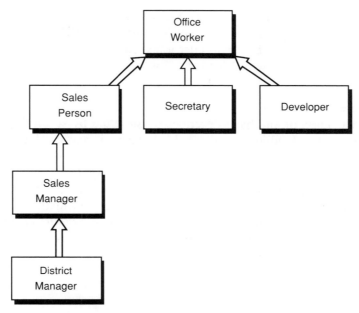

Figure 2.8 Inheritance hierarchy of office workers.

In fact, the class SalesPerson can have its own additional methods, such as

TotalOrders (returns the total number of orders)
TotalAccounts (returns the total number of accounts)

In turn, these methods would be inherited by the SalesManager and DistrictManager subclasses of SalesPerson. The class inheritance hierarchy of object-oriented languages provides an excellent means of organizing complex code bases. Some object-oriented languages such as Smalltalk come with a comprehensive initial class hierarchy. The users of the language can specialize some classes in the initial class hierarchies to create classes for their applications. Smalltalk programmers spend a substantial amount of time familiarizing themselves with the workings of the initial class hierarchy of the Smalltalk programming environment.

In summary, class inheritance has two main aspects:

1. *Structural.* Instances of a class such as SalesPerson, which is a subclass of OfficeWorker, have values for instance variables inherited from OfficeWorker such as Name, Address, Salary, and so on.

2. *Behavioral.* A class has methods such as AccumulatedVacationLeave, GiveRaise, and ChangeAddress, which are inherited by its subclasses such as SalesPerson and Secretary. As a result, a message can be sent with selector GiveRaise to an instance Margaret of Secretary in order to execute the method GiveRaise in Office-Worker with Margaret as the target object.

Inheriting Instance Variables

The class of an object describes its structure by specifying the object's instance variables. In all object-oriented languages, instances of a subclass must retain the same type of information as instances of their superclass. One way to achieve this is to inherit the instance variables of the superclass directly and allow methods in the subclass to access and manipulate the instance variables of its superclass(es) without any constraints. This is the strategy in Smalltalk.

In this scheme, each subclass declares the *additional instance* variables that it introduces (as specialization or extension). Thus, if class C_1 declares

```
Class C₁
Instance Variables: X₁,
                     X₂,
                     X₃
```

and class C_2 is a subclass of C_1, then C_2 declares just the following additional instance variables that it introduces:

```
Class C₂ subclass of C₁
Instance Variables: X₄,
                     X₅,
                     X₆
```

The state of each instance of C_1 is stored in variables X_1, X_2, and X_3. The state of each instance of C_2 is stored in variables X_1, X_2, X_3, X_4, X_5, and X_6. This is illustrated in Figure 2.9 for class Person and its subclass OfficeWorker. The figure also demonstrates the state of OfficeWorkers. In general, the instance variables of a class is the *union* of the instance variables of all of its super-classes.

Redefining Instance Variables

When the object-oriented language specifies the types (classes) of the instance variables, it is possible to *redefine* (and thus override) the type declaration of an instance variable in a subclass. This overriding can be arbitrary or constrained. For example, we can have class C_2 declared as

```
Class C₂ subclass of C₁
Instance Variables: X₂: CT₇
                    X₄: CT₄,
                    X₅: CT₅,
                    X₆: CT₆
```

where the type of X2 in C2 (CT7) is *totally* unrelated to the type of X2 in C2 (CT2). For example, assume that the instance variable Address in the class Person is of class Address, that is,

```
Class Address:
Instance Variables
        StreetNumber: integer
        StreetName:   String[Char]
        Apartment#:   integer
        City:         String[Char]
        State:        String[Char]
        ZipCode:      integer
```

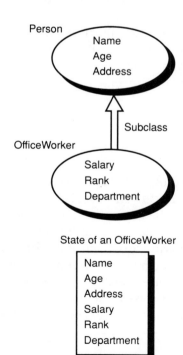

Figure 2.9 Instance variables of an OfficeWorker.

With arbitrary overriding, the subclass `OfficeWorker` of `Person` can redefine `Address` and declare it to be of type `String[Char]`.

The tradeoff between arbitrary and constrained overriding is between flexibility and type-safe programming: Arbitrary overriding provides more flexibility. However, inherited methods in the superclass that *assume* the type of the object to be as declared in the superclass can generate type errors if the type of the object is changed in a subclass. For example, if we have a method `PrintAddress` defined in class `Person` that *assumes* the class `Address` representation, then this method *must* be overridden in class `OfficeWorker`. Otherwise, invoking `PrintAddress` on an instance of `OfficeWorker` will generate a type error.

Inheriting Methods

As indicated earlier, a class defines both the structure and behavior of a collection of objects. The behavior is specified in the methods associated with the instances of the class. Methods are operations that can either retrieve or update the state of an object; the object's state is stored in its instance variables.

In an inheritance hierarchy, a method defined for a class is inherited by its subclasses. Thus, the inherited methods are part of the interface that manipulates the instances of the subclass.

For example, a `Text Document` and an `Image Document` both inherit from the `Document` class. The "generic" (or abstract) `Document` class has several methods, such as

```
OPEN
CLOSE
SAVE
SAVE AS
```

that are inherited by both `Text Document` and `Image Document`.

In the `Text Document` subclass, more specialized methods for editing and modifying font, character size, and so on for text strings are defined. These methods are not (or not necessarily) defined for just any document. They are applicable to (primarily) text documents. Similarly, `Image Document` has specific methods such as zooming and rotating, which are applicable to image documents.

Similar to instance variable definitions, the collection of methods applicable to an instance of a class is the union of all methods defined for the ancestors of the class plus the methods defined in the class definition.

Method Overriding

A subclass can override an inherited method. In other words, a method called *M* in class *C* can be overridden by a method also called *M* in a subclass

C' of C. Thus, when a message with selector M is sent to an object O, the underlying system binds M to the method with the same name in the most specialized class of O.

For example, consider the hierarchy of OfficeWorkers, with Sales-Person a subclass of OfficeWorker and SalesManager a subclass of SalesPerson. Assume that the formula for evaluating the end-of-year bonus for salespeople is completely different from that of regular employees. In particular, the formula to evaluate the bonus of a regular employee is a function of the ranking given by the employee's manager (a number between 1 and 5) and the number of years the employee has worked for the firm:

EvaluateBonus code in class OfficeWorker:

```
Bonus : Rank*1000 + NumberOfYears*100
```

The formula to evaluate the bonus of salespeople is a function of the total sales and the number of years the salesperson has worked for the firm:

EvaluateBonus code in class SalesPerson:

```
Bonus := TotalSalesAmount*0.01
         Rank*1000 + NumberOfYears*100
```

Finally, the formula to evaluate the bonus of a sales manager is a function of the following:

1. the total sales of all salespeople under the sales manager's supervision
2. the total amount of direct sales made by the sales manager
3. the number of years the sales manager has worked for the firm

The following statements reflect these factors:

EvaluateBonus code in class SalesManager:

```
Bonus := TotalSalesForceSales*0.005
         + TotalDirectSalesAmount*0.01
         + Rank*1000 + NumberOfYears*100
```

Since there are several codes, what determines which piece of code is used when the method EvaluateBonus is invoked? To see how code is selected, consider, for example, the following:

> Mary is an instance of SalesManager
>
> John is an instance of SalesPerson

Note that in addition to her position as a SalesManager, Mary is also a Sales-Person and an OfficeWorker. Similarly, John is a SalesPerson and an OfficeWorker. However, Mary is created as an instance of SalesManager. If a message asks Mary what her class is, the answer is SalesManager.

When the following message is sent, the search for a method called EvaluateBonus starts at the class SalesManager:

Mary EvaluateBonus

Since such a method is found in the declaration of this class, the search stops there; the appropriate method has been found and can be executed.

2.3.5 Multiple Inheritance

So far all of the inheritance examples have used *single* inheritance; each sub-class has had one and only one immediate superclass. In many situations, it is convenient to allow a subclass to inherit from more than one immediate superclass. In the Person class hierarchy, for example, there can be people who are both office workers and students. In Figure 2.10, a BorderedTextWindow allows editing of text in a bordered window that inherits from both TextWindow and BorderedWindow.

The mechanism that allows a class to inherit from more than one immediate parent is called *multiple inheritance*. With multiple inheritance we can combine several existing classes to produce combination classes that use each of their multiple superclasses in a variety of ways and for a variety of functions. As

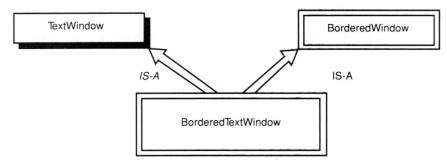

Figure 2.10 Examples of multiple inheritance.

opposed to a single inheritance, for which the class inheritance hierarchy is a tree with the most general class (typically the class object) at the root of the tree, the class inheritance hierarchy for multiple inheritance, for which a class can have more than one immediate predecessor, becomes a directed acyclic graph (DAG).

It was shown earlier that the set of instance variables for the subclass is the union of the instance variables of its immediate superclass and the additional instance variables defined in the subclass. Similarly, the set of methods for the subclass is also the union of the methods of its immediate superclass and the additional methods defined in the subclass. Methods in the subclass can override methods in the superclass.

With multiple inheritance these strategies are extended to the union of all immediate parents. More specifically,

(Instance variables of C) =

(local C instance variables) $\cup$ (C_i instance variables)

where each C_i is an immediate predecessor of C. Similarly, the methods of C are defined by

(Methods of C) = (local C methods) $\cup$ (C_i methods)

Suppose a `Rectangle` has two instance variables, `LowerLeft` and `UpperRight`, representing the coordinates of the lower left corner and upper right corner. A `ColoredRegion` also has two instance variables, `Color` and `Brightness`. A `ColoredRectangle`, therefore, will have

`UpperRight, LowerLeft, Color, Brightness`

Unfortunately, combining instance variables or methods of immediate predecessors is not that simple. The problem is that predecessors could have instance variables or methods with the *same name* but with totally unrelated semantics. For example, a `TechnicalConsultant` and a `Manager` can have values for `Skill` that are totally unrelated. For the technical person `Skill` reflects the technical abilities and experience in a particular technical domain. For a manager it reflects people management skills, knowledge of project management techniques, and so on. Therefore the "units" and domains of the values of `Skill` in these two classes are unrelated. It is necessary to consider what happens when a class such as `TechnicalManager` inherits from both. In other words, what happens when there is a conflict? The term *conflict* here means that different methods or instance variables with the same name are defined in a totally unrelated way by two or more superclasses.

Most of the problems of multiple inheritance deals with conflict resolution strategies. There are many such strategies, and each object-oriented language that supports multiple inheritance provides a slight variation of a basic strategy in its implementation. For more details see pp. 133–141 of Khoshafian and Abnous (1990).

2.3.6 Inheriting the Interface

Inheritance is used to *specialize*. For example, salespeople are specialized office workers involved in selling items, sales managers are salespeople who manage the quotas of sales people, and so on. However, characterizing inheritance as specialization has caused some confusion. A class C_1 inherits from class C_2 but the *interface* of C_1 (the subclass) is a *superset* of the interface of C_2.

The confusion is illustrated in Figure 2.11. Viewing class types as sets of objects with the same structure and behavior, SalesPersons is a subset of the set OfficeWorkers. The set of Secretaries is also a subset of the set of OfficeWorkers. Though not illustrated in the figure, the set of SalesManagers is a subset of the set of Salespersons, and the set of DistrictManagers is a subset of the set of SalesManagers.

With respect to interfaces and the representation, the inclusion hierarchies are reversed. For example, the set of attributes of sales people includes all of the attributes of OfficeWorkers as well as such attributes as Accounts and Orders, specific to SalesPerson. The interface of SalesPerson is also a superset of the interface of OfficeWorkers and includes additional methods such as TotalAccounts and AddNewOrders.

Thus, in addition to providing specialization, inheritance can also be viewed as an *extension*: When a class C_1 inherits from a class C_2 it provides additional interface routines (methods) and/or attributes to the external environment. For example, if the end-user license for a commercial software program is viewed as a contract between the designer of a class (the software) and its "clients" (the software users who create instances of the class), inheritance extends the contract with additional "terms" and "clauses" of execution. These contractual addenda can be viewed as restrictions (specialization) or additional capabilities (extension).

2.3.7 Deep Extensions

Class extensions and their relevance to object-oriented databases were discussed previously. Briefly, the extension of a class is the set of all existing instances of the class. When we have class hierarchies, it is useful to distinguish between the set of all instances of a class and the set of all instances of the class and its subclasses. The following example illustrates this difference.

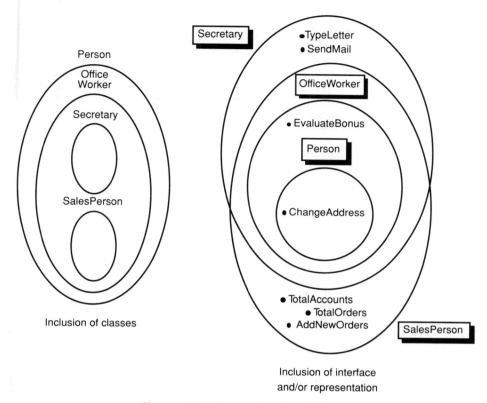

Figure 2.11 Class and interface inclusions.

Consider the class hierarchy of `OfficeWorkers` in Figure 2.12a. The class hierarchy is rooted at class `OfficeWorker`. As the inheritance hierarchy illustrates we have subclasses `MarketingWorker`, `DevelopmentWorker`, `AdministrationWorker`, and `SalesWorker` as immediate descendants. These classes have subclasses for various management and skill categories. What is the extension of, say, `DevelopmentWorker`? There are two possible definitions: that of extension and that of deep extension.

1. The extension of the class could indicate the set of all instances that are instances of the class proper. For `DevelopmentWorker` this would represent all developers who are neither managers nor QA personnel nor documentation personnel.

2. The deeper extension of the class (Straube and Ozsu, 1990) consists of all instances of the class plus all instances of its subclasses. In this

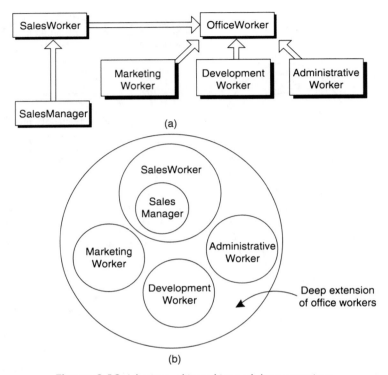

Figure 2.12 Inheritance hierarchies and deep extensions.

case the deep extension of DevelopmentWorker would include all development (managers, documentation, QA, "real" workers, and so on). The deep extension of OfficeWorker is illustrated in Figure 2.12b.

Deep extension is a powerful and useful concept, especially in the context of object-oriented databases. It enables the user to traverse or query the instances of entire class hierarchies rooted at a particular superclass. In fact, the more general strategy would be to support both the *extension* and the *deep extension* and to allow the user to have more control over the domain of the query.

Another important and interesting application of the deep extension concept is the population of the "database" through *INSERT*ing in the root. In Intelligent SQL, for instance (Khoshafian, 1991a; Khoshafian et al., 1991), the language allows the definition of subclasses though predicates on the attributes (or "columns") of tables. Thus, we could subclass RichWorkers as OfficeWorkers who earn more than $200,000. Then, if OfficeWorkers represents the deep extension of all employees (i.e., the extension of Of-ficeWorkers and all of its subclasses), when we insert an employee who earns more than $200,000, it will automatically be inserted into RichWorkers!

2.3.8 Generalization

Thus far the discussion of inheritance has concentrated on its *specialization* aspects. Most existing object-oriented systems allow developers to extend an application by *specializing* existing components (in most cases, *classes*) of their application. Software extensions are achieved by creating *subclasses* of existing classes. This is illustrated in Figure 2.13a, in which the classes with dashed frames are "older" existing classes and the classes with white frames are created by inheriting structure and behavior from existing classes. There-fore, specialization is a *top-down* approach to software development: We start with a general class hierarchy (the *top*-level superclasses) and extend it by the creation of subclasses (the classes that are the *leaves*, or at the *bottom* of the hierarchy). As was discussed earlier, specializing an existing class can be

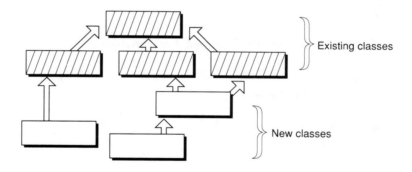

(a) New classes are specializations of existing classes

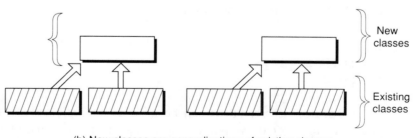

(b) New classes are generalizations of existing classes

Figure 2.13 Specialization and generalization.

achieved by adding instance variables, restricting existing instance variables, adding methods, overriding existing methods, and so on.

Generalization is the complement of specialization (Khoshafian et al., 1991; Chan et al., 1991). It uses a *bottom-up* approach by creating classes that are *generalizations* (or superclasses) of existing subclasses. This is illustrated in Figure 2.13b. Here the new classes (which are at the *top* of the hierarchy) are created by extracting common structure (instance variables and methods of existing, more specialized classes) from existing classes (which are at the *bottom* of the hierachy).

As an example of generalization, assume that we have two existing classes, `OfficeWorker` and `Student`. `OfficeWorker` has the following instance variables:

```
Name
SocialSecurity#
Address
Salary
EmployeeNumber
WorksFor
```

`Student` has the following instance variables:

```
Name
SocialSecurity#
Address
Major
Advisor
```

These *existing* classes have a common structure and behavior. In order to abstract this common structure and behavior, we need to *generalize* the two classes in class `Person` with instance variables

```
Name
SocialSecurity#
Address
```

Once `Person` is created, it can be used as a superclass of other classes that could be constructed by specializing `Person`. Thus, if the object-oriented system supports both specialization and generalization, software development would involve, among other things, a series of specialization and generalization tasks.

2.3.9 Advantages of Inheritance

Inheritance provides several advantages for modeling intelligent offices:

1. It offers a natural model for organizing information. For instance, inheritance directly captures the fact that sales managers are also salespeople.
2. It allows code and representation to be shared, thereby reducing the overhead of intelligent office systems.
3. It allows *new* classes and objects to be defined on top of existing hierarchies rather than from scratch. This increases the flexibility and extensibility of the intelligent office class hierarchies.

▪ 2.4 OBJECT IDENTITY

Whereas abstract data types and inheritance model and organize the *types*, or classes, of objects, object identity organizes the *objects* in the object space manipulated by an object-oriented program.

Object identity is the property of an object that distinguishes it from all other objects. The most common type of object identity in programming languages, databases, and operating systems is *user-defined names* of objects.

Using object identity, objects can contain or refer to other objects. This eliminates the need to use variable names that do not have the support of object identity, but it introduces some practical limitations. One limitation is that a single object may be accessed in different ways: Thus, an object may be bound to different variables that have no way of finding out whether they refer to the same object (Saltzer, 1978).

In conventional languages the limitations can prevent the use of object identity. For example, a salesperson identified by the name P1 may be characterized as the employee of the sales manager John Smith, who had the best sales in June 1988. The *same* salesperson bound to a different name P2 may be characterized as the salesperson who made three overseas trips during 1988. With the assumption that P1 and P2 can only be bound to objects (i.e., not to pointers), conventional languages do not provide predicates to correlate such identical objects directly.

In contrast, object-oriented languages provide a simple *identity test* with the expression $X == Y$, which is different from the *equality test* $X = Y$. The identity test checks whether two objects are the same. (The equality test checks whether the contents of two objects are the same.)

2.4.1 Operating System Path Names

One method used for identifying objects is path names for operating systems such as UNIX and DOS. Such operating systems have hierarchical directory structures in which each directory contains a collection of files and possibly other directories. The name of a file must be unique within a directory, and each file is accessible through a directory *path*, which is basically a concatenation of directory names.

For example, assume that an office has organized its computer inventory in software (Soft) and hardware (Hard) directories, as illustrated in Figure 2.14. Then all of the files that describe HP laser printers will be accessible through the path

```
ITEMS/COMPUTER/HARD/PRINT/HP
```

One problem with concatenated names is ambiguous file references. Often the users remember the names or attributes but not the location, that is, the path of the file. Another problem is that the object (file) space is often a tree. To store or access the *same* file within multiple directories the user must make multiple copies of the file. Besides replicating storage, users must maintain consistency. For example, if the information pertaining to a particular printer

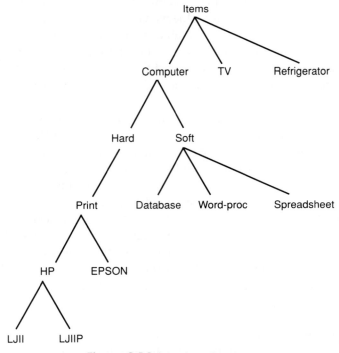

Figure 2.14 Items in an inventory.

is updated in the PRINT subdirectory, then *all* files that reference the printer must be updated by the user.

One way around this problem is by linking a file from one directory to a file in another directory. As will be shown later, this is similar to referential sharing with object-oriented systems that support object identity. However, although file linking provides some level of support for more general object spaces (more general than trees), it is not as general and powerful as full support of object identity.

2.4.2   Identifier Keys

Another method for identifying objects is to use *unique keys*, or *identifier keys*. This mechanism is commonly used in database management systems. For a database table storing OfficeWorker, for example, the identifier key would be a person's name (LastName_FirstName); for a database table storing items the identifier key would be the item number.

In the relational database model a relation is a set of records (tuples, rows) of the same type or structure. A relation can be viewed as a two-dimensional table of rows and columns, in which all elements in a column have the same base type (integer, character string, floating-point number, etc.). Each row is a tuple or a record. The column values of a row are its attributes. An identifier key is a subset of the attributes of an object that is unique for all objects in the relation. Figure 2.15 presents the OfficeWorker table, where the key is indicated as the concatenation of the LastName and FirstName attributes of a person.

Identifier key

Last Name	First Name	Age	Address
Adams	Tim	23	"12 Sutton..."
Brown	Jim	32	"43 Doloney..."
Ripper	Jack	70	"1 London..."
Silverman	Leo	34	"55 H Street..."
Smith	John	32	"1212 Main..."
Smith	Mary	32	"1212 Main..."

Figure 2.15 The OfficeWorker table.

There are three main problems with using identifier keys for object identity:

1. *Modifying identifier keys.* One problem is that identifier keys cannot (or should not) be allowed to change, even though they are user-defined descriptive data. For example, a sales manager's name may be used as the identifier key for the sales manager and may be replicated in salesperson objects to indicate for whom the employee works. But the sales manager name may need to change, for example, because of a change in marital status. This would cause a discontinuity in identity for the sales manager object.

2. *Nonuniformity.* The main source of nonuniformity is that identifier keys in different tables have different types (integer or character-string floating point) or different combinations of attributes. For example, the identifier key for the `Item` table is the `ItemNumber`, an Integer; for `OfficeWorker` it is (`LastName, FirstName`), a character string. Dealing with different collections/types of attributes for identification is inconsistent and causes added difficulty when working with several tables. A second, more serious problem is that the attribute(s) to use for an identifier key may need to change. For example, RCA may use employee numbers to identify employees, whereas General Electric may use Social Security Numbers. A merger of these two companies would require one of the keys to change, causing a discontinuity in identity for the employees of one of the companies.

3. *"Unnatural" joins.* A third problem is that with identifier keys joins are used in retrievals instead of simpler and more direct object retrievals as in GEM (Zaniolo, 1983), FAD (Bancilhon et al., 1987), and OPAL (Maier and Stein, 1986). For example, suppose we have an employee relation

```
OfficeWorker(Name, Age, Address, Salary, DeptName)
```

and a department relation

```
Department(Name, Budget, Location, ...)
```

and the `DeptName` attribute establishes a relationship between an office worker and a department. Using identifier keys, `DeptName` would have its own value as the identifier key of the department. A retrieval involving both tuples would require a join between the two tuples. Thus, using SQL, to retrieve all employees' names and the locations in which all employees work, we would use

```
SELECT OfficeWorker.Name, Department.Location
FROM OfficeWorker, Department
WHERE OfficeWorker.DeptName = Department.Name
```

This is *unnatural*; in most cases what the user really wants is the actual department tuple, not the DeptName. Tables in relational systems are in first normal form; they are *normalized*, or flattened. With normalization the user is restricted to a fixed collection of base types and is not allowed to assign and manipulate tuples, relations, or other complex object types of the attributes. Hence, normalization loses the semantic connectives among the objects in the database. In fact, relational languages such as SQL incorporate additional capabilities such as foreign key constraints to recapture the lost semantics.

2.4.3   Type-State-Identity Trichotomy

A class implements a *type* that describes both the structure and behavior of its instances. The structure is captured in the instance variables, and the behavior is captured in the methods applicable to the instances. An object O, for example, can respond to the following message by returning the name of its class:

```
O class
```

The values of the instance variables of an object constitute the *state* of the object. In other words, each instance variable value is an object. To see the relationship of type and state, assume, for example, that each OfficeWorker has the instance variables Name, Age, Address, Salary, Rank, Office, Department, Manager with the following types, where NAME, INTEGER, DOLLAR, OFFICE, ADDRESS, DEPARTMENT, and MANAGER are also names of classes:

```
Name:          NAME
Age:           INTEGER
Address:       ADDRESS
Salary:        DOLLAR
Rank:          INTEGER
Office:        OFFICE
Department:    DEPARTMENT
Manager:       MANAGER
```

The class NAME contains the following instance variables:

LastName: String of Characters
FirstName: String Of Characters

Similarly, the class DEPARTMENT contains the following instance variables:

Name: String of Characters
Budget: DOLLAR
Location: ADDRESS

Therefore, each instance of OfficeWorker contains several instances:

> an instance of NAME (the value of Name)
> two instances of INTEGER (the values of Age and Rank)
> an instance of ADDRESS (the value of Address)
> an instance of DOLLAR (the value of Salary)
> an instance of OFFICE (the value of Office)
> an instance of MANAGER (the value of Manager)
> an instance of DEPARTMENT (the value of Department)

Hence, the following are true about each object:

1. The object is the instance of a class (its type).
2. The object has a state, which is the value of its instance variables.

In addition, each object has a *built-in* identity, which is independent of its class or state. The identity of an object is generated when the object is created; it is permanent, whereas the state of an object (i.e., the values of its instance variables) can change arbitrarily; thus, an office worker's address can change, but the identity remains the same. Object-oriented systems that support *strong* built-in identity also allow the object to undergo *structural* modifications (i.e., change its class) without any changes in its identity.

As discussed earlier, identity formalizes the notion of pointers used in more conventional languages. Without identity or another means of referencing objects independent of their state, it is impossible for the *same* object to be the value of the instance variable of more than one object. This can be demonstrated by two examples:

1. *Same address:* Assume that the office worker Mary Smith is married to John Smith and they live at the same address. If we do not have a mechanism whereby the instance variable values of Address in both objects have the same address object as values, it will be hard, if not impossible, to maintain consistency across all occurrences of this address value. Here, the value of an instance variable is overridden by another object.

2. *Same department:* In some cases, the state of the object that is the value of an instance variable can be modified. For instance, assume that Jim Brown and John Smith work in the same hardware department. If John's budget is changed, the budgets of all employees of the hardware department need to be updated consistently. Object identity makes this unnecessary because the systems contains only one copy of the hardware department instance.

An object's state is constructed from base values such as integers, character strings, and floating-point numbers. Using only base values of instance variables (Integers, character Strings, Floats, etc.) *without identity or object references,* objects can be shared using two possible solutions:

1. The first solution is object replication, illustrated in Figure 2.16. The instance JohnSmith and the instance MarySmith each replicate the address information. The main problems with replication are wasting storage space and maintaining consistency. Whenever an instance variable is updated, as in a statement that changes the value of the Address instance variable to NewAddress, that is,

   ```
   JohnSmith ChangeAddress NewAddress
   ```

   the user has to make sure that all addresses that must be the same as John's address are updated. Thus, the user must create and maintain auxiliary structures in order to preserve the semantic consistency of two people having the same address. The same is true when the following statement changes the budget of John Smith's department:

   ```
   JohnSmith ChangeBudget NewBudget
   ```

   Here, the user must access and update the budgets of all employees who work in the hardware department.

2. The second solution is commonly used in "identifier key" systems (such as relational databases). Here, tables containing all addresses or all departments are constructed. A table must have an identifier key such that each object has a unique key value. The key value is then stored in the referencing object. For instance, we can use the department name as the key value

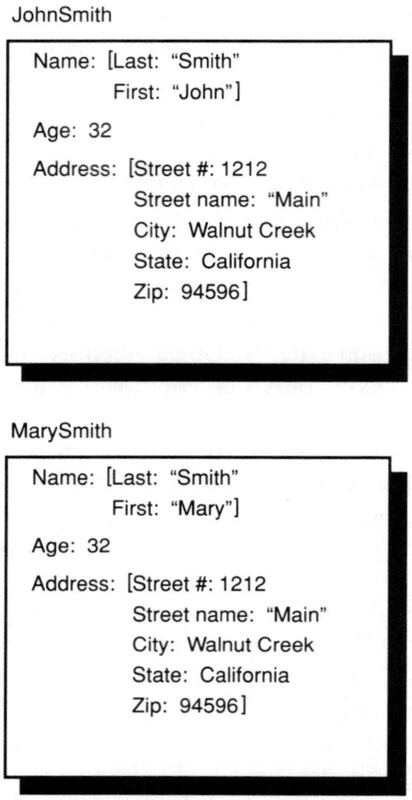

JohnSmith

Name: [Last: "Smith"
       First: "John"]

Age: 32

Address: [Street #: 1212
         Street name: "Main"
         City: Walnut Creek
         State: California
         Zip: 94596]

MarySmith

Name: [Last: "Smith"
       First: "Mary"]

Age: 32

Address: [Street #: 1212
         Street name: "Main"
         City: Walnut Creek
         State: California
         Zip: 94596]

Figure 2.16 Replicating the same address.

of a Departments table and store the same key value (i.e., the department name) in both John Smith's and Jim Brown's instances. This solution poses several problems. First, the Department instance variable is not storing an instance of class Department but rather a string of characters (the name of the department). Second, in order to retrieve or update any information for John's department, a "join" operation must be performed to match the name of the department stored in John's Department instance variable with a key value in the Departments collection or table. In other words, this scheme needs a declarative database query/retrieval sublanguage. This is *exactly* what happens in relational systems, in which the model imposes normalization constraints that force the retrieval of objects by matching key values in different tables.

Object identity does not require the overhead of replication and identifier key solutions. The use of identity allows a logical identifier (pointer) to be associated with each and every object in the system.

2.4.4   Object Spaces with Identity

Object spaces are built on top of base objects. The most common base object type, or class, is the integer. Other base object types are floating-point numbers, characters, and booleans. Objects that are instances of these types usually do not have instance variables. Instead, they are built-in object types, or classes, supported by the underlying system. In most cases, objects map directly onto object types that are directly supported by the underlying hardware.

Many object-oriented systems do not assign identities to base objects. For example, Smalltalk does not accept two different objects with the integer value of 5—only *one* integer 5 object can exist!

Smalltalk supports two equality predicates:

$$= =$$ to check for identical objects
$$=$$ to check for equality of object states

However, both of the following are true:

$$5 = = 5$$
$$5 = 5$$

Furthermore, the predicates

```
Integer new
```

and

```
Float new
```

generate errors.

The `new` message typically generates an identifier and associates it with the newly created object, but base objects don't have identifiers; their values are their identifiers.

Conceptually, an infinite pool of identifiers *I* exists such that

1. An identifier is associated with every nonbase object.
2. An identifier is associated with the object at object creation time *and remains associated with the object* regardless of any state or type modifications undergone by the object.
3. Each identifier can be associated with one and only one object. Furthermore, if there *is* an identifier in the system it *must* be associated with

an object. In other words, an object and its identifiers are indistinguishable. The identifier uniquely identifies the object, and the object remains associated with an identifier throughout its lifetime.

Therefore, each object has three properties:

1. The object is an instance of a class; this indicates the object's type.
2. The object has an identity; an identifier in I is associated with the object.
3. The object has a state; the state of an object is the object value of its instance variables. More specifically, if $A_{I1}, \ldots, A_{In}$ are the instance variables of an object O, the state of the object is

$$A_{I1} : i_1$$
$$A_{I2} : i_2$$
$$\vdots$$
$$A_{In} : i_n$$

where each `ij` is either an object identifier or a base object.

Figures 2.17 and 2.18 provide alternative graphical representations for objects. In Figure 2.18 identifiers are associated with nonbase objects (each object is framed in a rectangular box). Note that the identifier value of the `Department` instance variable for John Smith's department is a nonbase object. The identifier value of the `Department` instance variable for Jim

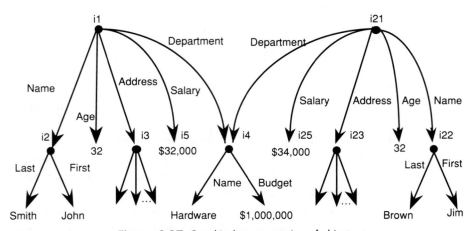

Figure 2.17 Graphical representation of objects.

Brown's department is the same. In other words, Jim and John *share* the same department value.

Figure 2.17 follows the representation of set and tuple models as in Bancilhon et al. (1987), Bancilhon and Khoshafian (1989), or Khoshafian (1989). Here, each object is labeled by an identifier, and for each instance variable (attribute in set and tuple models) there is a labeled and directed arc from the object to the value of the object. The label is the name of the instance variable, and the target is the value of the instance variable. As illustrated in the figure, the values of the Department instance variables of John and Jim are the same object. An alternative representation through rectangular boxes is illustrated in Figure 2.18.

The object space illustrated in Figure 2.17 is a *directed acyclic graph*. Actually, it is just as easy to represent graph-structured object spaces with arbitrary cycles. For instance, assume that each person has an additional instance variable Spouse. Then an office worker can reference his or her spouse and

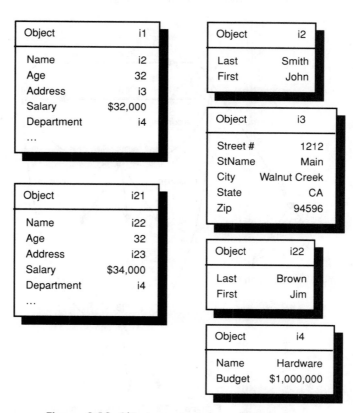

Figure 2.18 Objects represented as rectangular boxes.

be referenced back without constraints. This is illustrated in Figure 2.19. John and Mary also share their `Address` and `Children`.

As mentioned earlier, programming languages use virtual address pointers to achieve this object-referencing ability and to allow variables to point to the same object from multiple sources. In fact, pointers (or virtual memory addresses) can be used to *implement* object identity. The fundamental difference between object identity and virtual addresses, or pointers, is that identity is a semantic concept associated with objects whereas addresses represent memory locations of an underlying von Neumann machine.

▪ **2.5 OPERATIONS WITH IDENTITY**

Identity is the property of an object that distinguishes the object from all other objects in the computational environment. The type-state-identity trichotomy, discussed earlier, implies that there are several operations associated with object identity. The three most important categories of operations are

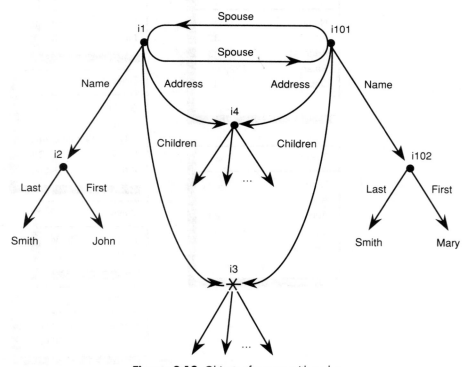

Figure 2.19 Object references with cycles.

- equality predicates
- copy operations
- merge and swap operations

2.5.1 The Different Facets of Equality

Understanding equality of the objects in an object-oriented system is fundamental to understanding the semantics of object states. Equality predicates partition the object space and determine when two objects can be treated as one or can be used interchangeably. As programming constructs, equality predicates are commonly used in loop structures (*WHILE* statements), *IF . . . THEN . . . ELSE* conditions, and *CASE* statements.

In conventional programming languages such as C or Pascal two types of objects can be compared using the equality predicate $=$:

- base objects such as integers, floating-point numbers, booleans, and characters
- references or pointers to records

Several languages have distinguished different forms of equality. A strongly typed language such as ML (Harper et al., 1986) provides a single overloaded predicate $=$ that indicates identity with references, equality with values, and recursive application of the record structure. In languages without strong typing, the distinction between predicates must be explicit. The Lisp family (Touretzky, 1984) traditionally provides *EQ*, which tests addresses and is hence implementation-dependent, and *EQUAL*, which tests for isomorphic structures.

Object-oriented languages must also provide predicates that distinguish between objects. Smalltalk (Goldberg and Robson, 1983) provides two predicates: an equivalence $= =$ that tests for the same object and an equality $=$ that is implemented separately for each class. The LDM (logical data model) of Kuper and Vardi (1984, 1985) distinguishes a "shallow" equality that compares the r-values of objects. So does FAD (Banreilhon et al., 1987).

With object-oriented systems that support object identity, a clean and rich collection of equality predicates can be supported. As described in Khoshafian and Copeland (1986), there are three facets of equality in object models: identity predicate, shallow-equality predicate, and deep-equality predicate.

Identity Predicate (Identical)

The identity predicate corresponds to the equality of references or pointers in conventional languages; it checks whether the object identities are the same.

With the semantics of object identity, if the object identities are the same, the objects are the same. Both SIMULA and Smalltalk support this predicate, which is indicated by $==$.

Consider Figure 2.20, where there are three instances of `Person`; for each instance the `Name`, `Age`, and `Address` are indicated. In addition, the object identifiers of only the structured person and address objects are indicated. Here the `Address` of John and Mary is the *same* identical object. In other words,

`O1.Address == O2.Address`

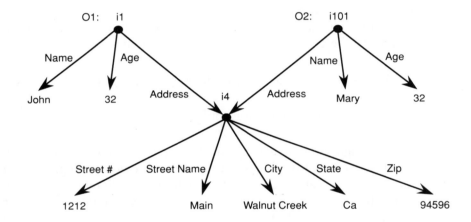

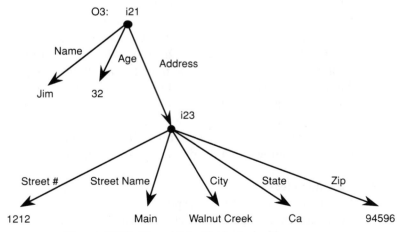

Figure 2.20 O1 and O2 with identical addresses.

is TRUE. Jim, who happens to live at the same physical address, has a *different* object value for O3.Address. In other words, although the *content* of the Address attribute of Jim is the same as that of John and Mary, the Address instance variable, or attribute value, of Jim is a *different* object (identifier i23) than the Address of Mary or John (identifier i4). Therefore,

O3.Address == O1.Address

and

O3.Address == O2.Address

are both FALSE.

Shallow-Equality Predicate (Shallow-Equal)

Two objects are shallow-equal if their *states*, or contents, are identical. In other words, two objects are shallow-equal if they are instances of the same class and the values they take on every instance variable are identical—corresponding instance variables cannot merely have the same object contents but must be identical objects. Two objects could be different but still shallow-equal. The syntax for shallow equality in SIMULA and Smalltalk is = .

Figure 2.21 illustrates two objects that have *different* objects as the values of their Children instance variables. Therefore, in this case

O1.Children == O2.Children

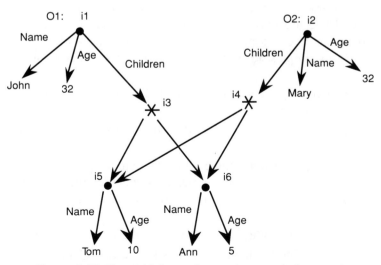

Figure 2.21 The Children of O1 and O2 are shallow-equal.

is FALSE. However, the *content* of O1 is identical to the content of O2; O1 and O2 have the *same* children objects. Thus,

O1.Children = O2.Children

is TRUE.

To demonstrate shallow equality with instance variables, consider the rectangles in Figure 2.22. Each rectangle has two instance variables representing its lower left and upper right vertices, respectively. In this example

REC1 = REC2

is TRUE. In other words, REC1 is shallow-equal to REC2. This is because the values of the corresponding instance variables of REC1 and REC2 are identical. That is,

REC1.LowerLeft == REC2.LowerLeft

and

REC1.UpperRight == REC2.UpperRight

are both TRUE.

Deep-Equality Predicate (Deep-Equal)

The third (and in a sense weakest) type of equality is value-based deep equality. There are two forms of deep equality, depending upon whether or not the predicate is checking for the isomorphism of the object graphs.

In its simplest form deep equality ignores object identities and checks whether

1. two objects are instances of the same class (have the same structure or type)
2. the values of corresponding base objects are the same

Figure 2.23 illustrates three arrays that are deep-equal to one another; all are one-dimensional arrays of three elements. Each element of each array is an instance of an *XY*-point. Furthermore, in all three arrays,

The value of the *X*-axis of the first element is 3.
The value of the *Y*-axis of the first element is 2.

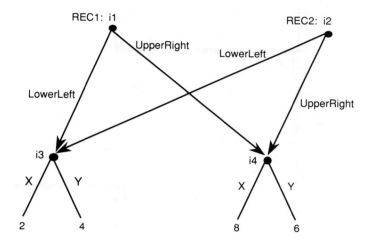

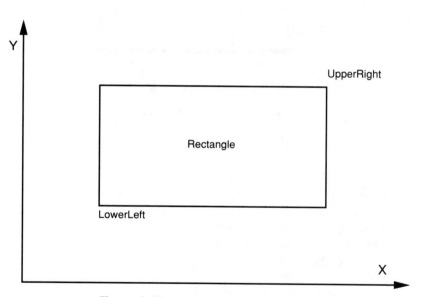

Figure 2.22 REC1 is shallow equal to REC2.

The value of the *X*-axis of the second element is 3.
The value of the *Y*-axis of the second element is 2.
The value of the *X*-axis of the third element is 4.
The value of the *Y*-axis of the third element is 6.

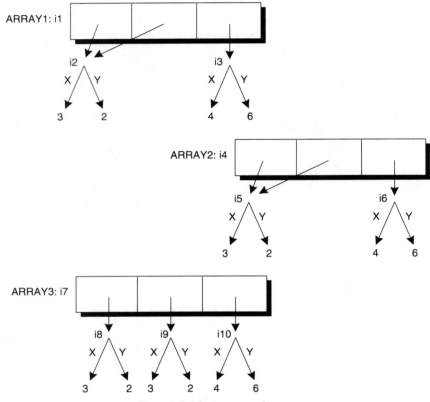

Figure 2.23 Deep-equal arrays.

Therefore,

```
ARRAY1 deep-equal ARRAY2
ARRAY2 deep-equal ARRAY3
ARRAY1 deep-equal ARRAY3
```

are all TRUE.

You may realize that ARRAY1 and ARRAY2 are more similar to each other; both arrays contain two objects rather than three. Furthermore, the first and second elements in both arrays are the *same* object. This is not the case for ARRAY3, which contains three different objects.

It is therefore possible to define a more restrictive form of deep equality and to require that the graphs of the two objects be isomorphic, preserving the sharing of references or the cycles in their corresponding subobjects. In this sense:

```
ARRAY1 deep-equal ARRAY2
```

is TRUE, but

```
ARRAY1 deep-equal ARRAY3
ARRAY2 deep-equal ARRAY3
```

are both FALSE.

Summary

In summary, there are three types of equality:

1. Identical, which checks whether two objects are the same.
2. Shallow, which goes one level deep and compares corresponding identities of the values of the instance variables or elements of the object.
3. Deep, which compares the contents of corresponding base objects. There are two forms of deep equality: a weaker one that checks only for equality of the corresponding base object and a stronger one that also checks for the isomorphism of the graphs of the objects.

Each predicate defines an equivalence relation on the object space. In other words, the following relationships hold:

1. *Reflexive:* Each object is (identical, shallow, deep) equal to itself.
2. *Symmetric:* If *O1* is (identical, shallow, deep) equal to *O2*, then *O2* is (identical, shallow, deep) equal to *O1*.
3. *Transitive:* If *O1* is (identical, shallow, deep) equal to *O2* and *O2* is (identical, shallow, deep) equal to *O3*, then *O1* is(identical, shallow, deep) equal to *O3*.

The strongest form of equality is identical. Shallow equality is stronger than deep equality. In other words, two identical objects are also shallow-equal and deep-equal (after all, they are the same object). Two shallow-equal objects are also deep-equal.

2.5.2 Facets of Copying

The previous section presented several facets of equivalence relationships between objects. The most powerful of these, the identical predicate, is used to check whether two variables refer to the same object. For instance, in Smalltalk/V we can create a new Complex number object as follows:

```
C1 := Complex new
```

and execute the variable assignment

```
C2 := C1
```

Then the value of C2 == C1 will be TRUE. C1 and C2 will be two global variables that refer to the same object.

Similarly, object-oriented systems that support object identity promote two facets of object copying: *shallow-copy* and *deep-copy*. Both operations create and return a new object.

Shallow-Copy

The shallow-copy message creates a new object that has instance variables with values *identical* to the instance variables of the target object. Hence, if

```
O2 := O1 shallowCopy
```

then O1 = O2 (i.e., O1 shallow-equal O2) is TRUE. However, O1 == O2 is FALSE: O1 and O2 are *different* objects. For example, either of the rectangle objects in Figure 2.22 could have been created through the shallowCopy operation. In other words,

```
REC2 := REC1 shallowCopy
```

would have yielded the REC2 object that shares its instance variable values with REC1, as illustrated in the figure.

If we have a collection object such as a set, the shallow-copy message will create a new object whose contents will be the same as the contents of the target object. For example, either of the sets of children illustrated in Figure 2.21 could have been created through the shallowCopy operation. That is,

```
O2.Children := O1.Children shallowCopy
```

would have generated the same sharing of children between John and Mary as shown in Figure 2.19.

Deep Copy

Conceptually, the deep-copy message creates a new object that has instance variables with entirely new values such that the new object is deep-equal to the target object. Every subobject that is reachable from the root of the object created as a result of the deep-copy operation will be a *new* object. The newly created copy does not share any component (or element, if the copy is either a collection or the value of an instance variable) with the original target object.

As mentioned earlier there are two facets of deep equality: one that checks for the isomorphism of the graphs of the objects and another weaker one that just checks for the equality of corresponding base objects. Corresponding to these two types of deep equality there are two types of deep-copy. For example, ARRAY2 of Figure 2.23 could have been created through a deepCopy message:

ARRAY2 := ARRAY1 deepCopy

which preserves the graph of the target object. In terms of implementation, it is easier to support the weaker form of deep-copy, which just traverses the object and creates copies of each subobject (values of instance variables or elements in collection objects). Thus,

ARRAY3 := ARRAY1 deepCopy

2.5.3 Merging and Swapping

Additional operations associated with object models support identity. One of the more interesting operations is *merging*. For example, two objects with separate identities may later be discovered to be the same and therefore need to be merged.

Codd (1979) has argued for a "coalescing" operator in RM/T that merges identity. This operator checks whether all corresponding instance variables of two objects are equal (=); if so it makes one object identical to the other, such that all references to either object are now to one and the same object. The support of object merging is useful in statistical databases when an attempt is made to merge information gathered by different sources. This is called record linking (Wrigley, 1973; Howe and Lindsay, 1981), in which records that contain different sorts of information about the same objects are coalesced.

Note that merging is an updating operation whose semantics and support could be tricky and difficult to implement. The simplest approach is to impose the following two requirements:

1. The two objects must be instances of the same class (and hence the same type).
2. The two objects must be deep-equal.

Then, all that we need to do is be sure that all of the references to the old objects and their subcomponents refer to the merged object and its subcomponents.

It is possible to make merging more sophisticated and to provide support for merging differently structured objects. Figure 2.24 illustrates the merging of tuples O3 and O6. Before the merge, O1.b and O2.c referenced the same object O3; similarly, O4.f and O5.g referenced the same object O6. Objects

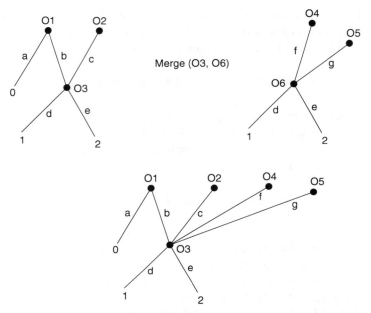

Figure 2.24 Merging O3 and O6.

O3 and O6 were different objects. After the merge, the objects O1.b, O2.c, O4.f, and O5.g all reference the same object.

Smalltalk does not support the merge operation as described here; instead it provides a become: method. That is, when the statement

```
O1 become: O2
```

is executed, the identifiers of O1 and O2 are interchanged. This means that objects that were referencing or accessing O1 (O2) will now be accessing O2 (O1). For example, assume that John is in office OF1001 and Tim is in office OF2002. If John and Tim swap offices, all we have to do is execute the statement

```
John getOffice become: Tim getOffice
```

If John is the assistant of his manager Mary and Mary has an instance variable, officeofAssistant, then *before* John's office became Tim's office, the statement

```
Mary getofficeOfAssistant officeName
```

would have returned OF1001. *After* the swapping, the same message to Mary would return OF2002. Similarly, *all* direct reference to John's old office would automatically refer to John's new office.

As another example, using rectangular boxes for objects, Figure 2.25 shows what happens when John's home address becomes Jim's home address (i.e., John and Jim interchange houses). In that case, objects such as Jim's children, spouse, parents, and friends, which were referencing his old address, will automatically reference his new address. The same holds for John. This scheme avoids all of the headaches of address changes and forwarding addresses.

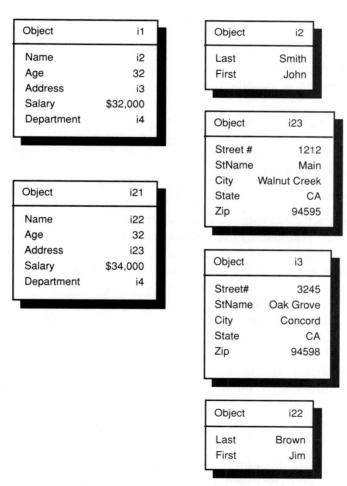

Figure 2.25 John's Address becomes Jim's Address.

2.5.4 Advantages of Object Identity

Object identity offers several advantages:

1. It allows the direct representation of graph-structured objects.
2. Users do not need to maintain referential integrity.
3. All memory or database-dangling reference problems are resolved.
4. The various operations (predicates, copying, etc.) associated with object identity provide powerful object manipulation functionalities for intelligent office objects.

■ 2.6 SUMMARY

The preceding sections have described the main concepts of object orientation and their applicability to intelligent offices. The main concepts of object orientation appear in its definition,

Object orientation = abstract data typing + inheritance + object identity

Each of these concepts provides advantages for the modeling and implementation of object-oriented database applications.

Abstract data typing models various *classes* of an application, where each class instance has a *protocol*; a set of messages to which it can respond. With abstract data types there is a clear separation between the *external* interface of a data type and its *internal* implementation. The implementation of an abstract data type is *hidden*. Hence, alternative implementations could be used for the same abstract data type without changing its interface.

In most object-oriented systems, abstract data types are implemented through *classes*. A class is like a factory that produces *instances*, each with the same structure and behavior. A class has a name, a collection of operations for manipulating its instances, and a representation. The operations that manipulate the instances of a class are called *methods*. The state, or representation, of an instance is stored in *instance variables*. The methods are invoked by sending *messages* to the instances. Sending messages to objects (instances) is similar to calling procedures in conventional programming languages. However, message sending is more dynamic.

Inheritance organizes the classes of object spaces in inheritance class hierarchies. Through inheritance we can build new software modules (e.g., classes) on top of an existing hierarchy of modules. This avoids redesigning and recoding everything from scratch. New classes can *inherit* both the behavior (operations, methods, etc.) and the representation (instance variables, attributes, etc.) from existing classes.

Inheriting behavior enables *code sharing* (and hence reusability) among software modules. Inheriting representation enables *structure sharing* among data objects. The combination of these two types of inheritance provides a powerful modeling and software development strategy.

Inheritance is achieved by *specializing* existing classes. Classes can be specialized by extending their representation (instance variables) or behavior (operations). Alternatively, classes can be specialized by *restricting* the representation or operations of existing classes. It is also useful to allow the *generalization* of existing class hierarchies and to build more general classes from existing, more specialized subclasses.

Inheritance also organizes the classes of object-oriented database applications. Object identity organizes the *instances* of persistent classes of object-oriented databases. Identity is a property of an object that distinguishes the object from all other objects in the application. In programming languages identity is realized through memory addresses. In databases identity is realized through identifier keys. User-specified names are used both in languages and in databases to give unique names to objects. Each of these schemes compromises identity.

In a complete object-oriented system, each object is given an identity that is permanently associated with the object, immaterial of the object's *structural* or *state* transitions. The identity of an object is also independent of the *location*, or address, of the object. With object identity users can *referentially share* objects. Object identity provides the most natural modeling primitive to allow the same object be a subobject of multiple parent objects. It allows objects to be referentially shared, and it supports the construction of complex/compound object spaces. These object spaces are most natural and direct in various object-oriented database applications such as CAD, CAM, CASE, and intelligent offices.

3

MODELING AND DESIGN FOR OBJECT-ORIENTED DATABASES

As discussed in Chapter 2, object orientation attempts to model the real world as directly as possible. In other words, the fundamental object-oriented concepts (abstract data typing, inheritance, and object identity) provide a framework whereby programmers can easily model, prototype, and implement real-world applications.

The goal of data modeling in database management systems is similar. In the context of database management systems a *data model* specifies the structure and operations for persistent databases. Depending upon the particular model, there are great variations in the representation and manipulation capabilities of the models.

Many times real-world conceptual paradigms are not mapped directly to structures supported by the data model of a database management system. For these cases there are algorithms available to map a real-world model to a database model. This mapping is illustrated in Figure 3.1. The transformation corresponds to the mapping. The real-world model is often called the *conceptual model* of a problem domain.

When designing database applications for a particular database management system, a designer goes through a number of steps. These steps map the conceptual model of the database management system onto constructs represented

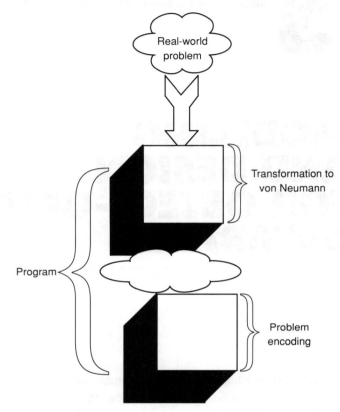

Figure 3.1 Conventional programming.

through the *data definition language* of the database management systems. The definition of the structure of a database for a problem domain is called the *schema* of the database.

■ 3.1 CHAPTER ORGANIZATION

The rest of the chapter is organized as follows. Section 3.2 discusses a three-layered architecture as it applies to object-oriented databases. Section 3.3 provides an overview of object-oriented analysis and design. Section 3.4 discusses the predecessors of object-oriented databases, namely network, hierarchical, and relational models. Section 3.5 concentrates on set-and-tuple complex object models. Section 3.6 presents some interesting algebraic operators for complex object models. With the background of Section 3.2–3.6, Section 3.7 goes deeper into modeling of object-oriented databases. Section 3.8 discusses all of the integrity constraints that *could* be incorporated into object-oriented databases.

■ 3.2. THREE-LAYERED ANSI/SPARC ARCHITECTURE FOR OBJECT-ORIENTED DBMSs

In database management system applications, the database professional (in most cases the *database administrator*, or DBA) is responsible for tailoring the conceptual structure, the physical auxiliary structures, the integrity rules, and the security control for particular applications and problem domains. Therefore, the database professional must be concerned with the *conceptual design* as well as the *physical design* of the database. The conceptual design is primarily concerned with the specification of the *enterprise* model, which is shared by all users of a corporation. The physical design is concerned with the placement of the database onto physical storage and the subsequent efficient access and manipulation of the database.

The ANSI/SPARC Study Group for database management systems has proposed an ANSI/SPARC architecture standard, as illustrated in Figure 3.2.

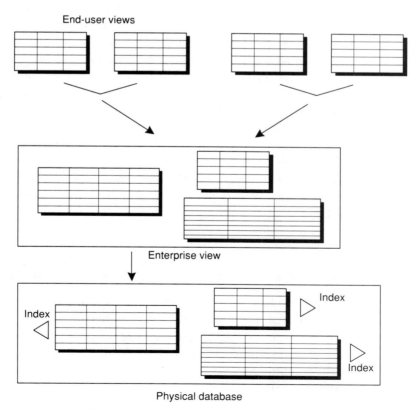

Figure 3.2 The ANSI/SPARC architecture standard.

Although initially proposed for network, hierarchical, and relational DBMSs, this architecture is neverless applicable to object-oriented database applications as well, especially intelligent office applications. The standard recognizes three user classes and levels:

1. **End users.** End users are nontechnical users who run programs that access specific components of a corporate database. These users access the external level of the architecture, also called a *logical view* of the database.

2. **Enterprise users.** The second class is the enterprise. The global conceptual corporate database is shared by all end-users. This corresponds to the *conceptual level* of the architecture. In some cases the conceptual level is obtained by integrating several individual views or external schemata. Corresponding to this level, the *conceptual schema* models the persistent objects in a business. In object-orinted databases both views and conceptual persistent object schemata could be used to construct the conceptual schemata. In a particular application the end-user external schemata are built on top of a common conceptual design.

3. **Database professionals.** The third class is the database professionals, or DBAs. In addition to designing the conceptual schema, the DBA designs and specifies different aspects of the *physical databases* (which are stored in persistent storage media). This corresponds to the *internal* (or storage) *level*. Mapping a conceptual schema onto an internal physical schema involves the following:

   - Additional integrity constraints
   - Specification of auxiliary structures such as indexes on collections
   - Specification of data placement and clustering strategies
   - Possible replication of data

■ 3.3 OVERVIEW OF OBJECT-ORIENTED ANALYSIS AND DESIGN

As stated earlier, object-oriented systems attempt to model and implement real-world problems as directly and easily as possible. To achieve this in an object-oriented development environment we need to define the problem (functional specification), perform object-oriented analysis, and create and implement the design. This section provides an overview of these phases of development for object-oriented systems.

3.3.1 Defining the Problem

Before solving any problems using an object-oriented database, we must have a *high-level requirement specification*, which, among other things, it is used to specify the following:

> *The functionality:* What capabilities do the different components of the system provide the user?
>
> *The paradigm:* What type of interaction-of-execution model does the system provide to the user?
>
> *The environment:* where or on what systems and platforms is the system supported?
>
> *The interfaces:* What are the user-interface paradigms used for the system?

3.3.2 Performing the Analysis

Once the high-level requirement specification is complete, the next step is to perform an *object-oriented analysis* (OOA) of the system. The analysis provides a detailed description, which is complete, consistent, readable, and reviewable by different interested people and can be tested against reality.

Object-oriented analysis provides a detailed description of the system using the symbolism and methodology of the system's object-oriented design. The object-oriented analysis will be incorporated into the object-oriented design (OOD) of the software. The object-oriented design phase provides detailed specifications for the classes of the problem/product domain and *specifies additional support classes for the implementation.* Hence, the classes and the class definitions will be used as the functional specification for the code base.

Object-oriented analysis is language-independent, and the classes defined in this phase are conceptual. Some classes will be implemented directly; others will need to be mapped to implementation classes in OOD. This is illustrated in Figure 3.3.

3.3.3 Designing Object-Oriented Systems

Although there are many proposals and strategies for designing object-oriented systems (see, for example, Wirfs-Brock et al., 1990; Booch, 1991; Coad and Yordon, 1991; and others), most experts agree on two aspects of the design of an object-oriented application: static and dynamic design.

The static aspects concern the definition of the entities (classes), their attributes (instance variables), their relationship (inheritance, one-to-one, one-to-many, and many-to-many), the static behavior of their instances (operations,

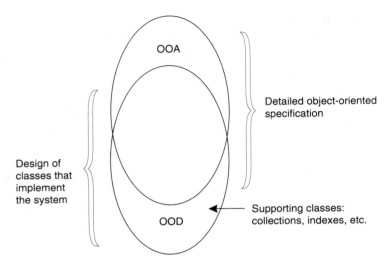

Figure 3.3 Object-Oriented analysis and design.

member functions), and so on. Dynamic aspects concern behavior of the objects during the operation of the system. Design of the dynamic aspects includes state transition, data flow diagrams, and dynamic relationships between objects. A complete specification and design of an object-oriented system must incorporate both of these aspects.

The Major Steps

Roughly, the top-down design of object-oriented databases involves the following steps:

1. Specifying end-user views and models
2. Merging external end-user views and models to generate the conceptual model
3. Mapping the conceptual model onto the persistent classes of the object-oriented databases
4. Implementing the physical design

Throughout this discussion *entities* and classes are used interchangably.

STEP 1: Identify Classes (Entities), Relationships, Operations (Methods and Behavior), and Integrity Constraints of the Problem Domain for End Users.

This step involves understanding the problem domain for particular users. In this step classes, relationships between classes, and operations of the problem domain are identified. Both static (definition of classes) and dynamic (interaction between objects, state transition, etc.) aspects of the behavior of classes are identified. All operations that need to be performed for each end-user entity are identified. All *constraints* specific to end-user needs are also identified. Through this step the object-oriented database designer models the problem domain of the individual user views or business functions; this step corresponds to the external level of the three-layered architecture. Therefore, this step lets you specify the following:

The classes, or entities, that is, the people, places, environment, objects, events, roles, etc., that correspond to the concurrently shared persistent object classes.

The operations, functions, or methods on these classes, such as the average salary of people and the area of a house.

The relationships, whereby classes could be related to one another through either *inheritance* relationships or *composition* relationships. As dicussed in Chapter 2, the former indicates that one class inherits both structure and behavior from another (e.g., `OfficeWorker` is a `Person`). The latter takes on many forms but basically indicates that an entity either contains or references other entities; it allows the definition of complex objects.

The integrity constraints, whereby a database management system (including object-oriented databases) maintains a database in a consistent state. Consistent states of databases are expressed through integrity constraints or business rules that reflect acceptable database values or states.

STEP 2: Merge Views.
The integration of the different user views into one global and consistent business entity-relationship (ER) model involves *merging* the different entities (class definitions) and relationships into one consistent model. The resulting model incorporates all of the individual user views. This step constructs the logic of the business and hence corresponds to the second logical level of the three-layered architecture described earlier.

STEP 3: Map the Object-Oriented Database Design onto the Underlying Object-Oriented Database.
Since object-oriented databases (in general) allow the representation of general graph-structured object spaces, the mapping of the entity-relationship diagram or object-oriented design (representing the classes and their relationship) onto the *schema* of the object-oriented database should be relatively straightforward. This mapping involves the definition of the *structure* (instance variables or

attributes) of the persistent object types as well as the *behavior*, or the operations (methods). Note that this is in sharp contrast with the *normalization* that needs to be performed for relational databases.

STEP 4:   Implement the Physical Design.

From the specifications of the problem domain and the different applications of the enterprise being modeled, the database professional subsequently needs to specify a number of performance-tuning constructs and auxiliary structures. These include storage clusters, indexes, and data replication.

3.3.4   Developing Front-Ends and Applications for Object-Oriented DBMSs

One of the most fundamental advantages of object orientation is the fact that object-oriented databases alleviate the mismatch between the host programming language and the embedded database language:

> One problem in developing database applications is the *impedance mismatch* between the data manipulation language (DML) of the database, and the general-purpose programming language in which the rest of the application is written. . . . There are two aspects of this mismatch. One is the difference in programming paradigms. . . . The other aspect is the mismatch of type systems. (Zdonik and Maier, 1990)

Setting aside solutions offered by, say, 4GL database languages, one important offering of object-oriented database management systems is the possibility of developing the entire application in *a single environment, using a single (powerful) programming language*. To perform this task, the database developer needs to incorporate a uniform mechanism for integrating the persistent and transient object types into the software design. In the application it is possible that the front-end component will use a substantial percentage of the code. Furthermore, just as the persistent object space of the object-oriented database management system (OODBMS) is in some cases defined through a C++ class hierarchy, the graphical user interface could be defined through a C++ class hierarchy.

The object-oriented design, therefore, should incorporate not only the persistent objects but also the entire application, including the front-end. Section 3.7 illustrates a graphical object-oriented design symbolism that identifies persistent classes and their relationships in a complete OODBMS application.

■   3.4   TRADITIONAL DATABASES AND DATA MODELS

Before discussing various models of object-oriented databases a brief overview of traditional data models is appropriate. This discussion is important since, even though object-oriented databases became commercial in the mid-1980s with products such as ServioLogic's GemStone, Graphael's G-base, and Ontologic's Vbase, the vast majority of commercial database management systems are based on the more traditional models and products in terms of both the installed base (existing DBMSs) and the purchase of new DBMSs. This trend is expected to continue, with new OODBMSs concentrating more on niche markets.

Another reason why "traditional" models, especially the relational model, are important is that, although there are a number of emerging object-oriented database companies, relational (as well as some network and hierarchical) DBMSs are starting to incorporate object-oriented features. In fact, because of the proven technologies, extensive standardization efforts, and large installed bases, it is likely that the application of object-oriented concepts and techniques will be more prominent through object-oriented extensions of these traditional models than through entirely new OODBMSs. This, of course, remains to be seen.

The next three sections give a brief overview of the three traditional database models, namely, hierarchical, network, and relational.

3.4.1 Hierarchical Data Models

DBMSs based on the hierarchical data model were perhaps the earliest database management systems that became commercially available. Among these DBMSs, the information management system IMS from IBM, which became commercially available in 1968, is perhaps the best-known and most popular hierarchical DBMS. IMS is primarily a mainframe DBMS running under MVS. Another popular hierarchical DBMS product is System 2000 from SAS Institute. System 2000 was originally marketed by MRI and then later by Intel Corporation.

The hierarchical data model represents the structure of the persistent database as a collection (forest) of trees, where each node of the tree represents a set of objects (records) of the same type. A *node* is either a *root node*, without a parent, or a *child node,* with one and only one *parent node.* Child nodes that are not at the leaves of the hierarchy are also parent nodes. The main restriction of the hierarchical model is that each child can have one and only one parent. Furthermore, the *relationships* between parents and children are *one-to-many.* Briefly, in a one-to-many relationship the *parent* (the one side of the relationship) contains or references zero or more children (the *many* side of the relationship). This is similar to a set-valued attribute in complex object models, which will be discussed in Section 3.5.

Figure 3.4 illustrates a hierarchical representation of intelligent office container objects, rooted at Desktop. The rectangle labeled Desktop represents

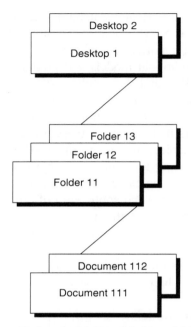

Figure 3.4 A hierarchical representation of desktops, folders, and documents.

all of the `Desktop` instances in the persistent database. Each of these desktops can contain a set of folders and a set of devices. Each folder contains a set of documents. Given the restrictions of the hierarchical model, each folder can belong to one and only one desktop. Similarly, each document can belong to one and only one folder.

Two representation restrictions of the hierarchical model are as follows:

1. Each child record type can have only one parent record type. For instance, documents cannot be elements of desktops *and* folders.
2. Only one-to-many relationships are supported. This means that the *same* document cannot be in more than one folder. In a model supporting many-to-many relationships directly a document will be contained in *many* folders, and a folder will contain *many* documents.

Several techniques and constructs have been introduced in hierarchical DBMSs to resolve the restrictions. The most notable is *virtual records*. By placing records in one place and *referencing* through virtual records one can represent many-to-many relationships and also have the same record type be a member in multiple "parent" node types. Figure 3.5 illustrates how virtual records can be used to represent the many-to-many relationship between `OfficeWorkers` and `Departments`.

Although hierarchical products support a variety of access modes, overall data manipulation is navigational. This means that the accessing of records of a *child* node is achieved by hierarchically traversing the parents of the nodes. For instance, to retrieve a particular document, we must

1. Retrieve a particular `Desktop` (say, `JohnsDesktop`)
2. Retrieve a particular `Folder` from the children of `JohnsDesktop`, that is, a folder that is contained in `JohnsDesktop` (say, a folder called `ResumeFolder`).
3. Retrieve the particular résumé document (say, for `RobertSmith`) contained within `ResumeFolder`

The sequence is

`JohnsDesktop` → `ResumeFolder` → `RobertSmith` résumé document

The key point is that (in the absence of virtual records and other techniques for *direct* references) the only way to retrieve and manipulate the `RobertSmith` resume document is through this path.

3.4.2 Network Model

In the 1950s and 1960s *data definition* products were developed by large companies such as IBM, General Electric, and Honeywell. These products

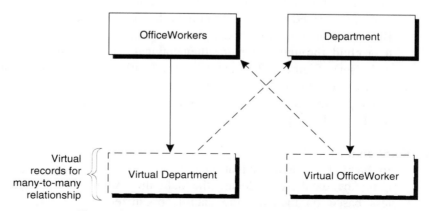

Figure 3.5 Virtual records for many-to-many relationship.

permitted the description of the structure of databases that were accessed by many users. The earlier data definition products eventually evolved into COBOL, developed by CODASYL in 1960. The COBOL language had a *DATA DIVISION* construct that separated the description of the data or the database from the routines that accessed and updated the data.

The CODASYL Language Committee eventually proposed an extension of COBOL for databases. The group commissioned for this task was the Data Base Task Group (DBTG). In 1969, DBTG defined the Data Description Language (DDL) and the Data Manipulation Language (DML) for databases. This laid the foundation for *network* database management systems. The DBTG specification was preceded and influenced by a product from General Electric called IDS (Integrated Data Store), which was available in the early 1960s. Other early network database products were IDMS from Cullinet (1970), DMS 1100 from Sperry (1971), and IDS-2 from Honeywell Information Systems (1975). Another popular network model is TOTAL.

The network model is more general than the hierarchical model. Although the only type of relationship supported by the network model is one-to-many, it is possible for the same record type to be a child, or a *member*, with multiple parent, or *owner*, record types.

In the network model record types represent the entities, and sets represent the one-to-many relationships. Keep in mind that the word *set* in this context is used for the one-to-many relationship between owner and member.

Figure 3.6 illustrates a schema that can be supported directly by the network model. Here, folders are members of not only desktops but also drawers of cabinets. Similarly, drawers are members of not only cabinets but also desktops.

Accessing particular objects in a network model is similar to accessing them in a hierarchical model. Again, although there are different access constructs supported by various products, the access mode is basically navigational. But with the network model the navigation is richer since we can navigate to a child through one path, then navigate to a parent (owner) from another path (set). Figure 3.7 illustrates a navigation from a particular desktop to a folder, then from the folder to a drawer and from the drawer to its owner desktop. Here a folder on John's desktop is contained in a drawer belonging to Mary's desktop.

3.4.3 Relational Model

In hierarchical and navigational databases the application programmers *navigate* the database to locate the data they want. The navigation is more or less based on the way the data is organized in the underlying system (in, say, secondary storage devices). This causes many problems; for example, any reorganization of the underlying data means that all application programs

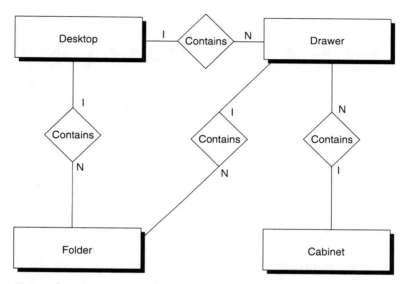

Figure 3.6 One-to-many relationships supported directly by the network model.

have to be rewritten. In other words, the hierarchical and navigational models do not support *data independence*, which isolates users from changes in the underlying physical storage structures of the databases.

Motivated by the needs of a more *declarative* data model, Dr. E. F. Codd in the early 1970s came up with the *relational data model*. Since then relational database management systems have mushroomed. In fact, in terms of *new* purchases and installation of DBMSs, relational databases dominate all other DBMSs combined. This trend is expected to continue well into the 21st

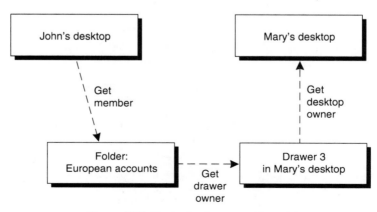

Figure 3.7 Navigation in a network model.

century. With "downsizing" and the emergence of client/server architectures many networked environments and applications are starting to use relational database servers (SQL servers) as their persistent repositories (Khoshafian et al., 1992a).

Relational databases are *declarative*. This means that they remove the burden of specifying how to access server data. Instead, applications concentrate on *what* they need from the database. Besides freeing the applications from possible modifications to the underlying physical databases, "data independence frees developers from having to perform complex query processing or having to spend countless hours tuning application code to run in particular configurations" (Khoshafian et al., 1992a).

In the relational world, a database structure is a collection of *relations*, or *tables*. Each table is organized into rows and columns. The persistent objects of an application are captured in these tables, as illustrated in Figure 3.8.

Three main components form a relational database: *structure*, integrity constraints, and instances (or rows of records) in each relation. The first and second components deal with the overall structure of the database (the meta-

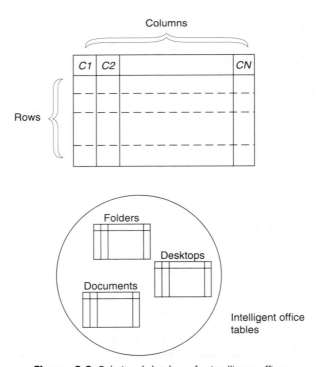

Figure 3.8 Relational database for intelligent offices.

data); the third component deals with the *population* of the database with data objects.

1. **Structure.** The database consists of a collection of tables, or *relations*, $R_1, \ldots, R_n$. Each table R_i has columns $C_{i1}, \ldots, C_{im}$. Each column C_{ij} has a *type* that represents a set of permissible values called its *domain*. This type indicates that the column values will be elements of the particular domain. Tables can be *base tables* or *view tables*. Base tables are the actual data stored in the database. View tables, also called views, are tables produced from relational commands that operate on the base tables. These virtual tables don't actually exist in the database. Rather, they are produced upon request by a user and are defined in terms of one or more base tables. The specification of the tables (base or views), their columns, and the types of the columns are part of the *schema* of the database. A database management system uses a data definition language (DDL) to *define* the schemata of persistent databases. Throughout this book, the terms *table* and *relation* are interchangeable; in some cases, the words *column* and *attribute* are also interchangeable.

2. **Integrity constraints.** The integrity constraints on individual relations (column values and row values) of an individual table or the *constraints on relationships* between values in multiple tables are defined in the schema by means of the DDL.

3. **Instances, or rows of records, in each relation.** Each relation in a populated database contains zero or more rows. The values and structure of these rows are determined by the schema of the database. If r is a row in relation R_i, then it will have values (some of which could be *NULL*) for columns C_{i1} through C_{in} of R_i. The dot "." notation $r.C_{ij}$ is used to indicate the C_{ij} column value of r. As mentioned earlier, the term *attribute* is used for C_{ij}; thus, r has attributes $C_{i1}, \ldots, C_{in}$, and its C_{ij} attribute value is $r\dot{C}_{ij}$. The actual querying, inserting, deleting, and updating of rows of relations is done through a *data manipulation language* (DML).

In a relational database, the same information can be structured in many ways. For instance, we can have a database $D1$ with 3 tables (relations) and a database $D2$ with 10 tables *both containing exactly the same information*. In fact, the number of tables containing the same persistent database information can range from one to almost the total number of columns in the database, as illustrated in Figure 3.9. Specification of the number and structure of the database tables is part of the database design and is typically done by database professionals.

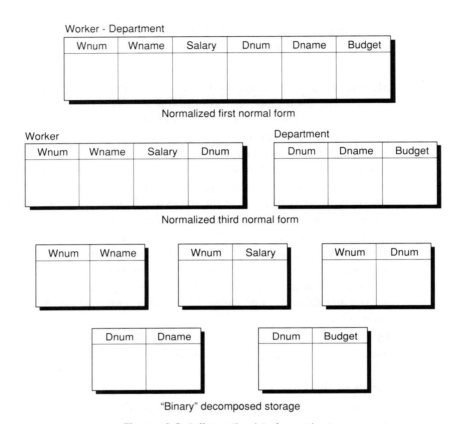

Figure 3.9 Different "levels" of normalization.

The relational model imposes the *first normal form constraint* on databases. The first normal form constraint of the relational model differs from the network and hierarchical models; it requires the attribute (column) values in a relation to be only atomic. More specifically, if *R* is a relation with columns $C_1, \ldots, C_n$, then the domain of each C_{ij} must be the domain of an atomic type (such as an integer, character string, or date). In particular, the C_{ij} values cannot contain *repeating groups* (i.e., sets of atomic values or sets of tuples).

Figure 3.10 illustrates the office automation example of Figure 3.6, which was modeled in accordance with the network model as a collection of tables. Unlike the previous examples in Figures 3.4 and 3.6, here some of the attributes or columns of the tables have been indicated. In particular, columns whose values are keys in other tables have been indicated. When a key of a table *T*1 (the *referenced* table) appears as column values in another table (say *T*2, the *referencing* table), it is called a *foreign key* in the referencing table. For instance,

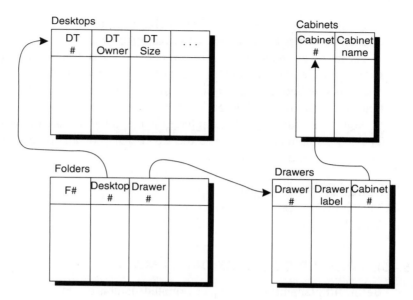

(a) Desktops, cabinets, folders, and drawers

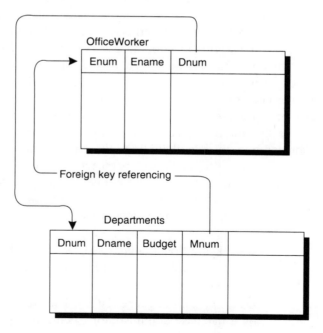

(b) OfficeWorkers and Departments tables foreign key references

Figure 3.10 Intelligent office tables with foreign keys.

Desktop # and Drawer # are foreign keys in the table Folders. Similarly, Cabinet# is a foreign key in the table Drawers.

As far as the manipulation of the persistent databases is concerned, the query language in relational database management systems is declarative, and the interrelationships between the various entities (tables) is achieved through predicates that perform *joins* on foreign keys.

SQL (Structured Query Language) is the defacto standard relational language. The SQL statement to retrieve the Category of all folders that are contained in John's desktop is as follows:

```
SELECT, F.Category
FROM Folders F, Desktops D
WHERE F.Desktop#  =  D.DT# and D.DTowner = "John"
```

■ 3.5 SET-AND-TUPLE COMPLEX OBJECT MODELS

Before implementing an object-oriented database application, it is necessary to *design* the application through an entity-relationship or object-oriented design mechanism. In fact, the starting point for implementing applications for *any* of the previously "traditional" models is the same. The advantage of an object-oriented database is that because all constructs and relationships are supported directly, almost *no* transformations are necessary to map an ER or object-oriented design diagram onto the schema of an object-oriented database. The data definition languages or mechanisms in most object-oriented database management systems provide constructs that directly capture the relationships in semantic or entity-relationship models. Thus, as far as the *definition* of the database is concerned, at least structurally, object-oriented databases are quite rich.

In addition to data definition, database management systems provide constructs for the manipulation of persistent database objects; in other words, *the data manipulation language*. Relational languages such as SQL provide a clear separation and a clean model for the data manipulation of relational databases. In fact SQL consists of three categories:

> Data Definition Language (DDL): The DDL constructs are used to create and/or destroy *TABLE*s, *INDEX*es, *VIEW*s, integrity constraints, and so on.
>
> Data Control Language (DCL): The DCL constructs are used primarily by a database administrator to enroll/drop users, to grant and revoke various privileges to users, and so on.
>
> Data Manipulation Language (DML): The DML allows users to *SELECT, INSERT, UPDATE*, and *DELETE* from persistent database tables.

Although SQL is the language of choice for most relational database management systems, the lack of a rigorous semantics for the language has resulted in a number of anomalies. Some of these are summarized in an article by the inventor of the relational model, Dr. E. F. Codd (Codd, 1970). In fact, although SQL continues to "grow" and gain popularity, the extensions to the language are often performed mostly as "ad hoc" extensions, either by standardization committees (e.g., SQL2 or SQL3) or by individual corporations.

For object-oriented databases, most commercial object-oriented database management systems provide ad hoc query languages and models without a rigorous model underneath. Interestingly enough, in many cases these ad hoc query languages are object-oriented extensions of SQL. This does not mean that rigorous models do not exist. As pointed out by Atkinson et al. (1992);

> We are not claiming here that no complete object-oriented data model exists, indeed many proposals can be found in the literature . . . but rather that there is no consensus on a single one. Opinion is slowly converging on the gross characteristics of a family of object-oriented systems, but, at present, there is no clear consensus on what an object-oriented system is, let alone an object-oriented database system.

Although the situation is somewhat better now than a few years ago, for object-oriented systems, we are still struggling for an agreed-upon powerful and simple object-oriented database data model and a standard endorsed by most vendors. Several interesting research and implementation efforts have elucidated complex object-modeling issues and alternatives for structurally object-oriented databases. Sections 3.5.1 to 3.5.3 provide an overview of alternative strategies for defining complex objects, concentrating on the distinction between identity- and value-based complex object models. Section 3.6 gives an overview of algebraic operations for complex objects.

3.5.1 Value-Based Complex Object Spaces

Several object models introduced "complex object" structure from set-and-tuple object constructors that are "value"-based (Ullman, 1987; Khoshafian, 1989; Ullman, 1988). The term *value-based* means that the uniqueness of an object depends solely on its *state*, consisting of atomic values (integer, float, character string) of instance variables. In other words, objects do not have "identities" independent of their state. The object spaces in value-based models are forests of trees. Although there is similarity with the hierarchical model, value-based models in database theory have rigorous mathematical foundations based on either logic, non-first-normal-form extensions of the relational model, or other formal models.

This section outlines a model given by Bancilhon and Khoshafian (1989) and Khoshafian (1989) called the Complex Object Database Language (CODL). It provides an overview of the object space definition in CODL. Section 3.6 then presents a number of algebraic operations that could be used with any of the models discussed in this chapter.

Based upon a collection of atomic objects (integers, floating points, character strings, etc.), CODL uses *set-and-tuple* object constructors to define the object space. The object space in any CODL program will actually consist of two subspaces: the *transient* and the *persistent* object spaces. The persistent object space is a tree rooted at the CODL key word **database**.

In order to identify persistent subobjects CODL utilizes the notion of a path. An object that is a path "points" to a persistent subobject of the database. All retrievals and updates of the persistent database are done through paths. For a tuple object we can get to the attributes of the tuple through an "extract" of an attribute. For a persistent set object we can get to an element of the set by specifying the value of a key. Hence, as we shall see, paths are basically sequences of attribute names and key values.

Objects in CODL

Assume that we are given a set of attribute names N and atomic values A (e.g., integers, floats, strings). Objects are defined (Bancilhon and Khoshafian, 1989; Khoshafian, 1989) recursively as follows:

1. Every atomic value is an object.
2. If $a1, a2, \ldots, an$ are distinct attribute names and $O1, O2, \ldots, On$ are objects, then $[a1 : O1, a2 : O2, \ldots, an : On]$ is a tuple object. Oi is called the ai attribute value of O.
3. If $O1, \ldots, On$ are objects then $S = \{O1, O2, \ldots On\}$ is a set object. Each Oi is an element of S.

The following are examples of objects:

Atomic objects	`25,John,1.3`
Set	`John,Mary,Susan`
Tuple	`[Name:Peter,Age:25]`
Hierarchical tuple	`[Name:[First:John,Last:Doe],`
	`Age: 25, Children: {Peter,Paul,Mary}]`
Set of tuples	`{[Name:Peter, Age:25],`
	`[Name:John, Age:7], [Name:Mary,Age:13]}`
Nested relation	`{[Name:Peter, Children:{Max,Suzan}],`
	`[Name:John, Children:{Mary,Frank}]}`

Object Equality

Object *equality* is defined as follows:

1. Two atomic objects are equal if and only if they are the same.

2. Two tuple objects are equal if and only if the values they take on each attribute are equal.

3. Two sets objects S and S' are equal if and only if for any element of S (S') there exists an element of S' (S) equal to it.

Examples of object equality are

$$[a : 1, b : 2] = [b : 2, a : 1]$$
$$\{1, 2, 3\} = \{2, 3, 1\}$$

Example of Value-Based Complex Object

Using dots to represent tuples and asterisks to represent sets, Figure 3.11 illustrates an example with value-based complex objects involving persons. The lines

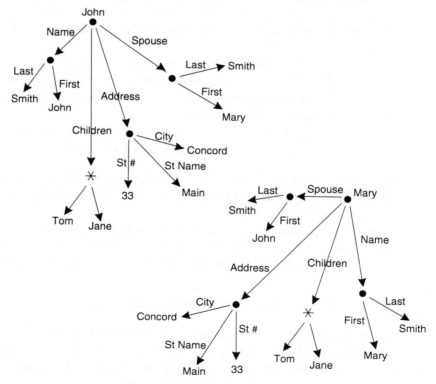

Figure 3.11 Value-based object space.

incident from set nodes represent set elements. The labeled lines incident from tuple nodes represent attributes.

3.5.2 Identity-Based Complex Object Models

Chapter 2 introduced object identity as one of the fundamental concepts of object orientation. Section 2.4 provided a detailed overview of the type-state-identity trichotomy and discussed various types of equality predicates and copying for object-oriented systems that support object identity.

Here, an overview of the definition of object spaces and object equality predicates for a *set-and-tuple* object model that supports object identity is provided. The similarity between this model and the one discussed in Section 2.4 is readily apparent. The main addition here is the introduction of sets and more rigorous definitions of object spaces with identity. The model here is based on FAD (Bancilhon et al., 1987).

Object Spaces

As usual, we start with a set of identifiers I and a set of attributes A. The definition is similar to the type-state-identity model except that, as stated earlier, sets are incorporated into the model. An object O is a triple (identifier, type, value), where the identifier is in I. The type is either atomic, set, or tuple. The value of an object depends on its type and is represented as follows:

> Atomic type: an element of a user-defined domain of atomic values.
>
> Set: $\{i1, i2, \ldots, in\}$, where the ij are distinct identifiers from I. The value of a set represents the mathematical notion of a set as an unordered collection of identifiers.
>
> Tuple: $[a1 : i1, a2 : i2, \ldots, an : in]$, where the ai are distinct attribute names from N and the ij are identifiers from I.

The value of a tuple represents a collection of identifiers labeled by attribute names. The value taken by the tuple object O on attribute aj is ij and is denoted $O.aj$.

An object system is a set of objects. An object system is consistent if and only if identifiers are unique for each object and for each identifier present in the system there is an object with this identifier (Bancilhon et al., 1987).

Equality

Section 2.5 discussed the different facets of equality:

1. *Identical*. The first is equality of identifiers. Two objects have equal identifiers if and only if they are the same object (i.e., objects are distinct if their identifiers are not equal). This is similar to the equality of pointers or references.

2. *Shallow-Equal.* Two objects are Shallow-Equal if they have the same types and equal object values. Equality of object values is defined as follows:

- Two atomic object values are equal if they denote the same element in the domain of base values.
- Two sets are Shallow-Equal if their contents are identical.
- Two tuples are Shallow-Equal if the values they take on every attribute are identical. Intuitively, the objects might be different, but their types and contents are identical.

3. *Deep-Equal.* Finally, the third (and, in a sense, weakest) type of equality is value-based deep equality, which is defined recursively as follows:

- Two atomic object representations are Deep-Equal if and only if they are Shallow-Equal.
- Two set objects are Deep-Equal if every element of one is Deep-Equal to an element of the other.
- Two tuple objects are Deep-Equal if the values they take on every attribute are Deep-Equal.

It is possible to define a restrictive form of deep equality and require that the graphs of the two objects be isomorphic, preserving the sharing of references in their corresponding subobjects.

Example of Identity-Based Complex Object

Using asterisks for sets, dots for tuples, and identity labels for objects, Figure 3.12 illustrates the same example as Figure 3.11. Note the *referential sharing* of the set- and-tuple objects, as well as the cycles in the graph-structured object space that is supported through object identity.

3.5.3 Hybrid Models

Although identity-based models are general, in some cases it is neither necessary nor desirable (because of the overhead) to generate an identifier for every object. In fact, even object-oriented languages such as Smalltalk do not generate an identity for *every* datum; small integers, for instance, do not have a separate object identifier. Similarly, some structures in databases do not need to be identified separately from an "owner," or enclosing object.

Object types that do not need to have an identity independent of their value are the atomic objects, or the objects that are the instances of the base types of

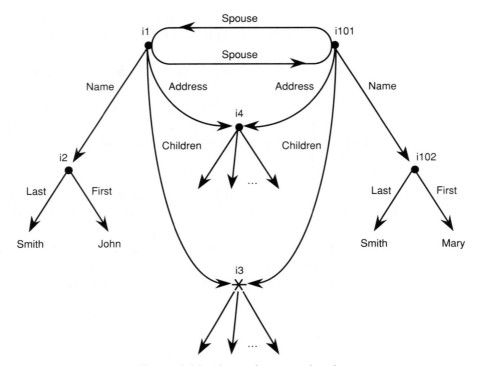

Figure 3.12 Object references with cycles.

the object-oriented database system. Examples of "base types" (these are called atomic objects in some models) are

Integers
Floating-point numbers
Fixed-point numbers
Booleans
Character strings
Bit strings
Timestamps
Dates

Having an identity for any object (atomic or otherwise; i.e., "base" or "set" and "tuple") provides a uniform and simple model. In many cases, however, these atomic values are not shared referentially. For instance, the

Social Security number of a `Person` represents a key in the set of `Persons` (or the extension of the class `Person`). Allocating an identity might not be relevant. Furthermore, assigning an object identifier for each atomic (or base type) value could be expensive in terms of both space and access time. The underlying system will need to allocate a separate identifier for each object, and these identifiers need to be stored in the database. The searches will be based on identifiers; this could incur an extra level of indirection for accessing each atomic object.

Designers of object-oriented database applications should have the freedom to specify whether they would like to have an identity for a particular field or attribute in a tuple. In addition to saving space and access time, specifying the fact that a particular attribute in, say, a tuple needs to have values as opposed to objects is also an integrity constraint specification.

For instance, for a `Person` the `Name` can be a tuple consisting of

> `First` : Character string
>
> `Middle` : Character string
>
> `Last` : Character string

Here, the `Name` tuple structure (although it does have structure) does not need to have an identity and can be a value. As the previous example involving `Person` suggests, `Persons` are referentially shared and hence must have identities. In other words, within the same application there are tuple structures, sets, or set elements that are not referentially shared and whose existence depends on the existence of a parent object (e.g., the `Name` of a `Person`). These attribute values or set elements do not need object identity and hence can be values.

With a pure identity-based model such as FAD, for which each object (atomic or otherwise) has an object identity, we need additional referential and existential constraints to indicate "values." In a richer hybrid model, it will be up to the database designers to decide when they have objects that are values and when objects must be used.

Intelligent SQL

The previous sections have provided an overview of various alternative value-and identity-based complex object models. How are these expressed in an object-oriented database language? To illustrate these concepts in the context of a language, the tuple and identity constructs in In Intelligent SQL are presented here in greater detail.

In Intelligent SQL to declare a tuple we can either create and name a tuple type or directly declare an attribute to be of type

$$\text{TUPLE (} < \text{tuple attribute declarations} > \text{)}$$

To create a named tuple type the syntax is

$<$ tuple definition $>$: : $=$ CREATE TUPLE $<$ tuple name $>$
$(<$ tuple elements $>)$
$<$ tuple element $>$: : $= <$ column definition $>$
$<$ column definition $>$: : $= <$ column name $>< $ date type $>$
$| <$ column name $>< $ tuple declaration $>$
$<$ tuple declaration $>$: : $=$ TUPLE($<$ tuple elements $>$)

For example, we can create a tuple-valued address attribute through the following statements:

```
CREATE TUPLE ADDRESS (
     Number              INTEGER,
     StrtName            CHAR (20),
     AptNumber           INTEGER,
     City                CHAR (20)
     State               CHAR (20),
     Zip                 INTEGER)


CREATE TABLE Persons (
     Name                CHAR (20),
     Age                 INTEGER,
     HomeAddr            ADDRESS)
```

Alternatively, we can have

```
CREATE TABLE Persons (
     Name                CHAR (20),
     Age                 INTEGER,
     HomeAddr            TUPLE (
                         Number        INTEGER
                         StrtName      CHAR (20),
                         AptNumber     INTEGER,
                         City          CHAR (20),
                         State         CHAR (20),
                         Zip           INTEGER))
```

Extended Dot Notation

In SQL columns are referenced by their name either directly or, if there is an ambiguity, preceded by a table name. The value of a column (attribute) in a row is a base type. Since in the proposed extension the value can be a row (tuple), we must have a way to access the columns of this row directly.

The extended dot notation would modify the "column-ref" production to

<column ref>::= [<column quantifier>.]<column-sequence>
<column sequence>::= <column name>
          |<column sequence>.<column name>

Thus, to retrieve the city in which Jerry lives we have

```
SELECT HomeAddr.City
FROM Persons
WHERE Name = "Jerry"
```

Note that a nested tuple can contain other nested tuples. For example, the City attribute can itself be a tuple that city. Thus, we can have

```
CREATE TUPLE CITY (
        Name            CHAR (20),
        Population      INTEGER,
        Mayor           CHAR (20)
        Elevation       FEET)
```

We declare the attribute type of city in Address to be CITY as follows:

```
CREATE TUPLE ADDRESS (
        Number          INTEGER,
        StrtName        CHAR (20),
        AptNumber       INTEGER,
        City            CITY,
        State           CHAR (20),
        Zip             INTEGER)

CREATE TABLE Persons (
        Name            CHAR (20),
        Age             INTEGER,
        HomeAddr        ADDRESS)
```

The street name of Jerry's address and the name of the city's mayor could be retrieved through

```
SELECT HomeAddr.StrName, HomeAddr.City.Mayor
FROM Persons
WHERE Name = "Jerry"
```

Tuple Expressions

The extended dot notation is used to retrieve tuple- or scalar-valued attributes of table rows. Tuple expressions are an additional construct for assigning and searching with tuple-valued attributes. The general form of a tuple expression is

$$TUPLE \ (\ < value \ list > \ )$$

where the <value list> contains a list of scalar and/or tuple expressions separated by commas. For example,

```
TUPLE (1322, "Spring", NULL,
         TUPLE ("San Simon", 10000, "Billy Joe",
               20000) )
```

is a tuple expression that can appear in a data manipulation statement (as demonstrated in the next section) or in a search condition, as in

```
SELECT Name, Age
FROM Persons
WHERE HomeAddr = TUPLE (1322, "Spring", Null,
                  TUPLE ("San Simon", 10000, "Billy Joe",
                        20000) )
```

Tuple expressions can also be used in other DML (data manipulation language) expressions. For example, we can modify the entire address of John Smith through:

```
UPDATE Persons
SET Address - TUPLE (1322, "Spring", NULL,
                TUPLE ("San Simon", 10000, "Billy Joe",
                      20000) )
WHERE Name = "John Smith"
```

Similarly, the Intelligent SQL *INSERT* statement also allows tuple expressions to be inserted into tables that have tuple-valued attributes. For example, we can have

```
INSERT
INTO Persons (Name, Age, HomeAddr)
Values ("John Smith", 22,
        TUPLE (1322, "Spring", NULL,
        TUPLE ("San Simon", 10000, "Billy Joe",
               20000) ) )
```

Identity in Intelligent SQL

The main extension in the data (or schema) definition language of SQL is the provision for an object identity of a row from a table as a column data type, a tuple type, or a user-defined abstract data type. Thus, in the extended SQL grammar we'll have

$$< \text{column definition} >: : =$$

$$< \text{column name} >< \text{data type} >$$

$$| < \text{column name} >< \text{tuple declaration} >$$

$$| < \text{column name} > \text{OBJECT} < \text{object type} >$$

$$< \text{object type} >: : =$$

$$< \text{data type} >$$

$$< \text{tuple declaration} >$$

$$\text{ROW} < \text{table-name} >$$

Note that if we do not have the keyword OBJECT we will actually get a value of the indicated type (e.g., a tuple). Thus, if we have a Department table declared as

```
CREATE TABLE Department(
    DeptName        CHAR (20),
    DeptNum         INTEGER
    Budget          FLOAT (2) )
```

then, assuming each office worker works in exactly one department, we can declare an OfficeWorker table as

```
CREATE TABLE OfficeWorkers (
    WorkerName      CHAR (20),
    WorkerAge       INTEGER,
    WorkerSalary    INTEGER,
    WorkerRank      INTEGER,
    WorkerDept      OBJECT ROW
                    Department)
```

With object identity the attribute or column value of a row is a tuple. Hence, the extended dot notation can also be used here to access the attributes of the nested tuples. So with the schema of OfficeWorkers and Department, we can retrieve the department name of Joe's department through

```
SELECT WorkerDept.DeptName
FROM OfficeWorkers
WHERE WorkerName = "Joe"
```

As far as retrieval is concerned, extended dot notation is basically what we need.

As mentioned earlier, there are several types of equality associated with object identity. In Intelligent SQL the predicate " = " means

1. Identical if the two arguments are Objects
2. Shallow-equal if the two arguments are tuples
3. Comparison of atomic values, otherwise

For instance, to retrieve the names of all of the workers who work in the same department as Joe, we have

```
SELECT AllWorkers.WorkerName
FROM OfficeWorkers AllWorkers, OfficeWorkers Joes
WHERE Joes.WorkerName = "Joe" and
      AllWorkers.WorkerDept = Joes.WorkerDept
```

For updates, we need a mechanism to allow the same object to be referenced by multiple parent objects. To this end an *ASSIGN* operation is introduced whose general form is

ASSIGN < object expression > TO < object expression >

where <object expression> is a select statement that identifies a single object, that is,

$$< \text{object expression} > \ ::= \ < \text{select statement} >$$

This means that the <select clause> of the <select statement> is a concatenation of attribute names separated by periods. For instance, to ASSIGN the address of Mary to Joe we have

```
ASSIGN SELECT Address From Persons WHERE Name = "Joe"
     TO
         SELECT Address From Persons WHERE  Name = "Mary"
```

There must be one Joe and one Mary in Persons.

Figure 3.13 presents another Intelligent SQL schema that incorporates both values and identity.

Values, Identity, and Intelligent SQL

Intelligent SQL was neither the first nor the only model to incorporate both values and objects with identity. As mentioned earlier, a number of object-oriented databases already assume that instances of some common base types do not have object identity. Other models make this distinction explicit for other types (such as tuples).

```
CREATE TABLE ADDRESS
(
    St Number     INTEGER
    St Name       CHAR(20),
    App #         INTEGER,
    Zip           CHAR(12)
    City          CHAR(20)
    State         CHAR(20)
    Country       CHAR(20)
)


CREATE TABLE Person
(
    Name          CHAR(32)
    Date of Birth DATE,
    Home Address  OBJECT ADDRESS,
    Phone Number  CHAR(14)
)
```

Figure 3.13 Intelligent SQL schema with identity.

	Shareable	Nonshareable
Mutable	General objects	Private objects
Immutable	Nonupdateable objects	Values

Figure 3.14 Mutability and shareability.

In fact it is possible, through integrity constraints, to capture the semantics of values from an identity-based model.

One notation was introduced by Khoshafian and Briggs (1988). As illustrated in Figure 3.14, we can introduce nonshareability and immutability properties and basically obtain "values." These concepts are discussed in more detail in Section 3.8; briefly, a node has nonshareable instances if an element in an instance of the node cannot be the attribute value of two distinct tuples or the element of two distinct sets, or if it cannot be the element of a set and the attribute value of a tuple. Similarly, an immutable object is one whose "value" cannot be modified through one of the operations of the object-oriented database data manipulation language.

It should also be noted that identifiers and even various properties and operations on identities could be incorporated into a value-based model through keys and unique key integrity constraints. If the underlying database management system generates unique identifiers and assigns them to each object that is created, the resulting system can achieve many of the advantages of an identity-based system (even though the "identities" are visible to the user and object identifiers become foreign keys that need to be traversed through joins to obtain the referenced object).

▪ 3.6 ALGEBRAIC OPERATORS FOR COMPLEX OBJECT MODELS

The previous section presents strategies for defining complex object spaces. These strategies are based on set-and-tuple object constructors. Roughly, a *tuple* is similar to the structure (instance variables and their types) of a class, and sets are collections of objects in object-oriented systems.

Here, the definition of object models for object-oriented databases is discussed. The first step in defining an object model is defining the object spaces. The second step is defining the operations, that is, the algebra that applies to the object spaces. Typically, these operations are the basis of a query language for the underlying object-oriented database language. Queries expressed through algebraic operators tend to be procedural in the sense that the query indicates the order of execution of the operators. A *calculus* provides a set-forming notation for the algebraic operations, as is typically done for relational systems. In fact, a number of proposals for non-first-normal-form and object-oriented query systems introduce both the algebra and calculus of the query system and have proven their equivalence (e.g., Straube and Ozsu, 1990).

Typically, query languages in database systems (object-oriented or relational) tend to be based on the calculus. For instance, relational database query languages, such as SQL or QUEL, define syntax and semantics based on the relational calculus. Query languages such as SQL are "declarative." They allow users to specify *what* they need to retrieve from the database without specifying how the results of the queries must be evaluated. In most relational database management systems, the SQL query (or the query expressed in a language based on relational calculus) is "translated" onto a relational algebra query tree. The underlying query optimizer of the relational database management system then decides on an "optimal" query execution plan, using optimization rules and cost estimates for the query.

Some object-oriented databases also perform query optimizations. At the very least, if a query specifies a select criteria and an index is available on the selected attribute of a collection, the underlying system will attempt to use the index in its optimizer.

Unlike relational systems, the calculus and algebra for object-oriented databases is not so clear. Many proposals and operations exist for such a model. This section discusses commonly agreed-upon operations of object-oriented databases. The discussion is based primarily on the proposals given by Bancilhon et al. (1987), Khoshafian (1989), Shaw and Zdonik (1989), and Straube and Ozsu (1990).

3.6.1 Set Operations

Object-oriented databases inevitably have "collection" objects. The most commonly understood or used collection object is the *set*. Other useful collection objects are *bags* ("sets with duplicates"), lists, arrays, queues, and stacks. The operations defined here could be defined for these collection types in addition to sets.

Union: If *S1* and *S2* are set objects, the union of *S1* and *S2* is defined through

$$\{s \mid s \in S1 \text{ or } s \in S2\}$$

Intersection: If *S1* and *S2* are set objects, the intersection of *S1* and *S2* is defined through

$$\{s \mid s \in S1 \text{ and } s \in S2\}$$

Difference: If $S1$ and $S2$ are set objects, $S1 - S2$ is defined through

$$\{s \mid s \in S1 \text{ and } (\text{not } s \in S2)\}$$

3.6.2 General Selection

The basic relational operators are *Select*, *Project*, and *Join*. Models and algebras for object-oriented databases have attempted to generalize these three fundamental operations for object-oriented object spaces in different ways. For instance, Shaw and Zdonik (1989) have *Select*, *Project*, and *Ojoin* algebraic operators.

Here, a more generalized select that is similar to the filter operation in FAD, which is more general than the *Select*, *Project*, and *Ojoin* given by Shaw and Zdonik, is given. To define the generalized *Select*, a definition of lambda abstractions is first provided:

$\lambda(x1, \ldots, xn)e$ is an n-ary operator abstraction with parameters $x1, \ldots, xn$. The body of the operator abstraction is the expression e. The scope of the parameters is restricted to the body of the abstraction.

Using this definition, the following definition can be made:

$$GeneralSelect(S1, S2, \ldots, Sn, \lambda(x1, \ldots, xn)e) \text{ as}$$
$$\{e(s1, \ldots, sn) \mid s1 \in S1 \text{ and } s2 \in S2 \text{ and} \ldots \text{and } sn \in Sn\}$$

For example, the following is a generalized select statement to retrieve a set of tuples containing the `Name` and `Department` of all `OfficeWorkers` who earn more than 50K:

$$GeneralSelect(\texttt{OfficeWorker}, \lambda(x)x.\texttt{Salary} > 50\text{K}$$
$$\rightarrow [\text{Name: } x.\text{Name, Department: } x.\text{Department}])$$

3.6.3 Nest

The *Nest* operator, originally introduced for non-first-normal-form relational models, takes a set object and collects sets based on a given predicate (in most cases, equality of some of the attributes). In effect, this operator constructs equivalence classes based on the given predicate.

The simplest form of the *Nest* operator constructs the equivalence classes (in sets) with attribute values whose "complements" have the same value. A complement is defined as follows: If S is a set whose elements are tuples of type

$$[a1 : t1, \ldots, an : tn]$$

then if $N = \{a1, \ldots, an\}$ and if A is a subset of the attributes N, that is, $A = \{ai1, \ldots, aim\}$, then the complement of A is $N - A$.

To illustrate, let `Names` be a set of names containing tuples of type

`[Last: String, First: String]`

For example, let

```
Names={[Last: "Smith", First: "John"],
       [Last: "Smith", First: "Mary"],
       [Last: "Fisher", First: "Mark"],...}
```

Then,

```
Nest(Names, Last)=
       {[Last: "Smith", First: {"John", "Mary"}],
        [Last: "Fisher", First: {"Mark"}],...}
```

The semantics of *Nest* is given by

$$Nest(S, ai) =$$
$$\{[a1 : s.a1, \cdots ai : Sti, \cdots an : s.an] |$$
$$\forall r \exists s \ (r \in Sti \ \text{AND} \ s \in S \ \text{AND} \ s.ai = r)\}$$

As stated earlier, it is possible to have more general `Nest` operators based on predicates involving more complex functions. FAD, for instance, has a *group* operator that allows the partitioning of a set S into equivalence classes under application of a function abstraction. More specifically, the group operator in FAD is defined by

$$group(\lambda(x1, x2, \ldots, xn)f, S) =$$
$$\{(a, \{s\}) | s \in S \ \text{AND} \ all\_equal(a, f(s))\}$$

where "all_equal" is the deep-equal predicate in FAD.

3.6.4 UnNest

The *Nest* operation creates a set-valued attribute based on the equality of one or more other attributes. The *UnNest* operator basically "undoes" the effect of the *Nest* and reflattens the set.

Assuming that S is a set of tuples with a set-valued attribute Ai, we have

$$UnNest(S, Ai) = \{[A1 : s.A1, A2 : s.A2, \ldots, Ai : t, \ldots]$$
$$| s \in S \ AND \ t \in s.Ai\}$$

3.6.5. Flatten

In some situations the result of an operation is a set of set. For instance, if we are projecting on a set-valued attribute such as `Children`, then the result of the project will be a set of sets. Since a set of sets is awkward to manipulate and in many cases we are interested in the union of all set elements, it is useful to have a *Flatten* operation that returns this union.

Assuming that S is a set of sets, *Flatten* is defined by

$$Flatten(S) = \{t \mid \exists\, s \in S \text{ AND } t \in s\}$$

For instance,

$$Flatten(\{\{1, 5, 7\}, \{2, 3, 4\}, \{6\}\}) = \{1, 2, 3, 4, 5, 6, 7\}$$

■ 3.7 MODELING CLASSES IN OBJECT-ORIENTED DATABASES

The complex object models discussed in the previous sections primarily used set-and-tuple constructor types to construct object spaces. Value-based, identity-based, and more general hybrid models that incorporate both identities and values have been discussed. The object models presented so far, however, lack two fundamental features of object orientation:

1. Classes and methods to capture the behavior of objects
2. Inheritance

On one hand, object-oriented models provide the conceptual foundation for a precise semantics of the object space stored and managed by an object-oriented database management system. On the other hand, we need an object-oriented design mechanism to capture not only the complex object representations but also the static and dynamic behavior of classes and objects.

As pointed out earlier, the goal of object-oriented databases is to remove the impedance mismatch between programming languages and database management systems. Object-oriented databases provide a uniform development environment. In many cases this is achieved through database extensions of an object-oriented language such as C++.

Design is the first step of conventional, database, or object-oriented development. It is not surprising, therefore, that design methodologies have been developed for object-oriented languages and object-oriented databases. Section 3.3 provided an overview of the major steps involved in the design of an object-oriented database application. This section provides

1. An overview of semantic and entity-relationship modeling in databases
2. An overview of the node-and-link types needed for the object-oriented design of classes in object-oriented database applications

3.7.1 Semantic and Entity Relationship Models

The goal of semantic data models (and most data models, for that matter) is similar to the goal of object orientation: *to model the real world as closely as possible*. However, there is one fundamental difference between semantic data models and other models. Semantic data models do not incorporate behavioral abstraction (or abstract data typing); they model *structural abstractions*. This is similar to AI knowledge representation. Semantic data models capture the semantics of the objects (entities) and relationships of an underlying object space. They are primarily used as design tools for underlying relational or network databases.

Semantic data models are not semantic *networks*. There are, however, common elements. Semantic data models use the *node-and-link* representation schema of semantic networks. Each node is an *entity type*. Similar to types in programming languages, an entity type represents a set of objects (entities) that all have the same attributes. An attribute is a function that can apply to an entity in the entity type. The name of an entity type identifies the *extension* (set of all instances) of the entity type. Entity types are analogous to classes, entities are analogous to instances, and attributes are analogous to instance variables.

Semantic data models also capture *inheritance* and incorporate various sorts of *attributes* (or slots in semantic networks). The fundamental difference, however, is that whereas semantic networks are used as an associative memory for the entire knowledge base, semantic data models are used to represent the structure of an underlying extensional database.

The forerunner of the semantic models was the famous entity-relationship (ER) model, introduced by Chen (1976). The ER model is considerably simpler than the more generalized semantic data model described in the following paragraphs; it does not incorporate the notion of *inheritance*. In particular, nodes in an ER diagram are either entity type notes, printable attribute nodes, or relationship (aggregate) nodes. The entity-relationship approach is a widely accepted technique for data modeling.

To illustrate the different node-and-link types of semantic data models, a portion of the sales office automation database using the Generalized Semantic Model (GSM) of Hull and King (1987) is presented. The GSM is a representative semantic model that incorporates concepts from alternative semantic modeling strategies. The different node (entity) and link (relationship) types in GSM are illustrated in Figures 3.15 and 3.16.

For node types an oval represents printable base types, such as integers, character strings, and floating-point numbers. A triangle represents *abstract*

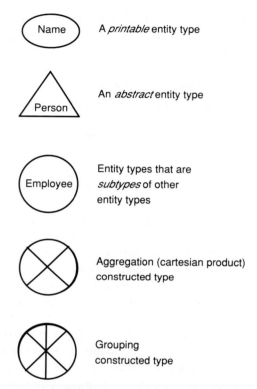

Figure 3.15 Different types of nodes in GSM.

entity types. The set of all instances of an abstract entity type is its *extension*. Entity types can inherit from one another. A circle represents an entity type that has an *IS-A* relationship (i.e., it is a *subtype*) to another entity type. Figure 3.15 illustrates two commonly used constructor types: the *aggregation* node type and the set, or *grouping*, node type. These roughly correspond to tuple and set

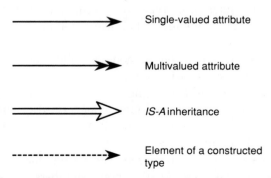

Figure 3.16 Different types of links (relationships) in GSM.

object types in complex object models, discussed in the previous section. The instances of an aggregation node type are elements of the Cartesian product of its children—the Cartesian product of sets $S_1, \ldots, S_n$ is $\{(e_1, \ldots, e_n) \mid e_1 \in S_1, \ldots, e_n \in S_n\}$. Grouping node types have one child. An instance of a grouping node type is a set whose elements are instances of the node type's child.

Figure 3.16 represents the different types of links, or relationships, that can exist between the nodes of a semantic model. Entity types have *attributes* that could be single- or multiple-valued functions. Single-valued functions are indicated by single arrow heads; multiple-valued functions are indicated by double arrow heads. These functions map instances of one entity type to instances of the pointed-to type. Another important relationship is the *IS-A* inheritance relationship, which is represented by a thick white arrow. Finally, constructed types point to their children through dashed arrows.

Using these node and link types, Figure 3.17 illustrates a portion of the intelligent office example in GSM. `SalesPerson` inherits from `Office-Worker`, and `OfficeWorker` inherits from `Person`. `Name` is an aggregate. `Age`, `Name`, `Salary`, and `Address` are single-valued attributes of `Person`. A specific set of accounts is assigned to each salesperson. Each salesperson also has a set of pending orders. Thus, both `Accounts` and `Orders` are sets. To illustrate two choices for representing sets, different constructs for `Accounts` and `Orders` have been used. `Accounts` is a multivalued attribute (or function) of `SalesPerson`; `Orders` is a single-valued attribute of `SalesPerson`, where the value is a group (set) of `Orders`. If the value of an attribute is a set, we can perform set operations on it.

Different constructs have been used here for `Name` and `Address`. For `Name` an aggregate was used, and for `Address` an entity type was used. The basic difference is that only abstract entity types (or subtypes) have distinguishable object identities. In other words, if an aggregate, or grouping, object is the attribute value of an entity and the entity is deleted, the aggregate object is also deleted. On the other hand, if an entity (object) is the attribute value of another entity, it will not be deleted when the entity referencing it is deleted. It has an existence (object identity) of its own. Entities can be shared between entities (i.e., can be the attribute value of more than one entity). For example, the *same* address could be referenced by the `Address` attribute value of each `Person` living in the same house. The distinction between aggregates and entity types is similar to the distinction between objects with identities and values (discussed in Section 3.5).

Some semantic data models emphasize constructor types, whereas others emphasize attributes. The Functional Data Model (Kerschberg and Pacheco, 1976) is attribute-based. Attribute values are entities, and attributes can be single- or multivalued. The data language DAPLEX (Shipman, 1981) was one of the earliest languages that supported the Functional Data Model. It provided both a

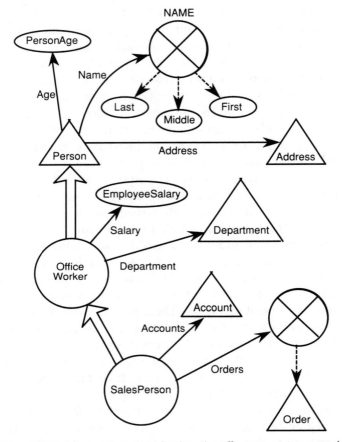

Figure 3.17 A semantic model for the sales office automation example.

data definition language and a data manipulation language based on attributes (functions).

At the other end of the spectrum is the aggregation-based entity-relationship model mentioned earlier. A schema in an ER diagram consists of

1. Rectangles representing entity types
2. Ovals representing ranges of attributes
3. Diamonds representing relationships (i.e., aggregation)

Relationships can be one-to-one (e.g., each person has one spouse), many-to-one (e.g., a person has many children), many-to-many (employees can work in different departments, and many employees work in the same department). Figure 3.18 illustrates a portion of the intelligent office example using an ER diagram.

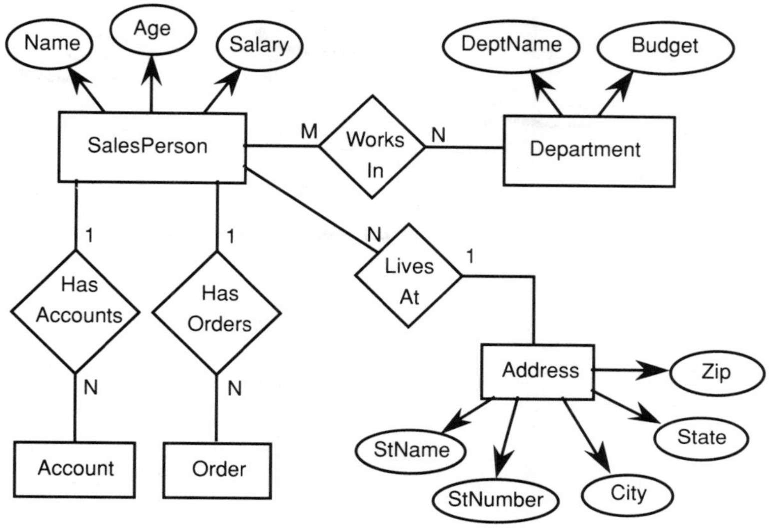

Figure 3.18 An entity-relationship model for the sales office automation example.

Alternative Constructs and Extensions

The basic node and link categories for ER modeling have just been introduced. Here, additional constructs and extensions to the basic ER modeling are discussed. Some of these constructs were illustrated in the previous examples.

1. **Keys.** In Figure 3.19, the italicized `SocialSecurityNumber` attribute of `Person` is a key. Similarly, the composite `<StreetNumber, StreetName>` is a key of `Address`.

2. **Weak Entities.** Sometimes an entity is entirely dependent on the existence of another entity. The dependent entity is called the "weak" entity. For instance, in the intelligent office example, each worker has a number of desktops. The desktops *pertain* to office workers and hence are weak entities. This is illustrated in Figure 3.20 by a double rectangle. This is similar to existential constraints discussed in Section 3.8.3.

3. **Inheritance.** An extension to the entity-relationship model is the incorporation of the second fundamental concept of object orientation, namely inheritance. This is an incremental extension to ER. In some cases, it is useful to have an entity type inherit attributes from one or more existing entity types. For instance, both real estate `Agents` and `Clients` are `Persons`. Semantic data models have traditionally had inheritance incorporated into them. An ER model with inheritance is similar to a semantic data model.

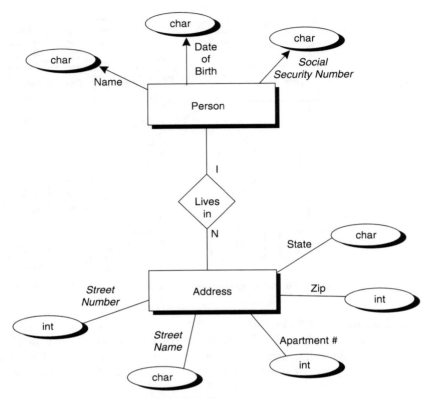

Figure 3.19 Keys in ER diagrams.

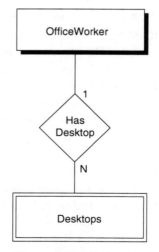

Figure 3.20 Weak entities.

The above constructs are only a sample of those that have been introduced and defined for ER modeling. Researchers have developed many other variations and extensions to the original ER model introduced by Chen (1976). The most significant extension remains the inheritance relationship.

Graphical representation alternatives for ER models have also been developed. For example, *Database Modeling and Design* by Toby Teorey (1990) follows a representation developed by Reiner et al. (1985). Figure 3.21 illustrates some entity types and their relationships using this alternative representation. Note that the cardinal nature of the relationship is indicated by the color of the diamond. A one-to-one relationship is white, a one-to-many relationship is white on the one side and black on the many side, and a many-to-many relationship is black.

A third alternative uses a "crow's foot" representation for the many side of the relationship (Everest, 1986). In this model diamonds are not used to represent relationships. Rather, the relationship name is a label on the link between two entities. Oracle's CASE·METHOD product uses this method (Barker, 1989). Figure 3.22 illustrates a portion of the intelligent office schema using this alternative representation.

The alternative representations are equivalent. Entity types and relationships can be represented using any of these schemes. Standards do not exist, and different CASE and database data modeling products will choose one or the other of these strategies.

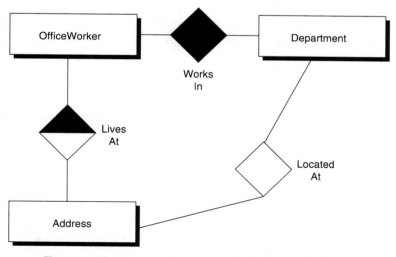

Figure 3.21 Alternative ER representation (developed by Reiner).

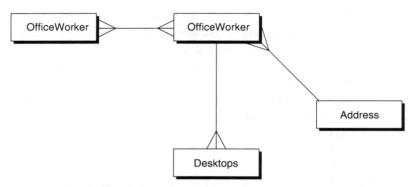

Figure 3.22 Crow's foot ER representation.

3.7.2 Object-Oriented Database Design

The previous section provides an overview of semantic and entity-relationship modeling techniques. This section outlines some of the nodes and links needed to design object-oriented databases. Node types, each of which reflect a particular object-oriented concept or an aspect of object-orientation, are described. To reflect the relationships between classes, this section also introduces link types.

The various node-and-link types are used to design classes (persistent, abstract, transient, etc.), and their relationship reflects the overall structure of the objects used in the object-oriented system, that is, the structure of the classes. To comprehend the *dynamic* behavior of the *instances* of the classes (the "objects"), this section also provides an overview of state transition diagrams and other constructs that capture the dynamic relationships between objects. Note that this symbolism and methodology have been used successfully in a number of projects in office automation. Several examples for the classes used in complex office automation systems are illustrated in *Intelligent Offices* (Khoshafian, et. al. 1992b).

Designing Classes

The object model used for both OOA and OOD incorporates constructs from a number of object-oriented models used in existing object-oriented databases and languages. Specifically,

1. It is built on top of a collection of *base* (or *printable*) object classes such as integers and character strings.
2. It incorporates the notion of a class with instance variables (attributes), which roughly corresponds to the concept of a *tuple, entity*, or *frame* in databases, entity-relationship models, and AI knowledge-representation models, respectively.

3. It incorporates the notion of *collection* classes, which corresponds to sets, lists, sequences, and so on in object-oriented languages and databases.

4. It allows each object to have an identity independent of its type. This corresponds to the notion of object identity of "pointers" in object-oriented programming languages and databases. We can associate identity with base object types, classes (tuples), or collection objects (sets).

5. It provides links for representing *inheritance relationships* between classes.

The entire design of the classes and their relationships is represented by a node-and-link diagram. Here we present a subset of the model.

Node Types

In most cases nodes represent types or classes. To distinguish whether it is a value or a reference (i.e., has object identity) we use dashed lines and solid lines. Thus, values have dashed-line perimeters, and classes, or object types with identity, have solid-line perimeters.

Figure 3.23 illustrates a rectangle representing a user-defined class and an oval representing a base class.

Both of these examples illustrate classes with solid lines, indicating that references to the class will incorporate object identity (similar to *reference to*, *object of type*, or *identity of*). This is the default. However, there are many cases (especially for the base types) in which the references are to instances that are values. To indicate this, dashed lines are used as illustrated in Figure 3.24.

In terms of the set-and-tuple models, the ovals represent what are often called the "atomic" types. With a hybrid model (one that incorporates both identities and values), solid ovals represent atomic objects with identities. Solid rectangles represent tuples with identities. Similarly, dashed ovals represent atomic values, and dashed tuples represent tuple values.

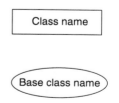

Figure 3.23 User-defined and base classes.

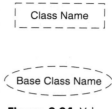

Figure 3.24 Values.

Collection types are represented by circles with labels inside. Keeping a consistent symbolism whenever possible and following the graphical representation given by Bancilhon et al. (1987) and Khoshafian (1989) as well as the GSM described above, an asterisk is used to represent a set. We can use an L inside the circle to represent a list, an A to represent an array, and so on. As usual, a solid perimeter represents sets with identities. This makes the set referentially shareable. These notions are illustrated in Figure 3.25.

In most applications there will be classes that serve solely as common ancestors of a number of subclasses without ever being instantiated. These classes are called *abstract classes*. Thus, abstract classes are used as superclasses of classes that have common behavior and structure. However, we never create instances of abstract classes. As illustrated in Figure 3.26, abstract classes are represented by rectangles with rounded edges.

As indicated earlier, with object-oriented databases applications could be developed through the same environment and language. This is in contrast to, say, relational database development, in which the design of SQL databases and the application that embeds them are more or less independent. Therefore, for object-oriented databases it is useful to indicate classes that are persistent.

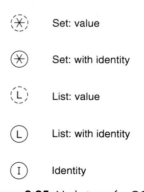

Figure 3.25 Node types for OOD.

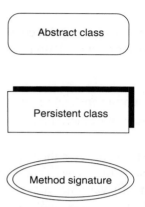

Figure 3.26 Nodes for abstract classes, persistent classes, and methods.

This is achieved by having shadowed rectangles represent classes, as illustrated in Figure 3.26.

Methods

So far the emphasis has been on the structural representation of classes (types). The methods of a type or a class can be represented as attributes of the class. This is the case, for example, with C++, for which methods are captured in member functions (as opposed to member variables).

In order to be consistent with the structural representation, symbolism may be used for which

1. The name of the method (attributes) labels the line that emanates from the class.
2. The line points to a node that represents the type of the attribute.

The *type* of a function (or method) is the *signature* of the function. The signature of a function is the type of its input parameter and the type of its result. In general, it is of the form

$$T1 X T2 X \ldots X Tn \rightarrow Tr$$

where $T1, T2, \ldots, Tn$ are the types of the input parameter and Tr is the type of the result.

In this methodology, the first argument will always be the same type as that of the class to which the method (function) pertains. As indicated in Figure 3.26, the node for a signature is two concentric ovals.

Link Types

The object-oriented design for object-oriented databases also incorporates links. Links are used to represent relationships between classes. The most important link types are

1. Links representing instance variables or attributes
2. Links representing inheritance relationships

Here, the GSM notation for these links is more or less followed. Figure 3.27 illustrates the various link types. The single arrow with a labeled attribute name represents an instance variable; a white arrow represents inheritance; an arrow with a circle as its vertex represents a composition link (for sets and identity).

Examples

Using the node-and-link object-oriented design notation, Figures 3.28 and 3.29 provide examples of the OOD of intelligent office objects. Figure 3.28 illustrates the (persistent) class OfficeWorker with instance variables SocialSecurityNumber and Name. Social Security numbers are integers. Names are instances of class WorkerName, consisting of First and Last names. The figure illustrates candidate keys for the OfficeWorker extension.

Figure 3.29 provides the object-oriented design of a portion of the folder and document classes. As illustrated, both word processor documents and compound documents inherit from General Document. Folders have creator, type, and I.D.; they contain documents. The documents contained in a folder can be instances of any of the subclasses of GeneralDocument. Folders have methods such as "Number of documents," which returns the number of documents in the folder.

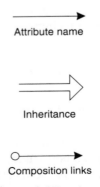

Attribute name

Inheritance

Composition links

Figure 3.27 Link types.

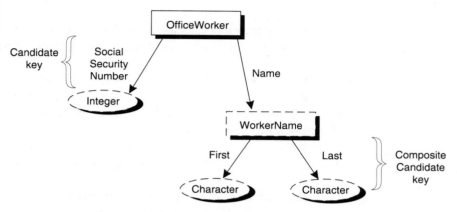

Figure 3.28 Candidate keys for OfficeWorkers.

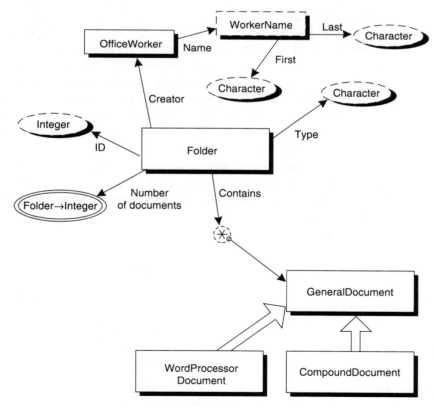

Figure 3.29 OOD in intelligent offices.

Dynamic Model

A dynamic model presents the standards for describing dynamic behavior of classes and objects in the object-oriented design. Specifically, it describes

1. The methodology and symbolism for state transition diagrams;
2. The methodology and symbolism for the inter-object relationships by indicating the control threads to which object instances belong and the messages that objects send to one another
3. The methodology and symbolism for the dynamic relationships between the objects, by specifyiing the order of execution of the messages

Here again we provide a brief overview of various dynamic model constructs.

State Transition Diagrams

The instances of each class will have a well-known collection of states. The states of the instances of a class are typically captured by the values of the instance variables of the class. Each state of a class instance will have a (unique) name. The "events" that cause the state transitions are primarily the protocols, or the interface of the class. In other words, in most cases the events correspond to the messages (especially the update messages) that could be sent to the object.

As illustrated in Figure 3.30 dashed rectangles are used to indicate the states in state transition diagrams. Dashed rectangles are used to represent intermediate states, and solid rectangles enclosing a dashed rectangle are used to represent an initial or final state. Arrows labeled with the name of the event or method that causes the state transition are also used.

Figure 3.31 represents a state transition for folders. Each folder has an initial and final state of being *Closed*. As a result of a click or open message, the folder state switches to *Open* (not searched). After a search is performed the folder state switches to *Open* and *Searched*.

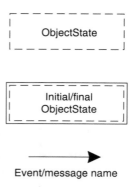

Figure 3.30 State transition diagram nodes and link.

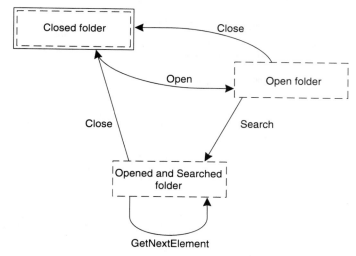

Figure 3.31 State transition for folders.

Note that at each state transition the arrows emanating from the state correspond to those messages that the state could accept or respond to. For instance, it does not make sense to send an *Open* message to a folder that is already open.

Object Instance Diagrams and Dynamic Relationships between Objects

The next type of symbolism deals with the messages sent between objects. Basically, this corresponds to the messages sent *from* an object to either the instance variables of the object or other "external" objects.

Since messages have arguments, each message will have a number of "slots" that will be pointed to by object instances. Sometimes a message *returns* a value. To distinguish between input and output slots, dashed slots are used for input and solid slots for output. In some cases a double rectangle (a solid enclosing a dashed slot) indicates an object that is both input *and* output. A dashed arrow emanating from an object points to one of these slots.

Each target object of a message is indicated by a rectangle. Since the *same* object could be the target of multiple messages, the object instances and *all* of the messages (which basically constitute the "protocol," or the interface of the object) pertinent to the execution of a method are separated by a line. In fact, on a single diagram we can depict messages emanating from multiple methods pertaining to the same instance.

Figure 3.32 illustrates the notation for objects, their protocols, and how they send messages to each other. Using the node-and-link model for

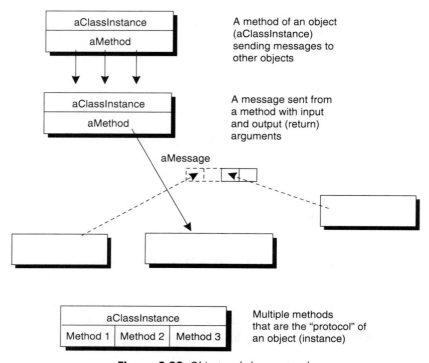

Figure 3.32 Object and class protocols.

the dynamic interaction of objects, the object-oriented design consists of the following:

1. There is a specification of the messages that are sent to other object instances from a particular method of an object. For a more precise specification as to how a particular method is implemented, we also specify the *order* of the messages emanating from a method. The order number labels the origin of the message arrow.

2. There is a label of a message and the name of the "protocol,"or method of the object, to which the message is sent (which should match).

3. If the message has an *output* or returns an object, the output is indicated by a solid box.

4. An arrow emanates from the object to the solid box. Since these are *object instance diagrams*, the arrows emanating from the same box indicate the same object. The argument arrows emanating from objects to input or output arguments are dashed.

5. An object that is an argument of a message (input) is indicated by a dashed box.

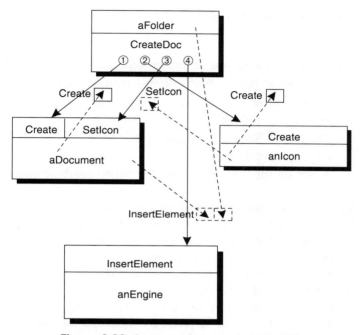

Figure 3.33 Creating a document dynamic OOD.

Figure 3.33 illustrates the creation of a document in a folder. First, the folder sends the message *Create* to the document class to create a document. Similarly, an icon is created for the document. Then, with the icon as an argument a message is sent to the document just created to set its icon. Finally, assuming that we have an "insertion engine" object, the document and folder are arguments of the *InsertElement* message sent to the engine.

▪ 3.8 INTEGRITY CONSTRAINTS FOR OBJECT-ORIENTED DATABASES

Through transactions, database management systems map one *consistent* (correct) database state onto another. The consistency of the database is typically expressible through *predicates*, or conditions, on the current state of the database. Predicates can also apply to objects or attribute values in the database. The predicates that capture the consistency of a database are called *integrity constraints*. Generally, a number of integrity constraints must be enforced on a database state to guarantee its consistency. The following are some examples:

- The age of a person cannot be a negative number.
- An account balance must be less than or equal to the sum of the deposits.
- If an employee works for a department, a record for that department must exist in the database.
- The Social Security number of each employee must be unique in the set of all employees.
- A person must have a name; the Name attribute cannot be empty or null.

As these examples suggest, many types of integrity constraints must be imposed on a database to maintain its consistency.

Relational database management systems have several categories for integrity constraints, such as referential integrity constraints, domains, and *NOT NULL* constraints (Khoshafian et al., 1992a). Most of these constraints are also valid in object-oriented databases, although due to the object-oriented constructs and the expressive power of the underlying model some constraints are either no longer relevant (such as referential constraints) or take on a different form (such as domains). In fact, the object-oriented concepts in object-oriented databases introduce other types of integrity constraints or integrity constraint specifications.

The integrity constraints for object-oriented databases discussed in this section include the following:

1. Unique/primary key constraints
2. Referential to existential constraints
3. *NOT NULL* constraints
4. Integrity rules
5. Triggers
6. Pre- and postconditions for methods
7. Specialization constraints
8. Disjointness constraints
9. Covering constraints

3.8.1 Key Constraints

In relational databases the specification of keys, in which one or more keys are specified for various database tables, is common. In object-oriented databases keys are also relevant for any type of collection of tuples or class instances.

Sets of instances of a class can be the class extension or a set object whose elements are specified to be instances of the class. In either case it will be useful to identify one or more attributes as keys, both as a constraint and as a hint to provide faster searches when key values are specified.

Therefore, a *key* is one or more attributes of a class that uniquely identifies an instance of the class in a collection. If a key consists of more than one attribute (column), it is called a *composite key*. Typical examples of keys include the SocialSecurityNumber of a person, the Unique Vehicle Identification Number of a car, and the ProjectNumber in a department. The class OfficeWorker in Figure 3.34 illustrates two (candidate) keys: the tuple with attributes <Last, First> and the column SocialSecurityNumber (by itself).

3.8.2 Referential Constraint

In any value-based model (for instance, the relational model) the most frequently used mechanism for establishing the relationships among the tables and columns is the *referential*, or *foreign key*, constraint. A referential constraint indicates that the attribute value in one table or column is actually a key value referring to another object in a collection.

The following are some examples from relational databases:

- The ManagerID (e.g., Social Security number) of a department's manager is a foreign key of an OfficeWorker record (row) in the relation OfficeWorker.
- Similarly, the DepartmentID in the OfficeWorker relation is a foreign key of a record (row) in the table Departments.

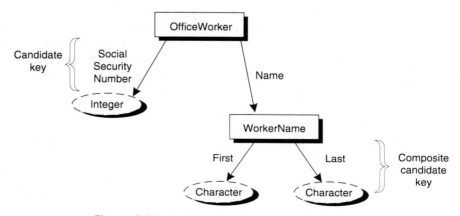

Figure 3.34 Candidate keys for the OfficeWorkers.

Each of the foreign key values is actually a "surrogate" of a foreign object, that is, a logical pointer or an identifier of the object. Therefore, the referential integrity constraint specifications attempt to guarantee that "dangling" references to objects do not exist. For the above examples, the implications are as follows:

- For each `ManagerID` in `Departments` there must exist an `Office-Worker` row whose primary key value (i.e., `SocialSecurityNumber`) is that `ID` appearing in `Departments`.
- For each `DepartmentID` appearing in the `Employees` table, there must exist a `Departments` row with that `ID` as key.

If a database management system supports referential integrity constraints, it will disallow the insert or modification of a foreign key value with no corresponding object in the "foreign" table.

With object-oriented databases that support object identity there is no need for "foreign key" or "referential" integrity constraints. Object identity solves the problem of dangling references and the need for referential integrity constraints. Thus, a powerful and important property of object identity is the ability to reference objects or entities directly. For example, if an `OfficeWorker-Department` database is implemented in an OODBMS, the department of an office worker is referenced and accessed directly by its (tuple) identity instead of an indirect and semantically void number such as `Department-Number`.

3.8.3 Existential Constraint

There is another type of constraint for identity-based models, which is related to referential integrity constraints: the *existential integrity constraint* (Khoshafian and Briggs, 1988). The purpose of existential constraints is to indicate that if an object is referentially shared (which can happen only if the system supports object identity), then it has an "active" domain, that is, a particular collection of objects of the same class that are currently in existence. The existential constraint indicates that the object must always exist in its active domain. The most natural active domain of the object is the extension of the object's class.

Figure 3.35 illustrates this for an `OfficeWorker DayPhoneNumber`. This number is also the phone number associated with an office. Notice that although a phone number is atomic (it can be implemented as a character string or integer), the example illustrates that it is sometimes useful

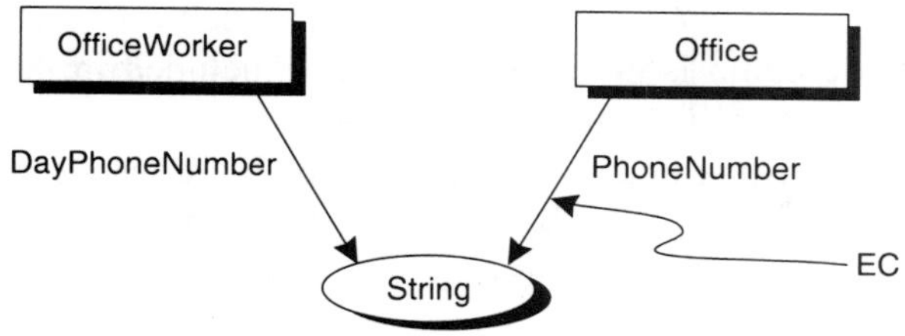

Figure 3.35 Existential constraint.

to have an *object identity* associated even with atomic objects. In this example the string-valued phone numbers referenced from both `OfficeWorker` and `Office` have identities. It is useful to have an existential constraint and, assuming that all day phone numbers are office phone numbers, to require that the active domain of a `DayPhoneNumber` attribute of `OfficeWorker` be the `PhoneNumber` of an `Office` object. In Figure 3.34 this existential constraint is indicated by EC, as given by Khoshafian and Briggs (1988).

3.8.4 *NOT NULL* Constraints

The concepts of a *NULL* value and a *NOT NULL* constraint are useful in object-oriented databases. To support the *NOT NULL* constraint the object-oriented database must support *NULL* values. A *NULL* value represents a "missing" attribute value. The string "NULL" actually indicates an object that is included in the domain of any attribute (instance variable).

In many applications *NULL* values are essential to support statistical analysis. For example, suppose you wish to obtain the average test scores of all students in a class. Some of those scores will be *NULL*, that is, either missing or unavailable for privacy reasons. Although the underlying system must support *NULL* values and three-valued logic, in many cases values of some attributes (instance variables) must not be empty or *NULL*. For instance, each office worker must have a salary, every person must have a name, and each department must have a budget.

In general, when an attribute or a column is declared to be of type T, then the attribute values in the class can be T-values or NULL. For example, if `Age` is of type `Integer`, then the `Age` of a person can be an integer value greater than or equal to zero or NULL. Remember that the *NULL* value represents missing or unknown information. Thus, a NULL for the `Age` of `John` indicates that we do not know what the age of John is. Therefore, when we declare that attribute A is of type T (e.g., attribute `Age` is of type `INTEGER`), then the permissible values of A are all T-values in the system plus NULL (e.g., the permissible values of `Age` are all `Integer` values—0, ± 1, ± 2, ...—plus NULL).

When a *NOT NULL* constraint is specified for an attribute, the range of values for that column is given by the values included in the type of the attribute only (that is, the *NULL* value is not valid).

In object-oriented databases *NOT NULL* constraints and the support of *NULL* values are applicable to both base types (such as integers, floats, character strings, etc.) and user-defined classes (such as `Person`, `Office`, `Folder`, etc.).

3.8.5 Integrity Rules

The integrity constraints discussed so far are special types that apply to attributes (or instance variables). That is,

- Key constraints indicate that the values of particular attributes must be unique within a collection.
- Non-null constraints are used to indicate that attribute values cannot be *NULL*.
- Existential constraints are used to restrict the active domain of attributes.

Whereas these constraints are quite common and useful, many situations are not covered by them. For example,

- Assume that we have two classes with extensions, `OfficeWorkers` and `Departments`, where office workers have salaries and departments have budgets. The following is a constraint on the database:

  - The sum of the workers' salaries must not exceed 50 percent of their department's budget.

- Assume that we have two classes with extensions, `Clients` and `Properties`, in the database. Here are some nontrivial constraints on the database:

  - If the client is not a U.S. citizen, he or she cannot own 50 percent of California's beaches.
  - If a property is co-owned by many clients, the total assets of all of the co-owners must exceed the property value.

It is not practical to have a special integrity constraint category for each constraint. Rather, we need a general mechanism whereby users can express integrity rules. This general mechanism must provide the constructs for the following actions:

1. **Defining the integrity.** The integrity rule will be declared as a predicate that must not be violated. Typically the sublanguage used to define the integrity constraint is the data manipulation language (DML) of the underlying database management system plus a number of constructs for defining the integrity rule itself (e.g., *ASSERT*).

2. **Specifying the actions to be taken when an integrity rule is violated.** In most cases when an integrity constraint is violated, the system will raise an exception that will probably end up aborting the transaction that caused the violation.

The general integrity constraint mechanism is more flexible than the special integrity constraints discussed in the previous sections. For instance, if we have a general integrity constraint definition mechanism, we will be able to define the key, *NOT NULL*, and existential constraints. The difference between the constraints is that *the special integrity constraints are supported by the system* whereas the general integrity constraint mechanism is user-defined. It could be argued that one does not need the system-defined "special" integrity constraints at all. There is some merit to this argument; however, supporting *some* integrity constraints explicitly by a DBMS has at least two advantages:

1. It provides the users with a clear and useful list of the most frequent integrity constraint categories. In most cases, the users do not need to worry about defining the integrity constraint explicitly each time they need it for an application. In a sense, it is similar to code sharing. The system supports these special integrity constraints, and all applications can use them without needing to recode from scratch each time.

2. Since the integrity constraints are "system-defined," there is the *potential* of better performance in supporting or checking the integrity constraint by the underlying system.

Because of these advantages and the need for expressing more general integrity constraints, future systems will most likely support both mechanisms. That is, provide a number of integrity constraint categories as well as allow users to define special integrity constraints by means of an integrity constraint definition sublanguage.

3.8.6 Triggers

The integrity constraints discussed so far are primarily predicates or assertions that should not be violated for a correct or consistent database. If a database operation violates an integrity constraint, the system will probably raise an *exception* (or error condition). The most reasonable response to this exception is the abortion of the transaction that violated the integrity constraint.

Triggers are somewhat different from the integrity constraints discussed so far. They are activated upon the execution of certain database operations or when certain conditions are satisfied. Therefore, conceptually, a trigger consists of a *condition* component and an *action* component. The condition can be either a particular state of the persistent database or the execution of a database operation. The action is a database program that attempts to ensure the integrity of the database state when the condition is satisfied.

Database management systems that support triggers often use the execution of database operations as the condition for activating the trigger. In object-oriented systems that support abstract data typing there are two categories of methods that deal with the *state* of objects: the *accessor* and *update* methods. Briefly, an accessor is a method that accesses a value of an instance variable. If the instance variable is a set, the accessor method can *select* objects from the set. An update method updates the values of instance variables of an object. If the instance variable is a set or collection object, the update might *insert* or *delete* elements from the set.

Given a consistent and correct state of a database, the only way integrity constraints could be violated is by the operations that modify the state of the database (i.e., updates, inserts, and deletes). If the condition is one of these operations, the trigger mechanism could be used to enforce integrity of the database through programs that make sure that integrity constraints are maintained. Note that unlike the previous declarative schemes that let the system enforce integrity constraints (and raise exceptions when constraints are violated), the trigger mechanism allows the database application developer to ensure that integrity constraints are maintained by means of the action that is activated upon the condition.

Triggers could also support other types of integrity constraints, such as domain constraints and non-null constraints. In fact, the trigger mechanism could allow the user to support *all* of the integrity constraints on the database. Triggers are complementary to other integrity constraint mechanisms because they allow database designers and application developers to program the enforcement of the integrity constraint explicitly. For instance, the user could declare an existential constraint either by special existential integrity constraint supported by the system or by a declarative assertion or integrity rule expressed by the designer. As for enforcement of the existential constraint, integrity constraints raise exceptions only when the constraint is violated. It is the responsibility of the programmer or application developer to realize that the object must exist in its active domain.

3.8.7 Pre- and Postconditions for Methods

The persistent classes in an object-oriented database will have accessor, update, and other methods that either retrieve aggregate values from the database or modify the state of the database. Pre- and postconditions with methods provide a powerful mechanism for both debugging and supporting integrity constraints.

Preconditions let us introduce certain constraints on the instance variables that must be satisfied before a particular method is executed. For instance, before retrieving or evaluating an aggregate value, such as the average salary of employees, we want to make sure that all values are *NOT NULL*. This could be expressed through a precondition on the set of worrker's whose average salary we are attempting to evaluate.

Postconditions let us articulate other constraints that must be satisfied upon terminating the execution of the method. For instance, if we raised the salary of an employee and want to guarantee that the employee's salary is not greater than his or her manager's, we can express this as a postcondition of the `GiveRaise` function.

The decision about whether to use object constraints or conditions on methods is a matter of convenience and taste. The two approaches achieve the same effect. Both help the programmer express the semantics of the abstract data type as directly as possible. However, there is no magic in constraints and conditions on either objects or operators. The completeness or correctness of the abstract data type is still only as good as the completeness or correctness of the code used to capture its behavior. It remains the programmer's responsibility to use these constructs to express the semantics of the abstract data type explicitly.

3.8.8 Specialization Constraints

Chapter 2 discussed *constrained overriding* of instance variables. Briefly, if a class $C2$ inherits from a class $C1$ and class $C1$ has an instance variable $A1$ of type $T1$, that is,

$$A1 : T1$$

then $C2$, which inherits from $C1$, can override $A1$, that is,

$$A1 : T2$$

provided that $T2$ is a subtype of $T1$.

The above is inheritance through *restrictions*: A class *C2* inherits from a class *C1* by restricting the domain of its instance variables or methods.

In object-oriented databases for which the extensions of classes could be persistent, a "set inclusion" semantics (Khoshafian et al., 1991) of the class hierarchy allows elements of a superclass to automatically be made elements of the subclass as well, as long as they satisfy certain conditions (restrictions).

Recall the discussion of extensions and deep extensions in Chapter 2. Briefly, consider the class hierarchy rooted at OfficeWorker in Figure 3.36. As indicated, all of the classes are persistent. The deep extension of OfficeWorker is indicated in Figure 3.37. It illustrates the set inclusion semantics: If we traverse all office workers, we will also traverse all secretaries, developers, salespeople, and so on.

Now suppose we introduce *restriction* clauses and allow subclasses to be defined through specifying a *WHERE* clause on the instance variables of a superclass. For example, following the syntax of Intelligent SQL (Khoshafian et al., 1991; Chan et al., 1991; Khoshafian, 1991a) we have a class OfficeWorker defined through:

```
CREATE TABLE Office Worker(
   Name     CHAR(32),
   Salary   INTEGER,
   ...)
```

Now we can define HighlyPaidOfficeWorker through

```
CREATE TABLE HighlyPaidOfficeWorker
SPECIALIZES OfficeWorker
WHERE Salary >= 50,000
```

The WHERE clause is a specialization restriction that identifies the elements of the subclass. Every time we insert into OfficeWorker and the predicate of the WHERE clause is satisfied (in the example, Salary >= 50000), the element automatically becomes an element of HighlyPaidOffice-Worker.[1]

---

[1] Notice that although this mechanism looks very similar to views in relational databases, it is quite different since the sublcasses are materialized relations that, in addition to the restrictions, can have other attributes (columns and instance variables). For more details see the work by Khoshafian et al. (1991).

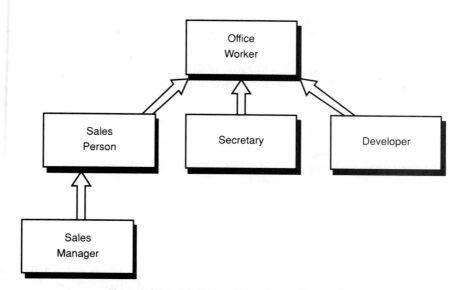

Figure 3.36 Inheritance hierarchy of office workers.

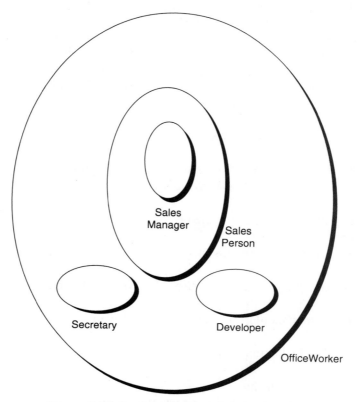

Figure 3.37 The deep extension of OfficeWorker.

Also note that we can have both *extensions* of the superclass through additional attributes or instance variables *and* specialization restriction constraints. For example, we can define

```
CREATE TABLE HighlyPaidManager
SPECIALIZES OfficeWorker
WHERE Salary >= 50,000 (
Rank        INTEGER,
Employees   SET[OfficeWorker]
...   )
```

3.8.9 Disjointness Constraint

The disjointness constraint specifies that two classes cannot have any element in common. In other words, if class *C1* and class *C2* are *disjoint*, we cannot have an element *c* that belongs to both classes. For instance, assume that we have the class hierarchy of Office Workers as illustrated in Figure 3.36. Now suppose we do not want to allow any worker to be both a Developer and a SalesPerson. In other words, Developer and SalesPerson, both of which inherit from OfficeWorker, must be *disjoint*. With this constraint the system will not allow the creation of a subclass (say, DeveloperSales) that inherits from both SalesPerson and Developer. For example, assume John is an OfficeWorker.

```
John = OfficeWorker new
```

(A Smalltalk-like syntax is used here to illustrate the constraint.)

Assume that John is made a Developer and saved in the database:

```
(Developer John) Save
```

Now, if we have the disjointness constraint

```
Developer and SalesPerson are disjoint
```

the system should raise an exception if we try to execute

```
(SalesPerson John) Save
```

3.8.10 Covering Constraint

The covering constraint indicates that a superclass cannot have instances that are *not* elements of a given collection of subclasses. As defined by Lenzerini (1987), "a covering relationship holds when a certain class [*the superclass*] is a subset of the union of other classes [*the subclasses*]." Consider again the example of the class hierarchy rooted at `OfficeWorker`. We have subclasses `SalesPerson`, `Secretary`, and `Developer`. Assume that we want to express the constraint that *every office worker must be either a salesperson, a developer, or a secretary*. One way to achieve this is through *abstract classes*. By making `OfficeWorker` an abstract class, we can never create instances of it, and hence all instances must be elements of one of the subclasses.

The support of covering constraints through abstract classes, however, is not always desirable. Covering constraints are different than abstract classes, since in some cases it will be desirable to create instances of the superclass. In other words, there are cases for which we would like to make the superclass a *nonabstract class* (i.e., a class that can be instantiated) but still have a covering constraint. For example, we might have methods that will instantiate office workers, update their instance variables, and so on and then make the office worker an instance of one of its covering subclasses. With covering constraints the system will complain only if the office worker that is created is not saved as an element of one of the covering subclasses of `OfficeWorker`.

∎ 3.9 SUMMARY

This chapter has provided an overview of various data modeling and object-oriented database design strategies for object-oriented databases. It has discussed strategies for constructing object-oriented database object spaces using *values* and *identities*. As pursued by various models such as Intelligent SQL, the most general scheme is to have a *hybrid* model that supports both. This chapter has also included useful algebraic operations for object-oriented databases such as set operations, generalized *Select, Nest, UnNest,* and so on.

The first step in developing any object-oriented application is providing the object-oriented design. The object-oriented design allows the *classification* (definition of classes) of the project. In object orientation, the design phase is perhaps the most important phase of development. This is especially true for object-oriented databases. This chapter has introduced strategies for designing databases and has discussed a node-and-link object-oriented design mechanism for object-oriented databases that explicitly captures persistence and object identity.

Finally, since database transactions map one consistent database state onto another, an overview of integrity constraints that are particularly applicable to object-oriented databases has been provided.

PERSISTENCE

In object orientation primitives are provided to create, instantiate, and manipulate *objects*. The internal *state* of objects is stored in instance variables. Each object has a *protocol*: the messages to which it responds. Given the fact that the "information hiding" and "encapsulation" of an object's state deal with the *protection* of the data stored in the instance variables of an object, it is not surprising that *object* orientation, even from its earliest days, has concerned itself with the *persistence* of objects between various program invocations.

To achieve persistence of the state of objects in a program, programming languages and environments rely on two basic strategies:

1. *Operating system files:* The most commonly used strategy to "store and retrieve" values is to use operating system files to store either structured text or records that do not contain memory addresses (or "pointers").
2. *Saving the image of a session:* The other strategy, which is used in some Smalltalk and Lisp environments, is to save the entire environment of a session. This saves the object states, the variables, and the environment parameters in one huge operating system executable file.

Each of these strategies has problems. The first allows persistence for only *some* types of objects. The second is potentially inefficient and has a limited ability to share objects concurrently.

The main philosophy behind persistent programming languages is to make persistence orthogonal to the type of objects. In other words, *any* type of object should be allowed to persist. The classical example of persistent programming languages is PS-Algol (Atkinson et al., 1983), which was one of the earliest languages to demonstrate how persistence of an "object" could be orthogonal to the type. *Any* object could persist, even if that object were a record with pointers. Pointer types (which represent in-RAM or virtual memory addresses) are the most difficult types to make persistent. Other examples of early persistent languages include Amber (Cardelli, 1984a) and Galileo (Albano et al., 1985). There have also been attempts to provide persistence for object-oriented languages.

In the context of object-oriented languages, there have been many attempts and products that have incorporated persistence into an object-oriented language. Servio's OPAL, for instance, extends the Smalltalk object-oriented language with persistence and other database constructs. Other systems have incorporated persistence into C++.

Other database concepts that have been incorporated into these object-oriented languages include transactions, querying for bulk data, recovery, and so on. In short, all nine of the features that represent the *database capabilities* discussed in Chapter 1 have been incorporated.

The advantages of extending an object-oriented language with database capabilities are many. One immediate consequence is that it alleviates the *impedance mismatch* that exists between programming languages and database management systems. For instance, in applications that use relational databases the data retrieved from the DBMS using a database query language such as SQL is manipulated using a host programming language such as C. SQL statements are often *embedded* in C programs to read database record values into C variables. Conventional programming languages such as C are procedural. Database query languages are higher-level and more declarative. Therefore, development environments that involve both types of languages mix (mismatch) these different programming paradigms. Furthermore, the data types in the different languages (SQL and C, for instance) are not the same and have to be mapped onto one another.

Extending an object-oriented language with database capabilities is one approach. An alternative approach is to extend a *database language* such as SQL with object-oriented and procedural constructs, an approach taken by some dialects of SQL. Actually, these are two of the approaches that are used to build object-oriented databases and support persistence in object spaces. As discussed in the following sections, there are several other approaches as well as slight variations of these two.

■ 4.1 CHAPTER ORGANIZATION

This chapter is organized as follows. Section 4.2 provides an overview of persistence in object-oriented databases. Section 4.3 discusses persistent object spaces and strategies for implementing object identity. Section 4.4 summarizes the strategies for object-oriented databases. Section 4.5 presents the "novel" database programming language approach, with examples from SIM. Section 4.6 extends an existing database language with object-oriented capabilities. It illustrates approaches that introduce object-oriented extensions to SQL. Section 4.7 presents another powerful approach in implementing object-oriented databases, namely extending object-oriented languages with database capabilities. It focuses on C++, including the means by which persistence can be incorporated into C++, the main software development phases in applications that use database functionality in C++, and different approaches to collection types that are containers of persistent objects. The section also discusses how in Servio's OPAL the "purer" object-oriented language Smalltalk is extended to become a database language. Section 4.8 briefly discusses the approach of embedding an object-oriented database in a host programming language. Section 4.9 illustrates how object-oriented database features can exhibit themselves through a specific application such as intelligent offices. Section 4.10 gives a summary.

■ 4.2 PERSISTENCE IN OBJECT-ORIENTED DATABASES

The term *persistence* is rarely used in the context of databases. Rather, the term used is *database*, which connotes the resilient, concurrently shared object space. The function of a database management system is to allow the concurrent access and update of persistent databases. In order to guarantee the long-term persistence of the data, database management systems employ various *recovery* strategies against transaction, system, or media failures.

There exists a fundamental relationship between concurrent sharing and persistence in databases. Transaction updates must persist, but since the persistent database is concurrently accessed and updated the database management system must concern itself with the consistency of the persistent data objects. As Chapter 5 will show, this is typically achieved by means of concurrency control and recovery strategies. The next section discusses levels of persistence in the context of *transactions*. The detailed definition of transactions will also be given in Chapter 5. For the purposes of discussion in this chapter, transactions are programs that are executed either entirely or not at all. For more details see Section 5.2.

4.2.1 Levels of Persistence

The data manipulated by an object-oriented database can be either *transient* or *persistent*. Transient data is valid only inside a program or transaction; it is lost once the program or transaction terminates. Persistent data, on the other hand, is stored outside of the "context" of a program and thus survives various program invocations.

Persistent data usually consist of the *databases* that are shared, accessed, and updated across transactions. For example, personnel databases, inventory databases, and databases on salespeople, accounts, or items all contain persistent data. However, there are several levels of persistence. The least persistent objects are those created and destroyed in procedures (*local data*). Next, there are objects that persist within the workspace of a transaction but are invalidated when the transaction terminates (aborts or commits). Transactions are typically executed within a session. The user establishes his or her login and sets different environmental parameters within a session, such as paths, display options, windows, etc. If the system supports multiprocessing, several transactions could be active within the same user session at the same time. These transactions will all share the session objects (i.e., the objects that persist for the duration of the session). When the user terminates the session, however, the session objects are invalidated. The *only* type of objects that persist across transactions (and sessions, for that matter) are permanent objects that are typically shared by multiple users. These objects (databases) persist across transactions, system crashes, and even media crashes (e.g., magnetic disk head crashes). Technically, these are the *recoverable* objects of the database. Still, the term *persistent objects* will be used here to identify this most persistent category of objects, with the understanding that there are actually several levels of persistence.

4.2.2 Alternative Strategies for Persistence in Object-Oriented Databases

There are several strategies to indicate which objects should become persistent. The following three strategies are used to create and identify persistent objects:

Persistent Extensions

The notion of a *persistent* extension has always been a fundamental assumption in database management systems. In conventional DBMSs (such as relational), when the user defines a schema using a data definition language (such as the DML of SQL), the definition incorporates both structure and extension. In object-oriented languages users define the structure of objects through the class construct. As mentioned in Chapter 2, a class is like a type in a conventional programming language such as Pascal, except that the class specifies the behavior (operations, or methods) of objects as well as their structure. Most object-oriented databases also use classes to define the structure of objects and their methods. The most essential function of a database management system is to allow users to store, manipulate, and iterate over bulk data. Since a class represents a category of objects that are all of the same "type," it is useful to have persistent class extensions and to treat the class as abstract data type constructor *and* as the container of all of its instances.

Object-oriented database management systems that support persistent extensions typically have *iterators* or other constructs to traverse (navigate) the persistent instances of the class. Object-oriented databases that support persistent extensions have at least three methods by which an object is created:

1. Every time an instance of a persistent class is created it is automatically inserted into the extension.
2. An object can be specified as persistent the moment it is created; this could be specified, for example in the *NEW* constructor of the object.
3. An explicit *Write* or *Save* operation can be required to save the object to the persistent database.

Persistence through Reachability

The second strategy is to have one or more persistent database roots and to make every object that is *reachable* from these roots persistent. This was the approach used in PS-Algol.

Programming or database languages typically incorporate different type constructors for tuples (record, aggregate, etc.) and collection objects (set, extension, group, etc.). Therefore, reachability can be defined transitively using this set-and-tuple model. The persistent object space has a root called `database`, and every object reachable from this database root is persistent. More specifically, the persistent object space is defined as follows:

- The `database` object is a persistent tuple object:

$$database = [S1 : \{\ldots\}, S2 : \{\ldots\}, \ldots, Sn : \{\ldots\}]$$

- If pT is a persistent tuple object then $pT.a$ (i.e., the attribute a of pT) is a persistent object.
- If pS is a persistent set object then every element e of pS is persistent.

Database and programming languages that provide persistence through reachability use a similar definition.

Figure 4.1 illustrates the transient and persistent object spaces accessible in transaction. Note that persistent objects can be subobjects of transient objects, but by the persistent object space definition above the converse cannot happen (any subobject of a persistent object is persistent). In other words, a persistent object can have multiple parents, some of which may be transient. The objects in the transient object space are visible only within the current transaction. When the transaction terminates the transient objects on the right-hand side of Figure 4.1 disappear.

Object-oriented database languages that use reachability to identify the persistent object space include FAD, O2, and OPAL. In O2 and OPAL, rather than one database root (as in FAD and PS-Algol), users can have multiple-named roots of persistent subspaces.

In OPAL, for example, each user has a `UserProfile` object instance that, among other user-specific information (e.g., passwords, access rights, etc.),

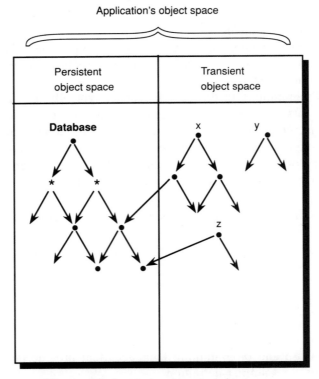

Application's object space

Figure 4.1 Persistent and transient object space.

contains an instance variable called `symbolList`. This instance variable contains the names of all of the objects that serve as the roots of the persistent object space. Objects specified through `UserProfile` can be shared and accessed through different transactions.

Persistent Instances

Another strategy is to render particular instances of a class persistent either by explicitly declaring them to be persistent or by making an existing object persistent through a function call. With this approach persistence is not a property of classes; rather, the user can construct databases and "place" objects in various databases. This is illustrated in Figure 4.2, where the set represents the set of all existing instances of the class `Folder` during run time. The user or application program developer has declared some instances to be persistent and others not. The specification of *which* objects (instances) are persistent is completely independent of the class definition.

This mechanism works well with the persistence-through-reachability approach. Some *entry point* (or *root*) objects will either have references to other objects or contain sets of other objects. These objects will also be persistent through reachability. For instance, if the sales person `John` is an entry point, or root, then objects reachable from `John` such as his customers or his office are all persistent. ObjectStore from Object Design uses such a strategy.

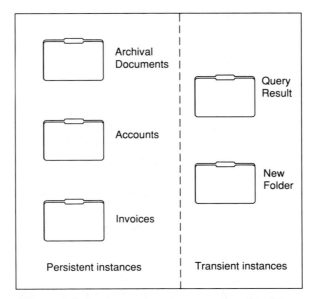

Figure 4.2 Transient and persistent instances of `Folder`.

Persistent Object Spaces

The term *persistent object spaces* primarily refers to the collection of all *instances* that are persistent. In an object-oriented system these are instances of classes. For *classes* and their relationship to persistence in object-oriented systems there are two approaches:

1. Persistent instances or objects must be instances of a *persistent class*. Thus, there is a category of classes that can instantiate persistent objects. Persistent classes can be defined explicitly as persistent or can be persistent by inheriting directly or transitively from a persistent root class, say, `PersistentObject`. The class extension mechanism uses this approach.

2. The system can support persistence without the need to designate explicitly some classes as "persistent" (i.e., it is able to instantiate persistent instances). In a sense this means that *any* or *all* classes can instantiate a persistent instance. The persistence is a property of instances or objects proper.

■ 4.3 PERSISTENT OBJECT SPACES: IMPLEMENTING OBJECT IDENTITY

One of the most fundamental aspects of persistence in programming languages and object-oriented systems is the ability to make *references* or *object pointers* persistent. Persistent languages such as PS-Algol can support persistence of any type, including pointer types. Pointers are useful in constructing graph-structured object spaces and allowing objects to be *referentially shared*. As mentioned in Chapter 2, object identity provides a consistent mechanism to support referential sharing. Thus, one of the most important aspects in understanding the implementation of a persistent object system is the implementation techniques for object identity.

Several implementation strategies can be used to support object identity, including the use of identifier keys and the use of a virtual or physical addresses as identity. These strategies can be used as the underlying implementation techniques that support the more complete object identity concept.

There are two important considerations in implementing identity: transient versus persistent object spaces and address versus indirection strategies.

4.3.1 Transient versus Persistent Object Spaces

The consideration for transient versus persistent object spaces is mentioned here for completeness. As indicated in the previous section, programming languages are being extended with persistence. The basic reason for having a persistent object space in the underlying implementation is to support persistent database and programming languages. Another reason for supporting persistent or secondary storage identifiers is to provide access to a much larger object space.

For instance, an earlier implementation of the Smalltalk-80 virtual machine was a memory-resident transient system that could accommodate only 64K objects (Goldberg and Robson, 1983). Other implementations attempted to extend this limitation and allow a larger object space. One of the earliest attempts was the LOOM (Large Object-Oriented Memory) virtual memory system (Kaehler and Krasner, 1983), which supported objects residing on secondary storage. LOOM achieved support for a much larger number of objects in the object space by implementing object identities using a 32-bit object pointer, as opposed to the 16-bit object pointers of the memory-resident implementations of Smalltalk-80. The basic idea underlying LOOM was to "trap" the object pointer references and transparently load them from secondary-storage-referenced objects on demand. It is interesting to note that ObjectStore from Object Design uses a similar strategy (Object Design, 1992a, 1992b).

4.3.2 Address versus Indirection

The second consideration—the use of an address versus an indirection—provides a more crucial categorization for distinguishing between the different implementation strategies. The address could be

- A virtual memory address
- A secondary storage address
- A structured name in a distributed environment

The indirection could be

- Through a memory-resident table
- Through an index for secondary-storage-resident objects

A fundamental tradeoff between an address-based scheme and an indirection-based scheme occurs between the ease and flexibility of object movements versus the overhead of accessing components of objects.

Indirection through an Object Table

Indirection through an object table involves an Object Table (or array). Each object identifier is an index or pointer to an entry in this table. That entry contains the starting address of the object. Figure 4.3 illustrates this for a person.

Earlier Smalltalk implementations (Krasner, 1983; Goldberg and Robson, 1983) used an object table to implement object identity. The pointers to the table were called *oops* (object-oriented pointers) instead of identifiers. In other words, an Object Table is used to map

Object pointer → memory address

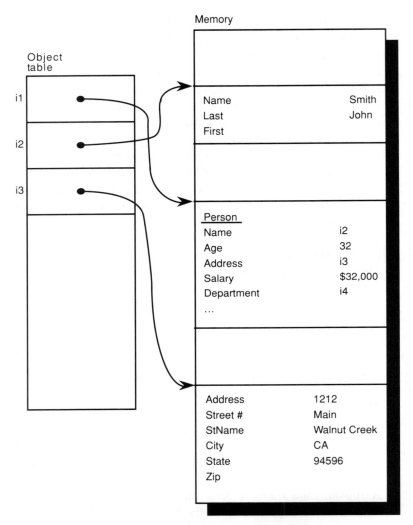

Figure 4.3 Identifiers as object table indexes.

Aside from the memory address, the indirection-based scheme is similar to the address-based scheme described next. Therefore, compared to the address-based schemes, indirection through an object table has to go through an extra level of indirection to access the object's state when using an object pointer.

Although the strategy of indirection through an object table involves an extra memory access and some processing overhead, its advantage is that the objects can be freely moved in memory without affecting their identity. Only the starting memory address of the object needs to be changed, and that is stored in only *one* place in the Object Table. The object-oriented pointer that implements the object identity remains the same. Moving objects is extremely important in garbage collection.

Indirection through an Object Table is used primarily for memory-resident objects. As with the LOOM implementation, the scheme could be combined with a virtual memory system to swap objects to and from secondary storage.

Identity-through-Address Schemes

Perhaps the simplest implementation of the identity of an object is to use the address of the object as its identity. As discussed earlier, this is the main option for reference in conventional languages such as C and Pascal as well as in object-oriented languages such as C++ and Eiffel. Some implementations of Smalltalk even avoid object tables and indirection. One example is the Tektronix 4044 Smalltalk implementation (Caudill and Wirfs-Brock, 1986), in which a large object space is supported by using object addresses directly as object pointers.

Using the virtual address as the identity of an object does not preclude persistence. There are two reasons for this:

1. *Dual representation:* It is possible to have an implementation-of-identity or an object-state representation for secondary-storage-resident persistent objects and a different representation when the object is read into the primary memory. In other words, one scheme of identity is used to support disk-resident objects. When the object is read into primary memory it gets *transformed* to an *in-RAM* representation. The easiest way to do this is to look at each variable in the object's state and replace each secondary storage identity with its primary storage identity, reading it in if necessary. This is the strategy used in LOOM. Since many objects could be transitively reached from an object, it is more convenient to perform the transformations *greedily*, in other words, to access and transform *only if* the object gets referenced.

2. *Persistent store:* It is possible to have a persistent store address space and use it like any other virtual address space. The persistent heap in PS-Algol (Atkinson et al., 1983) uses this approach. There is no difference in the use, referencing, or accessing of objects that are stored in the persistent address space as compared to normal in-memory addresses.

The use of a *virtual address* is just *one* identity-as-address alternative. With persistent collections three other schemes have been used to implement identity. These are *identity through record identifiers, identity through structured identifiers,* and *identity through surrogates.*

Identity through Record Identifiers

In some database management systems, such as System R (Astrahan et al., 1976) and INGRES (Stonebraker et al., 1976), internal record, or tuple, identifiers are introduced to identify individual records in a relation. A relation in these models is a set of tuple objects. A tuple identifier is the secondary storage address of the tuple. It consists of the pair

```
[Disk Page Number, Slot/Line Number]
```

The disk page number identifies a unique secondary disk page on the (logical) hard disk. Each page contains a slot array that contains the pointers to the actual records, or tuples, in the page. The slot or line number indicates the particular entry for the tuple pointer in the page. Strictly speaking, there is partial indirection in the record identifier scheme—the disk page number is direct; the slot array is indirect.

Identity through Structured Identifiers

This scheme is similar to naming conventions for paths in operating systems. Structured identifiers are useful in multiworkstation environments managed by a distributed file system. In some distributed systems, such as the Cambridge File Server (Dion, 1980) and the LOCUS system (Popek et al., 1981), the identifiers of files (the objects of the systems) are structured, such that part of the structure captures an aspect of the location of an object such as a disk or server. More recent distributed file management systems also use a similar strategy.

The structured identifier strategy relies on a *naming* convention: the name of the workstation, the name of the drive, the name of the directory, the name of the file, and so on. However, each name is mapped onto a physical unit or device. Therefore, there is some indirection in mapping the name onto the actual physical entity in accessing the object. This scheme provides full data independence in the sense that the structured identifier is unattached to the actual content of the object. However, as with any addressing scheme, it does not provide location independence; the identifier is a function of where the object is stored.

Identity through Surrogates

Another powerful technique for supporting identity is through surrogates (Abrial, 1974; Hall et al., 1976; Codd, 1979; Bancilhon et al., 1987). Surrogates are system-generated, globally unique identifiers, completely independent of object state or object address. Surrogates are *persistent* identifiers and can be used to access objects in persistent store.

Conceptually, an object identity associated with an object is independent of the object's name, state, type, or location address. The surrogate implementation strategy directly reflects the value, location, type, or name independence of object identity. With the surrogate strategy, each object (of any type) is associated with a globally unique surrogate at the instant it is instantiated. This surrogate is used to represent internally the identity of its object throughout the lifetime of the object.

The surrogate implementation strategy uses *indirection*: Given a surrogate we must still find the address of the object indicated by the surrogate. Unlike the identifier key approach or the object table entry approach, a surrogate is unique *throughout the system*, even if it is distributed. A database identifier key is unique only within the set of tuples or relations.

As illustrated in Figure 4.4, a surrogate is attached to the object as a self-describing special attribute. As long as the surrogate is stored with the object, the object can be moved to a different location, copied, replicated, fragmented, and so on. Leach et al. (1982) discuss several implementation issues involved in the nontrivial task of generating globally unique surrogates in a distributed environment. These issues will not be discussed here.

■ 4.4 ALTERNATIVE STRATEGIES FOR DEFINING AND MANIPULATING PERSISTENT OBJECT-ORIENTED DATABASES

Although standardization efforts do exist, there are currently as many strategies for defining persistent databases in object-oriented databases as there are object-oriented databases.

Chapter 1 summarized six strategies for implementing object-oriented databases. These strategies, which capture the essence of the definition and manipulation of persistent objects in an object-oriented database, are as follows:

1. Using a novel database data model/data language approach
2. Extending an existing database language with object-oriented capabilities
3. Extending an existing object-oriented programming language with database capabilities
4. Providing Extendible object-oriented database management system libraries
5. Embedding object-oriented database language constructs in a host (conventional) language
6. Using application-specific products with an object-oriented model and an underlying object-oriented database management system

The following sections expand upon these strategies with special emphasis on C++ class hierarchies, object-oriented extensions of SQL, and application-specific approaches (more specifically, *intelligent offices*). These three alternatives will likely become the most important and prominent strategies for the next generation of object-oriented databases.

Surrogate	Name		Age	Address					
	Surrogate	LastString	FirstString		Surrogate	Street #	StreetName	City	State	
S1	S2	Smith	John	32	S4	1212	Main	Walnut Creek	CA	
										...
										...
										...

Figure 4.4 Identifiers through surrogates.

■ 4.5 NOVEL DATABASE DATA MODEL AND DATA LANGUAGE APPROACH

The most aggressive approach is to develop an entirely new database language and database management system with object-oriented capabilities. Examples of research projects and commercial object-oriented databases that have pursued this approach are FAD (Bancilhon et al., 1987), Galileo (Albano et al., 1985), and SIM.

SIM (Unisys, 1987a, 1987b), which stands for Semantic Information Manager, is a Unisys Corporation commercial database management system based on the semantic data model. It is the core system of the InfoExec Environment of Unisys. Other products in InfoExec include a data dictionary system, an interactive querying facility, and language interface components.

The data model in SIM is based on the Semantic Data Model of Hammer and McLeod (1981). In SIM users can define entity types (classes) that can inherit from one another. Attributes of entities are like functions from one entity to another. Thus, complex objects and complex relationships between entities can easily be modeled. The attribute functions can be single- or multiple-valued. SIM also allows the specification of various forms of integrity constraints.

SIM introduces novel DML (data manipulation language) and DDL (data definition language) constructs for a data model based on semantic and functional data models. For example, the data definition of `OfficeWorkers` and `Managers` classes in intelligent offices takes the following form:

```
CLASS OfficeWorker
(Name :STRING[32];
WorkerAddress     :Address;
WorkerOffice      :Office;
ReportsTo         :Manager INVERSE IS Manages
);

SUBCLASS OfficeManager of OfficeWorker
(Title            :STRING[10];
 Manages          :OfficeWorker INVERSE IS Manager MV
);
```

Here `Address` and `Office` are also classes.

In addition to its data definition language (which is used to define the persistent classes), SIM also has a data manipulation language. SIM supports constructs to *RETRIEVE* objects from a persistent class's extensions, *INSERT* objects into a persistent class, and *MODIFY* the values of instance variables of an object.

■ **4.6 EXTENDING A DATABASE LANGUAGE WITH OBJECT-ORIENTED CAPABILITIES**

Several programming languages such as C++, Flavors (an extension of LISP), and Object Pascal have been extended with object-oriented constructs. It is therefore conceivable to follow a similar strategy with database languages. Since SQL is a standard and the most popular database language, it seems reasonable to extend it with object-oriented constructs. This approach is being pursued by many vendors of relational systems as they develop to their next-generation products.

After the earlier ANSI/ISO SQL standard became widely accepted, standardization efforts concentrated on an upward-compatible enhancement called SQL2. This standard was ratified in 1992 (Melton and Simon, 1993). Here are some of the extensions incorporated in SQL2:

1. It provides a richer type system, including *DATE, TIME, TIMESTAMP*, and *INTERVAL*.
2. It offers internationalization and better support of character strings.
3. It allows the user to create and name domains (specific ranges of values) using the built-in data types or other domains, which provides a restricted form of specialization.
4. It supports different levels of isolation that can be explicitly set through the <set transaction statement>. There are four levels of isolation: 0, 1, 2, and 3. Level 3 guarantees serializability. The other weaker levels could result in having transactions that read each other's intermediate result (nonserializable execution).
5. It introduces constructs that better capture the underlying relational conceptual model of the language. For instance, it enriches the referential integrity constraint through cascaded deletes.

The SQL2 extensions are primarily *incremental*. Concurrent with the SQL2 standardization effort there is an effort to define a SQL3 standard that will encompass *intelligent database* features. In fact, many "advanced" features originally proposed for SQL2 have been postponed with the intention of incorporating them into SQL3. The following are some object-oriented and intelligent database extensions that are being integrated into SQL3:

- Object-oriented extensions
- Integrity constraint extensions
- Support of recursion
- Roles as a security mechanism
- Savepoints

Object-oriented features proposed for SQL3 include the following:

1. *User-defined abstract data typing:* Most SQL systems come with a built-in collection of abstract data types: integers, floating-point numbers, character strings, dates, timestamps, and so on. To be more flexible and to satisfy user needs for extendibility, one trend is to enrich these abstract data types and support additional types. A more realistic approach is to allow users to develop *their own abstract data type* in a host language such as C. Subsequently, tables could be defined with column values that are user-defined abstract data types. The operations and methods of the abstract data types could be used in SQL statements. User-defined abstract data typing can be thought of as a generalization of *DOMAINs* supported in SQL2 and further enhanced in SQL3.

2. *Inheritance:* Inheritance hierarchies can be defined for domains or abstract data types and tables. The abstract data type inheritance is similar to inheritance of classes in object-oriented systems. Classes do not have extensions. Table definitions, on the other hand, define both structure and extension. SQL3 includes a proposal for table inheritance. Other object-oriented extensions that could be incorporated into SQL include *tuples* (structure-valued attributes) and *object identity*. These features and a more detailed description of how abstract data typing and inheritance could be incorporated into SQL will be discussed in the context of *Intelligent SQL*.

4.6.1   Intelligent Databases and Intelligent SQL

The incremental and radical extensions of SQL are elements of the next-generation databases, namely *intelligent databases* (Parsaye et al., 1989; Khoshafian et al., 1990b). Intelligent databases integrate the following:

- Object orientation
- Deductive rules (expert systems and AI)
- Information retrieval
- Multiple media

Figure 4.5 illustrates the features of intelligent databases. Some of these features are discussed in the next section, which deals with Intelligent SQL. Some elements of Intelligent SQL were discussed by the OODB task group in May 1990 (Khoshafian, 1991a). More detailed inheritance and generalization properties of Intelligent SQL are presented in works by Chan et al. (1991) and Khoshafian et al. (1991); features and architecture of intelligent database engines that support Intelligent SQL are presented by Khoshafian et al. (1990b). Deductive reasoning extensions to SQL systems are presented by Khoshafian and Thieme (1991).

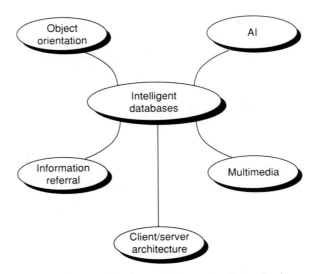

Figure 4.5 Some of the technologies in intelligent databases.

Note that Intelligent SQL is neither the first nor the only database language to incorporate object-oriented or other intelligent database constructs into a relational language. In fact, it has already been mentioned that object-oriented features such as user-defined abstract data typing and inheritance are being integrated into the next-generation SQL3 standard. Other examples include PROSQL (Chang and Walker, 1986), which interfaced PROLOG with SQL/DS, and the POSTGRES experimental database management system (Stonebraker and Rowe, 1986; Stonebraker et al., 1990b), which extended a relational system with abstract data types, constructed types (similar to *tuple* types in Intelligent SQL), and a rule system. Some object-oriented databases have even used object-oriented extensions of SQL as their query language. Iris (Fishman et al., 1987) from Hewlett-Packard supports an extension of SQL called Object SQL, which allows querying of an object-oriented database using SQL-like syntax. The ONTOS object-oriented database management system supports a dialect of SQL (ONTOS SQL) that incorporates object-oriented features (Ontologic, 1991).

4.6.2 Object-Oriented Constructs in Intelligent SQL

The three main concepts of object orientation are encapsulation, inheritance, and object identity. All three concepts are integrated into Intelligent SQL. Section 3.4 already discussed how tuples and object identity are incorporated into Intelligent SQL. This section focuses on other features such as abstract data types, inheritance, and multimedia types.

Abstract Data Types

For abstract data typing, methods and operations can be associated with

- User-defined data types, such as a stack
- Tuple types, such as an address
- Tables, such as employees and departments

The user-defined abstract-data-typing concept is an extension of another useful concept supported by several commercial databases, namely *user-defined functions*. SQL systems typically come with a built-in collection of aggregate functions: *AVERAGE, MAX, MIN, COUNT, SUM*, and so on. Many systems allow users to define their own functions (and to invoke these functions in SQL statements) using either a fourth-generation language (such as dBASE), a general-purpose programming language (such as C), or a procedural extension of SQL (such as TransactSQL). Abstract data typing extends this notion to types such that both types and operations could be constructed by a user and used in persistent SQL systems.

As mentioned earlier, there is a SQL3 proposal for user-defined abstract data typing. Consider a generic stack type example that can be used in Intelligent SQL tables. The generic *Stack* class has *Push* and *Pop* methods. The type parameter will allow us to create stacks of different types of objects:

```
CREATE CLASS Stack[T] (
INSTANCE VARIABLES (
        ARRAY StArr[M] of T,
        Top   INTEGER);
METHODS (
 Push
 Stack X T -> Stack
(St Stack, Value T
 St.Top = St.Top + 1
 St.StArr[St.Top] = Value
 RETURN St);

 Pop
 Stack -> T
(St Stack
 St.Top = St.Top - 1
    RETURN StArr[St.Top + 1]);))
```

Once the data type stack is defined, it can be used in Intelligent SQL tables:

```
CREATE TABLE Account
  AccountNumber      INTEGER,
  Location           CHAR(20)
  Payables           Stack[DOLLAR])
```

and Intelligent SQL queries:

```
SELECT AccountNumber, Pop(Payables)
FROM Account
WHERE Location = "New York"
```

Inheritance

Inheritance is a powerful object-oriented concept that can be used to organize the structure and instances of persistent tables. As stated earlier, the SQL3 next-generation standard supports inheritance through an *IS-A* construct. Here, *SPECIALIZES* is used instead of *IS-A*. In fact, it is also possible to start from existing tables, discover commonalities, and *GENERALIZE* to supertables. Specialization and generalization in Intelligent SQL are discussed by Khoshafian et al. (1991) and Chan et al. (1991).

The following is an example of table inheritance involving office workers in intelligent offices:

```
CREATE TABLE OfficeWorker(
  Name            CHAR(20),
  Address         CHAR(100),
  WorkerOffice    CHAR(10),
  Salary          FLOAT,
  DateOfBirth     DATE
)


CREATE TABLE Manager
  SPECIALIZES OfficeWorker(
  Title           CHAR(10))


CREATE TABLE VicePresident
  SPECIALIZES Manager(
  AdminAssistant  CHAR(20))
```

Then, to retrieve the name and address of all managers who earn more than $60 thousand, we have

```
SELECT Name, Address
FROM Manager
WHERE Salary > 60k
```

In other words, the table `Manager` inherits the columns `Name` and `Address` from `OfficeWorker`.

Since the definition of a table incorporates the definition of a *structure* and extension (the set of all rows of the table), table inheritance in Intelligent SQL has a *set inclusion* semantics. This means that if table $T2$ is a subtable of table $T1$, the elements (rows) of $T2$ are also elements of $T1$. This is illustrated in Figure 4.6. An important implication of the set inclusion semantics is that when we execute a query such as

```
SELECT Name, Salary
FROM OfficeWorker
WHERE DateOfBirth > 10/10/45
```

we retrieve the names and salaries of all regular office workers, managers, vice presidents, and so on. In other words, the query is over the *deep extension* of `OfficeWorker`.

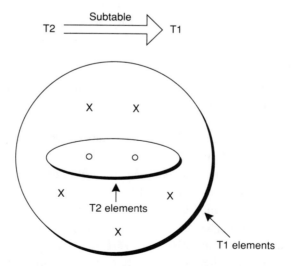

Figure 4.6 Set inclusion semantics of subtables.

Another implication of this is that upon any deletion or modification of a set of rows in a supertable, the corresponding rows are deleted or modified in all subtables. For instance, the statement

```
DELETE FROM OfficeWorkers
WHERE Salary >= 100,000
```

will delete vice presidents, managers, and office workers who earn more than $100,000!

Inheritance in Intelligent SQL can also be performed through *restrictions*. As described by Khoshafian et al. (1991), the general form of inheritance in Intelligent SQL is

```
CREATE TABLE <table name>
        SPECIALIZES <restricted table name list>
        [AS <column name list>]
        [<table elements>]
```

where

```
<restricted table name list>
        ::=<restricted table name>[, ... ]
<restricted table name>
        ::=<table name>
                [WHERE <restriction clause>]
<table attributes list>::=<table attributes>  [, ... ]
<table attributes>::=<table name> (<columns list>)
```

The rules for the semantics of inheritance in Intelligent SQL can be summarized as follows:

1. The graph of the table inheritance hierarchy is a directed acyclic graph (DAG); that is, there are no cycles.
2. If an *AS* clause is specified, the columns inherited from the supertables are renamed to the names in the *AS* clause.
3. The inheritance hierarchy has a set inclusion semantics.
4. For any supertable with a *WHERE* clause specified, the elements of the supertable that satisfy the *WHERE* clause are also elements of the subtables. This is another consequence of the set inclusion semantics and implies that a row that is inserted into a supertable will be "inserted" into any subtables having a *WHERE* clause that the tuple satisfies.

As an example of inheritance using restriction (the *WHERE* clause), consider the following definitions:

```
CREATE TABLE HighlyPaidWorker
       SPECIALIZES OfficeWorkers
       WHERE Salary > 60,000

CREATE TABLE AveragePaidWorkers
       SPECIALIZES OfficeWorkers
       WHERE Salary > 25,000 and <= 60,000
```

Then, with the above semantics, every time we insert an office worker (or a manager or vice president) who earns, say, more than $60,000, that worker is automatically an element of HighlyPaidWorker.

Although the restriction mechanism and certainly the examples look similar to the *VIEW* mechanism in SQL, they are actually quite different. The tables that specialize through restriction are materialized (physical) tables *that can also introduce additional columns and rows*. In other words, we can have specialization through extension and specialization through restriction in the *same* subtable definition. Furthermore INSERTs and DELETEs could be performed directly on tables that are specializations of other tables (through restriction or otherwise).

Generalization

Inheritance usually connotes *specialization*, and, as discussed in Chapter 2, specialization uses a top-down approach to database construction. Generalization is the complement to specialization; it uses a bottom-up approach. In generalization, supertables are constructed from existing tables; these supertables can then be used to create new specialized tables. The general form of generalization in Intelligent SQL is

```
CREATE TABLE <table name>
GENERALIZES <subtable list>
[AS <column name list>]
```

Assuming that we have students in the database defined through

```
CREATE TABLE Student(
  Name            CHAR(20),
  Address         CHAR(100),
  GPA             FLOAT,
  Advisor         CHAR(20),
  DateOfBirth     DATE)
```

we can define

```
CREATE TABLE Person
 GENERALIZES OfficeWorker, Student
```

This statement will introduce a Person table in the database with the columns Name, Address, and DateOfBirth (the common columns in Office-Worker and Student).

The generalized table Person is implicitly populated with the union of rows from the subtables OfficeWorker and Student. Once a table such as Person is declared as a generalization of existing tables (such as OfficeWorker and Student, the semantics of the inheritance relationship is the same as the declarations

```
CREATE TABLE Person

CREATE TABLE OfficeWorker
SPECIALIZES Person
⋮
CREATE TABLE Student
SPECIALIZES Person
```

Because generalization allows the "integration," or union, of *existing* tables into more generalized tables, it provides an excellent model for the bottom-up integration of existing distributed databases (Chan et al., 1991; Khoshafian et al., 1991).

Multimedia Data Types

There is a close relationship between multimedia objects and object-oriented databases. Some database management systems support multimedia data types, such as text, images, voice, and video that can be arbitrarily large. For instance, the Microsoft SQL server supports *TEXT* and *IMAGE* fields that can be up to two gigabytes in each row! Although long fields can be stored in operating system files, storing them in the database allows the multimedia data to be shared concurrently by many users under transaction control. In most relational database systems that support long fields (called *BLOB, LONG VAR-CHAR, IMAGE, TEXT*, and so on) the functionality is primarily that of storing and accessing the fields, without much consideration of *data typing (structure + operations)*.

Some extensions of SQL, including Intelligent SQL provide special operators and predicates to query and retrieve multimedia objects. They extend the *BLOB* or long data field object support of some existing relational database management systems with more *intelligent* multimedia types. The "intelligence" in the multimedia type support is exhibited through either *content searches* of multimedia objects or the association of attributes and different operations with multimedia object structures.

Text Data

Text documents are the most popular storage medium in the office environment. In the typical office automation environment, however, full-text management and record management are completely independent. Users must interact with two independent and unrelated products to perform table searches and searches for long text fields within table rows. This is because the typical office environment information management and database management are decoupled.

Intelligent databases integrate information and database management. There have been a number of proposals to integrate full-text querying capabilities into SQL. The most notable of these is the SFQL proposal (AIA/ATA, 1990).

Here an Intelligent SQL approach that allows users to create, update, and retrieve text fields based on full-text boolean expressions is described. The Intelligent SQL approach is similar to SFQL in many aspects, the most important being the provision of complex boolean searches. The boolean expressions can appear in SQL *WHERE* clauses in conjunction with the usual search expressions.

If T is a text-valued field, then an expression of the form

$$[\text{``}Term1\text{''} \ AND \ \text{``}Term2\text{''} \cdots AND \ \text{``}Termn\text{''}]IN \ T$$

can appear as a SQL predicate. This expression is a predicate that is true if and only if all of the terms *Term1* , . . . , *Termn* are in T. Other kinds of boolean expressions involving *OR* and *NOT* are also allowed.

The following query retrieves the `Author` and `Publisher` of all books about "Object Orientation" and "Databases" or "Semantic data models" published before 1986:

```
SELECT Author, Publisher
FROM Books
WHERE
["Object Orientation" AND "Databases" OR
   "Semantic data models"] IN BookText
   AND Year <= 1986
```

The schema of Books is

```
CREATE TABLE Books (
Author                  CHAR(20),
Publisher               CHAR(20),
BookText                TEXT,
Year                    INTEGER)
```

Another important aspect of the text retrieval is the *RANK* or *RELEVANCE* of the returned text. For instance, if we are searching for the occurrence of a particular term and that term occurs 10 times in one record and 100 in another, the second record is more relevant. That is, frequency of count is often used as a measure of relevance (Salton, 1983; Salton, 1989). If we want the same query to also return the rank or relevance we have

```
SELECT Author, Publisher, RANK(BookText)
FROM Books
WHERE
["Object Orientation" AND "Databases" OR
   "Semantic data models"] IN BookText
                AND Year <= 1986
```

Image Data

Image data can correspond to graphs, charts, moving video images, or two-dimensional bitmaps; in vector format it can correspond to groups of shapes at specific positions and with specific sizes, shades, and colors. In general, the memory requirements using vector format are less than for the bitmapped storage of the same image. However, vector format is not as general as bitmaps. Images can be generated by scanners or imported from external PCX, TIF, or other image files. Images can also be used to represent spatial or geographic data.

Each of these formats has relative advantages and functionalities, and Intelligent SQL supports both raster and vector images. Supporting tuple-valued attributes as in the object-oriented extension of SQL helps cluster the media-specific information with the multimedia field.

For vector images, Intelligent SQL has built-in data types such as *RECTANGLE* and *POINT*. Each of these data types is a tuple type that can be further specialized by the user. For example, *RECTANGLE* is given by

```
CREATE TUPLE RECTANGLE(
        LOW-LEFT        XY-POINT,
        UP-RIGHT        XY-POINT,
        SCALE           FLOAT,
        ORIGIN          POINT,
        PICTURE         OBJECT IMAGE)
```

Here LOW-LEFT and UP-RIGHT indicate the lower left and upper right corners of a rectangle; the scale and origin provide the necessary information to place the rectangle on the IMAGE. The IMAGE field stores either the image contained in the rectangle or the image of the environment in which the rectangle is contained (e.g., the rectangle contains a map, and the IMAGE is the map of Madison, Wisconsin).

Similarly, POINT is a built-in data type given by

```
CREATE TUPLE POINT(
     POINT              XY-POINT
     SCALE              FLOAT,
     ORIGIN             FLOAT
     PICTURE            OBJECT IMAGE)
```

where SCALE, ORIGIN, and IMAGE are as before, and XY-POINT is a tuple giving the X and Y coordinates of a point that is given by

```
CREATE TUPLE XY-POINT (
     X-COORD            FLOAT,
     Y-COORD            FLOAT)
```

Following the PSQL (Pictorial SQL) proposal (Roussopoulos et al., 1988) associated with the "spatial" data types *RECTANGLE* and *POINT*, Intelligent SQL has a number of "built-in" operations such as *COVERED-BY, OVERLAPS, CLOSEST, PERIMETER,* and *AREA.* For example, to retrieve the city name, state, and population of all cities a unit distance from the point [4,9] with a population greater than 1 million we have

```
SELECT City, State, Population
FROM Cities
WHERE Location COVERED-BY {4 +/- 1, 9 +/- 1}
   AND Population > 1,000,000
```

Here the schema of Cities is

```
CREATE TABLE Cities (

    City              CHAR(20),
    State             CHAR(20),
    Location          POINT)
```

Intelligent SQL can also perform a juxtaposition query of dissimilar information stored in multiple spatial objects. If REC1 and REC2 are rectangles we can specify predicates such as

REC1 OVERLAPS REC2
REC1 BORDERS REC2
REC1 COVERED-BY REC2

in SQL *WHERE* clauses.

Other Approaches

SQL is the most popular database language, and as the number of extensions to the SQL standard passing through the ANSI and ISO standardization committees testifies, there is a clear direction for incorporating object-oriented features into next-generation RDBMS products. In fact, several leading RDBMS companies either have already incorporated object-oriented features into their RDBMS products or are planning to do so in the near feature.

As mentioned earlier, some object-oriented database management system vendors such as Ontos, Versant, and HP are providing some "object-oriented SQL" support to query and, in some cases, to update the persistent object spaces. These are, however, primarily SQL-like query languages on top of object-oriented database management systems, and the approach is different from relational DBMSs that support powerful relational engines and models and *extend* them through object-oriented features. Usually, the object-oriented extensions of SQL supported by these vendors are intended to provide alternative convenient and familiar interfaces for querying the persistent object spaces. Furthermore, the successful incorporation and implementation of object-oriented features in SQL provides opportunities to utilize powerful object-oriented features on existing relational databases.

■ 4.7 EXTENDING AN EXISTING OBJECT-ORIENTED PROGRAMMING LANGUAGE WITH DATABASE CAPABILITIES

Another approach is to introduce database capabilities to an existing object-oriented language. In this case the object-oriented features (abstract data typing, inheritance, and object identity) will already be supported by the object-oriented language. The extensions will incorporate the database features of querying, transaction support, persistence, and so on.

There are (at least) two options for extending an object-oriented language with database libraries:

1. Use language extensions that enrich, or extend, the object-oriented language with database management capabilities. For instance, Servio's OPAL language extended Smalltalk with database management classes and primitives. OPAL introduced constrained collection objects to store bulk data of the same structure, as well as selection blocks to have quantified queries on the constrained collection objects.

2. Provide extendible object-oriented database management system libraries. Servio introduced new language constructs to an existing object-oriented language; Ontos, Versant, Object Design, Objectivity, and others introduced a C++ client library for database management. The distinction between a language extension that needs to be preprocessed and a library is often blurred, and more often *both* mechanisms are used to embed or incorporate database capabilities within the object-oriented language (this is especially true in the case of C++). The libraries include classes for aggregates (sets, lists, arrays) and types. They have methods for *start/commit/abort* transactions, exception handling, and object clustering. For instance Ontos, Object Design, Objectivity, and Versant all provide C++ libraries for object-oriented database application development.

4.7.1 C++ Classes for Database Management Capabilities

In terms of class hierarchies that support persistence and database capabilities, C++ class libraries are by far the most popular. The C++ language was designed by Bjarne Stroustrup at AT&T in the early 1980s (Stroustrup, 1986). Stroustrup's early experience with SIMULA, the first object-oriented language, influenced his design of C++. The language's acceptance spread from AT&T to major universities and other computer industry firms.

The first implementation of the C++ language was released as a preprocessor to C compilers. There, is however, nothing inherent in the design of the language that demands a preprocessor approach, and its release as a preprocessor was intended to ease the adoption of C++. Currently, there are several C++ compilers from major software companies such as Borland and Microsoft.

C++ provides some support of all object-oriented concepts: abstract data types, inheritance, and object identity.

1. *Abstract data types:* C++ provides two constructs for abstract data type definition. The first is an extension of the *struct* construct, and the other is through the new *class* construct. The *struct* construct in C allows structural definition of an object composed of several members. To enable this, C++ extends the ability of defining functions as attributes of an object definition. All properties of a class declared through this construct are public, with the C++ compiler backward-compatible with existing C code. To the *struct* construct,

C++ adds the new *class* construct. With it, the designer constructs classes conforming to the traditional object-oriented view that instance variables can be hidden.

2. *Inheritance:* C++ allows a hierarchy of class definitions to inherit methods and instance variables from existing class definitions. The first release of C++ allowed only a tree hierarchy (single inheritance) to be defined. C++ also allows multiple inheritance.

3. *Object identity:* C++ does not support the strong notion as in Smalltalk. However, C++ allows reference to objects by either name or address. The address of an object can be used as a reference in the definition of a complex object. For a user-defined class the language provides copy constructors automatically. No operations are provided to compare user-defined objects. The only system-supported comparison of objects is by the value of their addresses. Users can develop either comparison or copy operations as part of class definition.

4. *Polymorphism and dynamic binding:* C++ allows ad hoc polymorphism by allowing overloading of function names and operators. Function names can be overloaded to have varied numbers of arguments of different types. System defined operators such +, −, and * can be overloaded by user-defined classes. C++ also supports parameterized types. Through this mechanism, type constructors such as sets and lists can accept type parameters as in Set<OfficeWorker> and List<Office>.

Given these advantages and the popularity of C++ it is not surprising that many object-oriented database management system companies such as Ontos, Versant, ObjectDesign, and Servio provide either C++ language extensions (which need to be preprocessed) or C++ class libraries for defining and manipulating persistent databases.

4.7.2 Persistent Roots or Entry Points

Typically, the persistent classes are defined by their inheritance from a root persistent class, say, PersistentObject. This is illustrated in Figure 4.7. Every class that has persistent instances must be a descendant of this persistent root class. Thus, PersistentFolder, which is a direct descendant of PersistentObject and which represents the most generic class of folders, can have persistent instances. Transitively, so can ResumesFolder and AccountFolder. The classes that are reachable through the PersistentObject root using inheritance hierarchies, therefore, represent the templates of the persistent object space in the database.

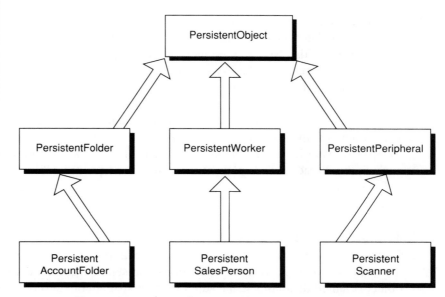

Figure 4.7 Persistent classes routed at `PersistentObject`.

In various database management system products the name or specific features of the root persistent class differ, but the main function is usually the same. Among other things, the `PersistentObject` class provides useful methods shared by all persistent objects. Some of these methods are described below:

1. Constructors called *new* with various parameters to instantiate ' and store persistent objects, including the location of the object (*where* the created object should be stored), access rights on the object, and so on

2. Methods to destroy the persistent object or remove it from the persistent object space

3. Methods to *Read* the instance variables of an object from the database and *Write* the current state of the object back to the database

4. Methods to *Lock* and *Unlock* the object to provide explicit concurrency control on the object by the user

5. Predicates to check whether the object has been modified

4.7.3 Extensions

Object-oriented databases that support C++ class hierarchies also allow the application developer to request that the *extension* (i.e., the set of all existing instances) be maintained explicitly by the OODBMS so that it can be traversed and otherwise manipulated by the application as a collection. Extensions were discussed in Section 4.2. The key point here is that the developer using the object-oriented database has (sometimes) the *option* of specifying whether the system *should* maintain the extension.

Since the instances of the class could be persistent, the notion of extension for the persistent class usually means, among other things, that the class can be treated as a collection object. For instance, if OfficeWorker should keep track of the set of all existing instances [i.e., all office workers—its (deep) extension], we can iterate over each office worker in some specific order such as by Name and display every office worker in a table; or we can iterate over all office workers to evaluate the average salary of all workers, and so on.

4.7.4 Collections and Relationships

Database management systems are used to manipulate bulk data. In most cases the data is stored in various collections, or sets. A common feature of most object-oriented databases is the support of persistent collections and one-to-many or many-to-many relationships. Object-oriented databases that support persistent collections typically support collection objects such as arrays, sets, lists, and dictionaries. Instances of these collection objects will be values of instance variables in persistent classes. In terms of the inheritance hierarchies there are many possibilities. Most of the time the inheritance hierarchies are *implementation hierarchies* and not subtype hierarchies. For example, behaviorally, a set could be a subtype of a bag because it introduces the restriction that the collection cannot contain duplicates. In terms of implementation, however, it is conceivable to have completely separate implementations of sets and bags.

Besides providing mechanisms to *insert, delete,* or *update* an object of a collection, collection objects typically provide operators (or *iterators*) to traverse the elements of the collection. In fact, an application might choose to provide a higher level of abstraction for navigating the elements of a collection and allow itself to modify the implementation later.

For example, assuming that each Folder contains a set of Documents, the persistent Folder class can support the following public methods:

```
Document* GetFirstDocument();
Document* GetNextDocument();
Document* GetLastDocument();
```

Then, the pseudo-C++ source code for navigating and printing the Name of every document in folder F1 is

```
Dp= F1.GetFirstDocument();
while (Dp != NIL)
{
    cout << Dp->NameOf();
    Dp = F1.GetNextDocument();
};
```

Collection Constructors

The following collection types are some *collection constructors* that can be used in persistent C++ classes. Note that support of collection types for C++ objects is not limited to *persistent* class hierarchies; collection types are useful for transient object collections as well.

Sets

Sets are collections of objects that in most cases do not contain duplicates. For instance, an OfficeWorker can have a set of degrees and a set of children. As discussed in Chapter 3 algebraic operators are sometimes supported by object-oriented, as well as relational systems; for example, SQL supports the *UNION* operator.

Bags

Bags are like sets, except that they can contain duplicates (i.e., the *same object* can occur more than once in the bag). For example, the result of the query "Without eliminating duplicates, find all documents in CabinetAccounts that deal with foreign accounts" might return the same document more than once since the document could be contained in more than one folder within the cabinet. Allowing duplicates is sometimes useful since it allows the user to *count* the number of occurrences of all returned objects, not just the distinct objects.

For sets (or bags) we can have operations to *iterate* over the elements, insert elements, delete elements, and check whether an object is contained in the set or bag (or any collection, for that matter).

Arrays

Arrays are collections that are populated and traversed by indexed accesses. For instance, the employees who are managed by an office worker can be represented as an array. Then, if the array is Employees, the first employee is retrieved through Employees[1], the second through Employees[2], and so on.

Dictionaries

Dictionaries are like arrays except that the retrieval is performed through a user-defined *name*, which (in most cases) is a character string. Dictionaries are useful, since they allow retrieval of objects based on user-defined key values. Thus, if in the previous example we had used a dictionary instead of an array to retrieve the employee John Smith, we would have used `Employees["John Smith"]` instead of traversing all of the employees and checking the `Name` filed to see which one is John Smith.

List

List is another ordered collection type whose elements are navigated in a particular order. Lists can be single-linked or double-linked, allowing users to navigate the ordered collection in both forward and backward order.

Implementing Collection Objects

There are several strategies for implementing collection objects. Here, the two most commonly used alternatives in C++ are presented. Note that these alternatives are *not* mutually disjoint (an implementation of an object-oriented database or a C++ class hierarchy might use *both*). The strategies are as follows:

1. Inheriting from the same root: For instance, as illustrated in Figure 4.8, if `Array`, `Set`, `List`, and so on all inherit from `Object` and are imple-

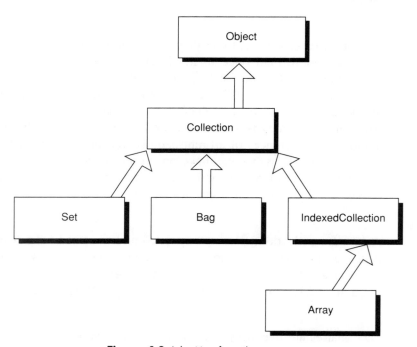

Figure 4.8 Inheriting from the same root.

mented as collections of instances of objects, they can be used to implement collections of any descendant of Object. In some implementations the constructors of the collection classes allow the user to specify the name of a subclass or subtype of Object. Thus, if the user is interested in collections in which all instances are of a particular type, he or she can specify the type name as a parameter.

2. Parametric types: C++ supports parametric types. The syntax is

$$\text{List<type>}$$

or

$$\text{Set<type>}$$

Object Design pioneered parametric types in C++. This approach is more convenient and at a higher level than the run-time type specification approach. Thus, if we want to specify an instance variable of the Department set of employees, where each element of the set is an Employee, we can do so through

```
Set<Employee> DepartmentEmployees;
```

Relationship Links

As described in Chapter 3, we can have one-to-one, one-to-many, and many-to-many relationships:

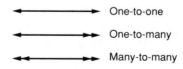

Recall that it is possible to implement one-to-one relationships as direct references and one-to-many or many-to-many relationships as set-valued attributes. For example, assume that we have a one-to-one relationship between Department and Manager:

This relationship could be implemented through a `ManagedBy` attribute of `De-partment` and a `Manages` attribute of `Manager`. It will, however, be up to the application programmer to guarantee the consistency of the relationship. In other words, in the absence of triggers or other integrity constraint mechanisms and given an instance D of `Department`, the application programmer must guarantee that

`D.ManagedBy.Manages`

is identical to D. This means, for example, that if the `ManagedBy` reference is modified to reference another manager, the application program must also modify the `Manages` attribute value of the previous manager (e.g., set it to *NULL*).

As mentioned earlier, if the OODBMS supports integrity constraints (e.g., triggers) the consistency can be maintained by the database system rather than the application program. In fact, rule 10 of Ted Codd's 12 rules for relational database management systems (Codd, 1985) is applicable here:

> **Rule 10:** Integrity constraints specific to a particular relational (*or object-oriented*) database must be definable in the relational (*object-oriented*) data sublanguage and storable in the catalog, not in the application programs.

An alternative approach to guarantee consistency of one-to-one, one-to-many, and many-to-many relationships, which is supported by a number of object-oriented databases including SIM, Versant, and Objectivity/DB, is the direct support of bidirectional links. For example, SIM supports the concept of *inverse attributes*. This notion was originally supported in DAPLEX (Shipman, 1981), and SIM is based on the functional and semantic models of DAPLEX.

We already saw one example of inverse relationships in SIM in Section 4.5. As a more extensive example, Figure 4.9 illustrates the definition of the OFFICE WORKER, `Department`, and `Manager` classes using inverse attributes. Using inverse attributes will guarantee that the system will maintain the referential consistency between the manager and the department. As indicated earlier, both Versant and Objectivity/DB support a similar feature through bidirectional links.

4.7.5 Transient C++ Pointers and Persistent Object Identifiers

C++ is a general-purpose programming language in which objects are referenced through *pointers*. Pointers represent virtual memory addresses. Object pointers

```
CLASS OFFICE WORKER

(Name                             :STRING(30);
 SocSecNum                        :INTEGER;
 DOB                              :DATE;
 Salary                           :NUMBER[9,2];
 Worker Department                :Department
                                  INVERSE IS
                                  Workers;


);

SUBCLASS Manager of OFFICE WORKER
(
Title                             :STRING(10)'
Manages                           :Department
                                  INVERSE IS
                                  Managed-by MV;


);

CLASS Department
(
DeptName                          :STRING(30);
DeptNumber                        :INTEGER;
Workers                           :OFFICE WORKER
                                  INVERSE IS
                                  Worker Department MV;

Managed-by                        :Manager
                                  INVERSE IS
                                  Manages;
);
```

Figure 4.9 SIM schema for OFFICE WORKER, Manager, and Department.

that are *transient* reference objects in-RAM (or in virtual memory) during the lifetime of the program and vanish once the program, objects, and references no longer exist.

When we deal with persistent object spaces in object-oriented databases we have the issue of *double representation*, which results from the on-disk storage and representation of the object and the in-RAM representation of the object. Double representation is illustrated in Figure 4.10. Figure 4.10(a) shows a

Page 5

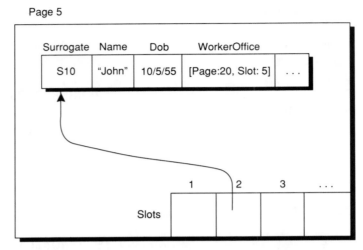

Figure 4.10(a) John's record's physical ID: Page 5, Slot 2.

secondary storage disk page where the object's physical address is the concatenation of the PageID and the SlotID. Figure 4.10(b) shows the same object in an in-RAM structure. Here, the WorkerOffice field of the object references an instance of Office. In Figure 4.10(a) this is represented as a PID (persistent object ID), which can be one of the following:

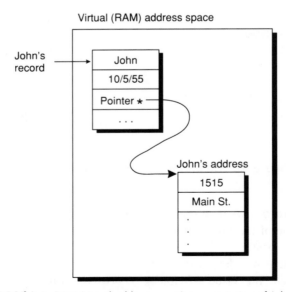

Figure 4.10(b) In RAM (virtual address space) representation of John's address.

1. The actual concatenation of [Page Number, Slot Number]. The main problem here is the lack of flexibility in moving the object. Some database management system implementations allow the object to be moved and leave a "forwarding address" when it moves, as illustrated in Figure 4.11. Then, when the object is to be read, if the object is moved the system can use the forwarding address to locate and read the object.

2. The "surrogate,"or object identifier, approach, as discussed in Section 4.3. Here the surrogate is completely independent of any physical address. It will be a system-generated unique identifier, which will be assigned to a single object. In this case, depending on a particular implementation, the system has to translate the surrogate into a memory address.

Other approaches besides these two have attempted to reduce the "two-representation" overhead and make the translation between the on-disk and in-RAM representations as smooth as possible. Of course, in the extreme case we

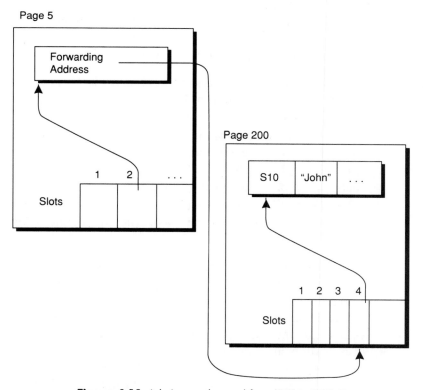

Figure 4.11 John's record moved from [5,2] to [200,4].

could just eliminate the dual representation and use the memory address as the object identifier if the implementation allows the concurrent sharing of virtual memory address spaces. One system that allowed this was Bubba, described by Copeland et al. (1990). ObjectStore from Object Design is a commercial DBMS with a similar approach.

4.7.6 Application Development Phases

There are a number of alternatives for developing applications for object-oriented databases that provide OODB extensions for C++. Specific products will have idiosyncrasies that must be addressed during the development phase, but this section provides an overview of the main phases commonly found in OODBMS products.

The assumption here is that the application developer has gone through the design phases as described in Chapter 3 and is ready to launch the implementation. Therefore, the main steps for implementing an application using an OODBMS that supports persistent C++ extensions or class libraries are as follows.

C++ Implementation Step 1: Data Definition

The user first defines the specific persistent classes either through a specific data definition language defined by the object-oriented database vendor or through a C++ header file. This definition includes the following:

- The *declaration* of the persistent class. If the OODB requires that the persistent class inherit from a `PersistentObject` root, then the class is declared as a subclass of `PersistentObject` directly or transitively.
- The member variables of the persistent class. In C++ the application developer can identify *Public* (accessible by all), *Protected* (accessible only by the subclasses; also known as *subclass visible*), and *Private* (can be manipulated only by the member functions of the class).
- The member functions of the persistent classes, that is, the operations that apply to the instances of the class. They define the *behavior* and *protocol* of the class.

There are other details and alternatives for object-oriented database implementations, but basically in this step the application developer implements the member variable and member function declarations of the persistent classes. Figure 4.12 provides a simple illustration of Step 1 by defining `Folder`, with `Name`, `Creator`, `Icon`, and sets of documents. The figure illustrates only the public accessor and update member functions of `Folder`.

Once these terms are defined, the declarations are processed through an OODBMS vendor-provided utility. As illustrated in Figure 4.13, the schema declaration processor utility does the following:

```
CLASS Folder: public PersistentObject{

public:
  Folder();
  ~Folder();

  char * getName();
  char * setName(char *);

  char * getCreator(){return Creator;}
  char * setCreator(char *);

  Icon getIcont(){return Icon};
  Icont setIcon(Icon I);

  Document * getFirstDocument();
  Document * getNextDocument();

  Document *insertDocument(Document *d);

};
```

Figure 4.12 Step 1 for defining Folders.

1. Creates a schema in the object storage module of the object-oriented database management system
2. Possibly rewrites or regenerates the data definition provided by the application programmer as a header file to be included in the developer's modules

C++ *Implementation Step 2: Implementation of the Persistent Classes*

As stated earlier, the data definition incorporates both the definition of the *structure* of the persistent database (i.e., the schema) and the *behavior*, or the operations, associated with these persistent classes. These are implemented in member functions; therefore, the application developer must implement the member functions of the persistent classes. Some of these member functions are *accessor* functions, which access the "hidden" member variables or instance variables of the persistent classes. Other member functions are *update* functions, which modify the state or values of the instance variables of instances of the persistent class. Still other member functions perform more sophisticated operations. For instance, it is possible for aggregate functions such as *average salary* or *total*

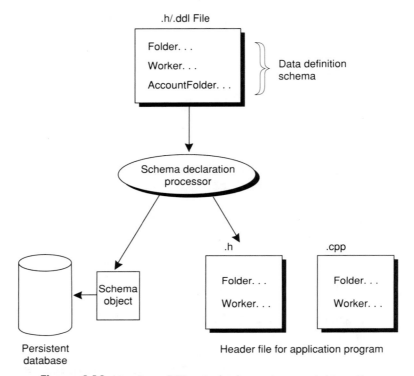

Figure 4.13 Mapping a DDL onto database schema and .h/.cpp files.

number of employees supervised by manager to be evaluated through member functions that are part of the protocol of the persistent class.

C++ Implementation Step 3: Implementation of the GUI Classes

Although it is conceivably possible to perform input/output through the persistent class implementations, a more reasonable approach is to have separate classes to deal with the end-user *graphical user interface* (GUI) interactions. Graphical user interfaces have been set apart here since, first, they have become common place, and most human-computer interaction now takes place through GUI environments; second, in database management systems and applications a considerable percentage of the code pertains to the front-end or the GUI environment (percentages as high as 60 to 80 percent have been quoted); and third, the main application domain discussed throughout this book is intelligent offices where graphical user interfaces are *the* interaction environment of choice for the users of the system.

The GUI objects include various types of *windows*, *menus* (pop-up, pull-down, etc.), *forms*, *dialogs*, *tool bars*, *buttons*, *list boxes*, and semantics of mouse movements. The values of the various items are, in many cases, retrieved from the underlying databases; therefore, in many cases the GUI objects reference and access instances of persistent classes. Chapter 8 of Khoshafian and Abnous (1990) provides a more detailed description of object-oriented GUI systems.

C + + Implementation Step 4: Compile and Link

Once the persistent classes and the front-end GUI classes are implemented, the next step is to compile and link these classes. This is illustrated in Figure 4.14. OODBMSs typically provide run-time libraries to be linked with the application programs. In some cases, GUI libraries support the GUI classes on a particular platform. These and other application-specific libraries are linked together to produce the application program executable.

4.7.7 Dynamic Data Definition

One of the major advantages of relational databases is the support of dynamic data definition. This means that relational database tables could be created at run time. For instance the user can create a Form for workflow to process

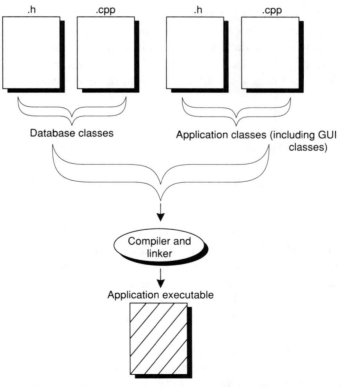

Figure 4.14 Last phase of OODB application development.

LoanApplications. The fields and their types could then be defined at run time, and the user can use the Form to populate and display the values of the variables. In relational databases this is achieved by executing the following at run time:

```
CREATE TABLE LoanApplication(
    Applicant  CHAR(32),
    Amount     DOLLAR,
...)
```

The application program that interfaces with the database calls the run-time dynamic SQL statement to create the table. If inheritance is supported, as in Intelligent SQL, the *CREATE TABLE* statement can specify supertables (corresponding to superclasses) from which the dynamically created table inherits. Relational database management systems that support object-oriented constructs will continue to support this powerful feature.

Some object-oriented databases such as ONTOS and Versant also allow dynamic definition of persistent C++ classes, thus providing the same advantages as dynamic table creation in relational databases.

In relational databases the table definitions are themselves stored in system catalogs, which are also relational tables. The fourth of Codd's 12 rules (Codd, 1985) for being a complete relational database system is as follows:

> **Rule 4:** The database description is presented at the logical level in the same way as ordinary data, so that authorized users can apply the same relational language to its interrogation as they apply to the regular data.

This rule means that SQL can be used to access the "system catalogs." Relational database management systems typically store the "meta-data" (that is, the descriptive data about the database) in relational tables as well. In other words, the information about the structure of the tables (the number of columns, the name and type of each column, and so on) are also stored in relational tables. One important advantage of this strategy is that SQL statements can be used to query and possibly even update these "meta tables." Depending upon the product or context, the tables that contain various types of information about the content and structure of the database are called *system catalogs*, *meta-data*, and *data dictionaries*.

Thus, in relational databases SQL can be used to query the system tables in order to obtain facts about the structure or content of the database. For instance, the user can query tables in the system catalog to answer the following:

- What are the names of the tables contained in this database?
- What are all of the integrity constraints defined for a particular table *T*?
- Which view uses a particular table *T*?
- Who has authorization to update tables *T*1 and *T*2?

Using the same language for data definition and data manipulation is an elegant and uniform approach to data access. The user needs to learn only a single language or mechanism for accessing the database content and structure.

There is a similar approach in some object-oriented databases. The "meta" information about the persistent C++ classes can itself be stored in persistent C++ classes that provide a functionality similar to system catalogs in relational systems. The descriptive "meta" information of persistent C++ classes consists of

- The superclasses of the persistent class
- The member variables of the persistent class
- The member functions of the persistent class

Assume that the class that contains all of the definitions of the persistent classes in the database is called `ClassCatalog`. `ClassCatalog` can provide the following methods:

> `getMemberVariableDefinitions` (for instance variables, attributes, properties, etc.). This method is similar to retrieving the column definitions of a table from the system catalog in a relational database management system.

> `getMemberFunctionDefinitions` (for methods). This method could retrieve the name of the member function and its *signature* (the types of its input/output parameters, the type of the return value, and so on).

> `getSuperClasses` (for class names). This method could retrieve the names of all of the direct superclasses of the class.

Other methods could also be defined to retrieve various status information or statistics about the class.

As for dynamic data definition, the `ClassCatalog` class will allow the user to *construct* and *save* (or write to a database) an instance of the class. Instances of class `ClassCatalog` are persistent classes. The constructor will allow the user to specify the various parameters that define a class: the member variables, the member functions, the superclasses, and so on.

The construction and saving of an instance of ClassCatalog will make a persistent class definition entry in the schema. The user needs to provide the object code of the methods that pertain to the dynamically defined class. These object codes can be dynamically linked with the rest of the system at run time.

4.7.8 OPAL: Making Smalltalk a Database Language

The GemStone object oriented-database management system from Servio Corporation of Portland, Oregon, is one of the influential next-generation database management systems. It was one of the earliest object-oriented database management systems to provide strong support of object identity, inheritance, and encapsulation, coupled with database capabilities such as persistence, transactions, and ad hoc querying. GemStone's data definition and manipulation language is called OPAL. The basis of OPAL is Smalltalk; therefore, the syntax of OPAL is similar to Smalltalk. However, OPAL incorporates many database-specific constructs and operations. For more information on OPAL and the GemStone database system, see Copeland and Maier (1984), Maier and Stein (1990), and Servio (1990a–1990e).

As illustrated in Figure 4.15, OPAL introduces a class hierarchy of objects rooted at OBJECT. As is the case with programming in Smalltalk, the OPAL object-oriented database developers spend most of their time specializing these hierarchies.

As far as the persistent object space is concerned, GemStone uses a User-Profile to store information about the user (name, password, privileges, etc.). In addition, the UserProfile contains an instance variable called symbol-List. Various *dictionaries* can be added to the user's symbol list. The user profiles and dictionaries are used to control the name spaces in GemStone. For instance, a user's symbol list can contain a dictionary for specific classes and/or objects accessed only by the user; there can be other dictionaries of objects shared by many users and still other dictionaries to hold system objects.

Defining and Manipulating Objects in OPAL

In Smalltalk the instance variables are typeless. Primarily for performance reasons, OPAL introduces constraints to restrict the types of the instance variables. Using constrained instance variables, the definition of OfficeWorkers follows:

```
Object subclass: 'OfficeWorker'
instVarNames: #('name', 'waddress',
          'workerOffice', 'salary', 'dob')
classVars: #()
poolDictionaries: #()
inDictionary: UserGlobals
```

```
constraints: #[
                #[#name, LastFirst],
                #[#waddress, Address],
                #[#workerOffice, Office],
                #[#salary, Float],
                #[#dob, Date],
                #[#wdepartment, Department]
                 ]
```

These constraints indicate that 'name' has to be an instance of the class Last-First (which contains instance variables 'last' and 'first' for the last name and first name of an employee, respectively) or an instance of any one of the subclasses of LastFirst; waddress has to be an instance of class Address or one of the subclasses of Address; workerOffice has to be an instance of Office or an instance of one of the subclasses of Office; and so on.

It is no secret that the run-time dynamic binding of messages to methods in languages such as Smalltalk is expensive. Motivated by performance considerations as well as by a desire to provide querying capabilities, OPAL introduces *selection blocks*. A selection block specifies a query that associatively filters the qualifying elements in a collection, similar to a *SELECT* clause in SQL. Selection blocks are delimited by { and } and sent through a select: selector.

As an example of selection blocks, assume that Workers contains a set of office workers. To obtain the subset of all employees in Workers who earn more than $60,000 the query is

```
richWorkers:= Workers select: {:aWorker!aWorker.salary> 60000}
```

The predicate in the selection block can be more complex and can involve conjunctions. For example, to retrieve the workers whose last name is Jones and whose age is greater than 21 we have

```
Jones:=Workers select:
                {:aWorker! (aWorker.age > 21 ) &
                (aWorker.name.last = 'Jones')}
```

Other Database Constructs

In addition to selection blocks, there are other constructs that are specific to the database management capabilities of the GemStone environment. Some of these are listed on page 223.

```
Object
   Association
      SymbolAssociation
   Behavior
      Class
      Metaclass
   Boolean
   ClampSpecification
   Collection
      SequenceableCollection
         Array
             InvariantArray
             Repository
             SymbolList
         String
             InvariantString
             Symbol
      Bag
         Set
             Dictionary
                IdentityDictionary
                SymbolDictionary
                   LanguageDictionary
             SymbolSet
             UserProfileSet
   CompiledMethod
   Magnitude
      Character
      DateTime
      Number
         Float
         Fraction
         Integer
             LargeNegativeInteger
             LargePositiveInteger
             SmallInteger
   MethodContext
      Block
          SelectionBlock
   Segment
```

Figure 4.15 Kernel classes in OPAL.

```
Stream
   PositionableStream
      ReadStream
      WriteStream
System
UndefinedObject
UserProfile
```

Figure 4.15 *(continued)*

1. Collection subclasses, such as bags, sets, dictionaries, arrays, and so on. An interesting extension introduced by OPAL is the concept of *constrained collections*. Here, users can create a collection *whose elements must all be instances of a particular class (or one of its subclasses)*.

2. Indexes. OPAL supports both the equality = and identical == predicates. Accordingly, it allows the creation of two types of indexes: identity indexes and equality indexes. Identity indexes are useful when the predicate in the selection block involves a == on the indexed instance variable. Equality indexes are useful in value-based comparisons such as = and >= .

3. Transactions and concurrency control. The OPAL language provides primitives for committing and aborting transactions. When a user logs in he or she is given a new workspace and a "copy" of the current committed database. All updates to the database are done in this workspace and are transparent to all other users. Therefore, unless the user commits, only the user sees his or her updates. GemStone supports both optimistic and pessimistic (locking) concurrency control mechanisms. Transactions and concurrency control are discussed in more detail in Chapter 5.

OPAL also supports constructs for *security and authorization*, for replication of databases to enhance the recovery speed, and to *cluster* objects for better I/O performance.

■ 4.8 EMBEDDING OBJECT-ORIENTED DATABASE LANGUAGE CONSTRUCTS IN A HOST LANGUAGE

Database languages can be embedded in host programming languages. For example, SQL statements can be embedded into PL/1, C, FORTRAN, and Ada. The types of SQL (i.e., relations and rows in relations) are quite different from the type systems of these host languages.

Some object-oriented databases have taken a similar approach with a host language and an object-oriented database language. For example, O2 (Deux et al., 1990) provides embedded extensions for C (called CO2!) and BASIC. The extensions include special type constructors and different embedded escapes to the object-oriented message-passing environment of O2. ObjectStore from Object Design provides a more seamless mechanism for incorporating persistence and database support in C.

■ 4.9 APPLICATION-SPECIFIC PRODUCTS WITH AN UNDERLYING OBJECT-ORIENTED DATABASE MANAGEMENT SYSTEM

Another interesting approach is the development of application/domain-specific tools and environments that either use object-oriented database technologies or provide an object-oriented database view for the application domain. The intention in application/domain-specific solutions is not to provide a general-purpose object-oriented environment but to provide only useful or application-specific constructs, possibly with object-oriented and database features.

One application that is becoming increasingly important and is discussed throughout this book as an important application domain of next-generation object-oriented databases is *intelligent offices* (Khoshafian et al., 1992b). Some recent products such as Office.IQ from Portfolio Technologies, Inc., provide persistent and concurrently shared object-oriented environments tailored to office objects. These products can be used to organize the massive heterogeneous information in office environments as well as the *flow* of information in offices.

The intelligent office environment contains at least four categories of objects:

1. Information: First and foremost is information from different sources, stored in different formats. Information is almost always persistent and should be under versioning and transaction control. Any *concurrently shared* information should also be under the transaction-based concurrency control provided by an underlying database management system. There are various container, collection, and aggregate types that reference or store the information. Container objects such as folders and compound documents contain elements that can be other containers, multimedia objects, or application files.

2. Office workers: Office workers hold certain relationships to other workers *and* to other office objects. Two fundamental relationships exist with respect to other workers: the *inheritance* relationship (e.g., a `SalesManager` is also a `SalesPerson`, and a `SalesPerson` is also an `OfficeWorker`), and the *organizational relationship* (e.g., the vice president *reports to* the president, and the president *reports to* the CEO). Office workers also have

various *ownership* and *access* privileges for other office objects such as documents and peripherals.

3. Office tools, resources, devices, and peripherals: The office environment includes tools such as an electronic mail system, resources such as storage space, devices, and peripherals, all of which are *objects*. Other intelligent office devices include scanners, FAX boards, and various multimedia I/O devices.

4. Policies and procedures: Intelligent offices also include policy and procedure objects that could be instantiated and executed in the office environment. A policy or procedure is an *object* in the sense that it has attributes (instance variables) that can be read, searched, or updated. Policies and procedures also have *operations* (methods) associated with them that can be used to *activate* the procedure or policy. Policies and procedures could be implemented as *workflow* objects.

Every category of intelligent office objects pertains to a class hierarchy of persistent objects. The intelligent office environment allows the user to

- Create instances of existing object classes such as `Folders`, `Workers`, and `Policies`
- Specialize templates or class hierarchies of existing classes (for instance, by using the system to provide general or generic `Folder`, `Document`, `Worker`, and/or `Policy` types to create specific types such as `Accounts-Folder` or `HiringPolicy`)
- Control the concurrent accesses through, for instance, a check-out/check-in mechanism
- Perform complex searches on object spaces

Figure 4.16 illustrates the organizational constraints on container objects. Here, each object at a lower level can be contained in an object that is its immediate predecessor. Thus, a `Document` contains a collection of multimedia objects or application files, a `Folder` contains a collection of documents or other folders, a drawer contains folders, a cabinet contains drawers, and so on.

Objects can be referentially shared, with the same object contained in many container objects. For instance, the same document can exist in many folders, the same folder in many drawers, and so on. Each object consists of the following:

- A collection of <attribute> <value> pairs.
- A collection of subobjects contained in the object. An object can contain subobjects of a lower level in the containment hierarchy.

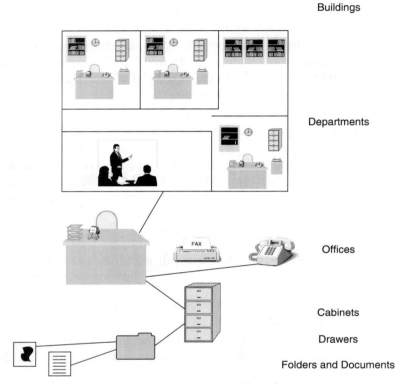

Figure 4.16 Organization of office information.

Object attributes, such as the following, are also common to all object types:

1. The Name of the object.
2. The Date the object was created.
3. The Label of the object, which appears under the object's icon.
4. The Owner of the object, which identifies who owns the object. This attribute is more complex than Name or Label (which are character strings). An Owner has many attributes itself, such as the *name* of the owner, the *picture* of the owner, the title, and the position.
5. Voice Annotation for the object, which can describe the purpose of the object.
6. The Lock State of the object, which indicates whether the object is locked, in what mode, and by whom.

The following sections describe some of the object types in the containment hierarchy.

4.9.1 Cabinets

In addition to common attributes, each cabinet contains drawers. When an office worker opens a cabinet, he or she will be presented with a sequence of labeled drawers. The cabinet object can respond to *search* requests to locate objects contained within it. These objects can be drawers, folders, or other documents. A cabinet also holds *indexes* containing an organized "table of contents" for all objects in the cabinet. Indexes can be organized by subject, date, category, owner, or any other user-specified attribute. Some of the operations applicable to cabinet objects are create, delete, and reorganize.

4.9.2 Drawers

Along with the attributes for its label, owner, and description a drawer can contain various types of indexes and folders. The following operations can be performed on the folders of a drawer:

- Create
- Delete
- Reorganize the folders in the drawer
- Check-out/check-in
- Modify the folder's attributes

The check-out/check-in protocol for folders enables office workers to perform operations on folders or objects in their desktops. In other words, to create, insert, delete, or manipulate the documents within the folder the office worker must check out the folder to his or her desktop, perform the manipulations, then check it back in.

4.9.3 Folders

Folders are contained in drawers or desktops. The folders on a desktop are the *active folders that the intelligent office worker is currently manipulating*. To access and manipulate the documents stored in a folder, the office worker must follow several steps:

1. Access the cabinet and the drawer containing the folder
2. Check out the folder to his or her desktop
3. Work on the documents in the folder
4. Check the document back in, creating a different version of the document

The following actions can be performed upon documents in a folder:

- Create
- Delete
- Reorganize documents in the folder
- Modify documents in the folder

Figure 4.17 illustrates a folder containing different types of objects in Office.IQ. The folder `Heterogeneous` contains a nested folder, an image, a voice answer, and other application files.

4.9.4 Documents

The lowest level of the containment hierarchy holds compound hypermedia documents. As explained in Parsaye et al. (1989), hypermedia documents are built by associating nodes through links. Thus, whereas a normal document is linear and

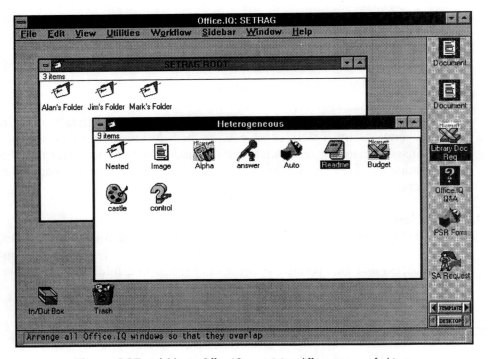

Figure 4.17 A folder in Office.IQ containing different types of objects.

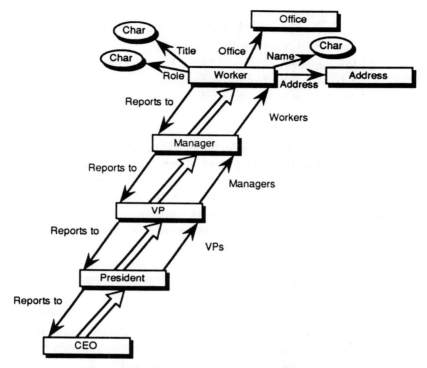

Figure 4.18 Hierarchical organization of office workers.

read from beginning to end, a hypermedia document is open-ended and can be read from node to node, depending on the reader's interests. The nodes in a hypermedia document could be text, images, voice, or any other media type.

An example of hypermedia is a thesaurus in book form. Each time a person consults a thesaurus, her or she enters it at a different location based on the word initiating the search. Hypermedia can be thought of as an enriched thesaurus, where instead of links existing between words, they exist between nodes of various types.

4.9.5 Office Workers

The office environment is organized by partitioning information and office objects, with privileges for manipulating the information or other objects assigned to different office workers as appropriate.

For example, consider the hierarchy of office workers illustrated in Figure 4.18. The figure illustrates two types of relationships:

1. Organizational relationships: `Workers` report to `Managers`; `Managers` report to `VPs`; `VPs` report to `Presidents`; `Presidents` report to `CEOs`; and `CEOs` report to their spouses.
2. Inheritance hierarchies: `CEOs` have the privileges and attributes of `Presidents`; `Presidents` have the privileges and attributes of `VPs`; and so on. Everyone has the attributes of `Workers`: `Name`, `Address`, `Office`, and so on.

In terms of privileges, office workers are assigned to various offices. An office thus represents the collection of all objects belonging to a worker in the corporation. Note that the same office worker can belong to different departments and thus have different offices. Figure 4.19 illustrates the assignment of privileges to various workers and groups. For instance, individual workers have privileges for their offices, whereas groups can access objects in a library.

Because organization hierarchies are much more elaborate than who reports to whom, the intelligent office environment also incorporates the notion of a *group*. Groups, which are also objects, have three important attributes:

1. Charter: a statement of the objectives and responsibilities of the group.
2. Privileges: Groups usually share common information bases in libraries, as illustrated in Figure 4.19. Individual group members have access to these libraries and can check information out.
3. Members: the office workers who belong to the groups and their respective roles.

Each worker can belong to one or more groups in one or more departments. Groups can also cross department boundaries. As a result, each office worker has several characteristics (attributes):

1. Several descriptive attributes: `Name`, `Address`, and so on.
2. His or her `Departments`.
3. His or her `Groups`.
4. Titles and roles: For the chief executive officer, the president, and the vice presidents the title and role are the same. The administrative assistant to the CEO, however, also plays the role of the corporate information coordinator of the CEO. Although his or her title is `AA`, as information coordinator he or she has *more* privileges than, say, the president and the VPs in accessing and updating information pertaining to the CEO.
5. Subordinates: those who report to him or her.

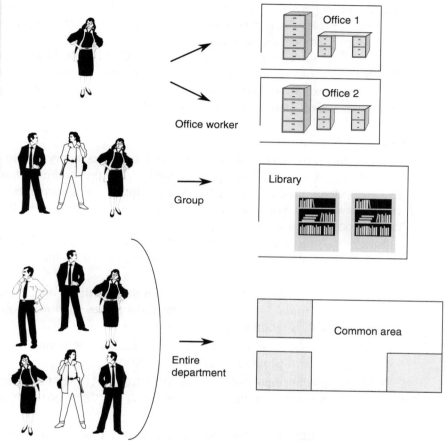

Figure 4.19 Access privileges to various localities.

6. An immediate supervisor in each group or department.
7. Responsibilities for various tasks, which correspond to the "protocol," or interface, of the office worker as an object. For instance, the protocol of an administrative assistant includes

   • Mailing packages
   • Making reservations
   • Updating the control calendar

8. Privileges to access or update office objects.

Office workers are also organized in inheritance hierarchies with respect to characteristics, protocols, and policies. These inheritance hierarchies reflect the structural sharing among the workers.

All office workers inherit from the root `OfficeWorker`. The `Office-Worker` root incorporates a number of attributes, including those just listed, that are common to all office workers. In addition, specializations provide more specific attributes (structure) and behavior for various workers in a corporation.

4.9.6 Policies and Procedures

In each corporation several policies and procedures apply to the enterprise as a whole (such as sick leave policies and hiring procedures set by the human resources department). The "text," or description, of a corporate policy or procedure can be presented through a workflow. When expressed in the proper form these procedures and policies can be *executed electronically*. In other words, a policy or procedure can be represented as an intelligent office node-and-link workflow "program" that shares the following attributes with computer programs:

- The nodes in the workflow can represent intelligent office objects such as workers, groups, and devices. The links represent flow or flow of control (as in most programming languages).
- An environment or a virtual machine that interprets and executes the policy/procedure "program" (i.e., the workflow).
- Descriptive attributes such as the `Author`, `Date` that the policy was issued, `Place` where the policy was issued, and the `Category` of the policy.

Therefore, `Procedures` and `Policies` are objects that have attributes (instance variables) and operations (methods). Based on the discussion in the previous paragraphs, the attributes of policy and procedure objects include

> `Name`: the name of the policy/procedure
> `Description`: the description of the policy/procedure, indicating *why* there is such a policy/procedure and *when* it will be activated
> `Author`: the department/office or office worker who created the policy/procedure
> The `Workflow`: captures the semantics of the policy or procedure through nodes, links, and relationships between nodes and links.

4.9.7 Intelligent Offices as Object-Oriented Databases

As the previous sections illustrate, many object types pertain to intelligent office applications. *All instances of these types are persistent.* Furthermore, the entire object space is under transaction control to guarantee consistency of the persistent object space.

In other words, although the end users interact with familiar objects such as folders and corporate procedures, there are underlying persistent database objects that implement these entities. Thus, the persistent object space is application-specific. There is also an underlying database management system that implements the persistent objects, class hierarchies, and concurrent accesses to the intelligent office objects. However, the object-oriented database functionality and the persistent object space support manifest themselves in application-specific objects and templates (classes).

■ 4.10 PERSISTENT COMPLEX OBJECT STORAGE STRATEGIES

The previous sections discuss various strategies for implementing object-oriented databases. Some of the sections also allude to a number of implementation techniques; for instance, Section 4.3 presented various approaches for implementing object identity. Section 4.7 discussed some of the issues involved in the representation and mapping of persistent objects in secondary and primary storage media.

This section provides further details concerning the implementation issues involved in *clustering* complex objects. The main idea of clustering is to allow objects that are accessed frequently together to be stored as close as possible to one another on the secondary storage medium. The idea is of course to improve the overall access from secondary storage.

Object-oriented databases often provide various constructs to allow the OODB application developers to specify how they want their persistent complex objects to be clustered on secondary storage. It is interesting to note that even some relational systems (such as Oracle) provide *CLUSTER* constructs to store records (tuples) that are often accessed together on the same storage extent (Khoshafian et al., 1992a).

Throughout this book complex object models have been discussed that construct object spaces from three constructs:

- Atomic objects
- Tuples
- Sets, or collections

In fact, most (if not all) object-oriented database systems do provide implementations of these constructs. Hence, understanding clustering amounts to understanding how objects composed of atomic, tuple, and set constructs that reference one another could be clustered on storage extents.

4.10.1 Object Size

In considering clustering alternatives the fundamental problem is size. Typically, database systems provide only limited support for objects that are larger than a few hundred bytes, or they restrict the number of levels of nesting allowed (the extreme case being relational systems that require tuples to be flat). These restrictions are too severe for many of the applications we wish to support. Object managers will be required to efficiently manage objects of arbitrary size and complexity. Objects can become large for a number of different reasons (Khoshafian et al., 1990a).

Sets with Large Cardinalities

Perhaps the most commonly recognized type of large objects in databases is a set with a large number of elements. Such large sets readily arise in clinical, census, geographical, and atmospheric databases. For example, in an experiment in atmospheric physics, atmospheric measurements were taken, using five instruments, four times an hour for 10 stations at six elevations and for every 6 degrees. During a period of five years the total number of measurements for the experiment was in the billions. This example could be extreme, but engineering and intelligent office applications do often involve sets with many elements.

Long Tuples

Though less frequent, there are some situations in which a tuple type has a large number of attributes. For example, Blum (1982) describes a clinical database based on the ARAMIS (American Rheumatism Association Medical Information System) database in which data for 1300 patients are recorded. Each patient tuple has 400 attributes corresponding to patient symptoms, physical exams, lab values, therapy, etc.

Large Atoms

Atoms (e.g., strings, integers) are the building blocks from which complex objects are constructed. There are numerous applications in which large atomic objects arise. For example, multimedia objects can consist of digitized audio, video, or text data. Objects of these types can be quite large. One minute of voice storage can consume up to half a megabyte. Bitmaps of digitized images can consume several megabytes of storage each.

Large Graphics

In some applications, such as CAD/CAM, a complex object may be large even though the set-and-tuple objects that it comprises each have a relatively small number of elements or attributes. Consider a VLSI chip that consists of 15 sections that contain a total of 134 cells. Each cell contains about 1500 transistors. In the representation of a transistor, a cell, a section, and the chip each consume about 100 bytes. However, note that the individual set cardinalities and the number of attributes per tuple type (usually less than 10 for chip, section, cell, and transistor) are not large.

As another example, consider the storage representation of a large software system. Assume that the system contains about 1000 modules, with each module represented as a tuple containing three set-valued attributes and a number (typically less than 10) of atomic attributes storing module ID, creator, time created, etc. The set-valued attributes are as follows: interface descriptors, which store the exported routines of the module; dependency modules, which store the module IDs of all modules from which the current module imports (or upon which it depends); and files containing the module source code, typically consisting of about 50 files of about five kilobytes each. The total system size is in excess of one-fourth of a gigabyte.

4.10.2 Alternative Storage Strategies

As discussed by Khoshafian et al. (1990a) and Valduriez, Khoshafian, and Copeland (1986), there are several alternative storage strategies for complex objects. The main goal of complex object storage strategies is to provide efficient retrieval and to update performance for complex objects. This section discusses three possible approaches to complex object storage: the direct storage model; the normalized storage model; and the binary, or decomposed, storage model (Copeland and Khoshafian, 1985).

Direct Storage Model

Consider the complex object with folders and documents illustrated in Figure 4.20. With the direct storage model an attempt is made to store complex objects as "directly" as possible, reflecting the way in which the complex objects are either defined or populated in the database. Thus, *subobjects* are stored close to their parent objects whenever possible. Of course, since we are dealing with hierarchies there are several alternative strategies (*depth first, breadth first*, etc.) for storing the complex object. However, the main approach is to avoid *decomposing* the complex object and storing all of the descendants and components of the complex object together. Figure 4.21 illustrates this for the complex object of Figure 4.20.

Of course, the primary advantage of this model is that retrievals of the entire complex object can be very efficient. The "joins" needed to recompose complex objects are avoided. However, the approach does have some drawbacks. For one thing, since with object identity the object spaces are *graphs* and not trees we might need to either replicate some objects or store the object with one of its parents with references in other parents. This goes back to retrieval through "joins" if objects are referentially shared.

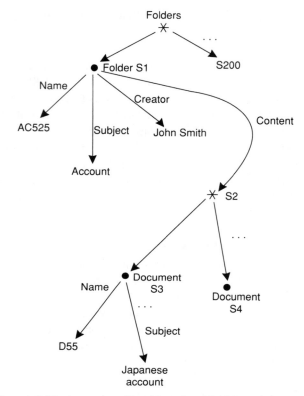

Figure 4.20 A complex object hierarchy of folders and documents.

Normalized Storage Model

The approach in the normalized storage model is similar to the approach of mapping a complex object model onto a third normal form relational database. (For more details about such mappings and third normal form relational schemata see the work by Khoshafian et al., 1992a.) Informally, this amounts to storing a homogeneous set of records for each record type. In order to capture the one-to-one, one-to-many, and many-to-many relationships, foreign keys are introduced in referencing tables.

Figure 4.22 illustrates the normalized storage for the example of Figure 4.20. Here a many-to-many relationship between folders and documents is assumed. One advantage of the normalized storage model is that it provides better performance in accessing object types that are contained in other parent objects. For instance, the documents that are referenced in folders can now be accessed and queried independent of folder objects. It also provides better support (or at least less complex and "fairer" support) of many-to-many relationships (referential sharing), since objects are neither replicated nor stored with only one of the parents (and referenced by others).

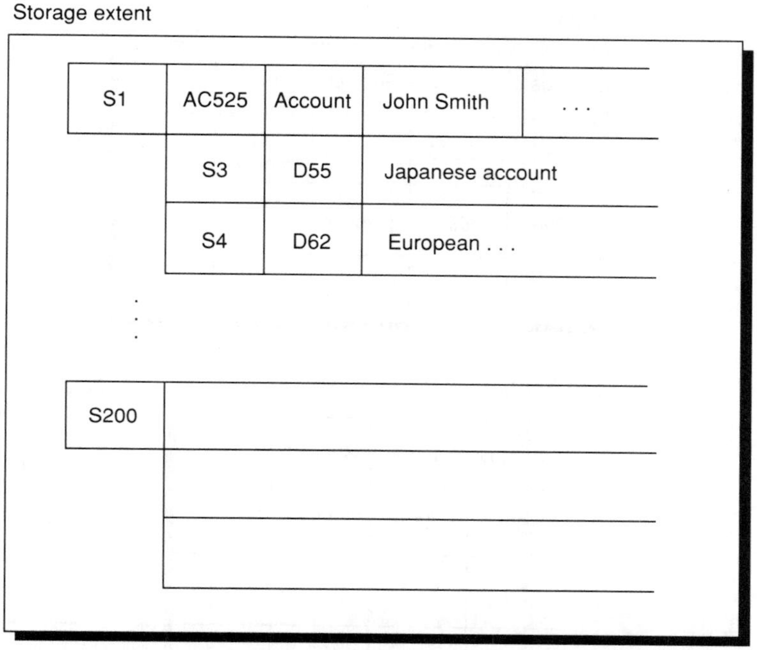

Storage extent

S1	AC525	Account	John Smith	. . .
	S3	D55	Japanese account	
	S4	D62	European . . .	

S200

Figure 4.21 Direct storage model: clustering the complex objects.

Decomposed Storage Model

The approach in the decomposed storage model (DSM) is to pair each attribute value of an object with the surrogate of the object. The original DSM proposal suggested that there be two copies of each attribute value: one copy clustered or sorted on the surrogate and the other on the attribute value. Figure 4.23 illustrates some of the "binary" storage of the DSM representation for the objects in Figure 4.20.

The main advantage of the DSM is simplicity and generality. The model provides a simple and elegant approach to storing arbitrary complex objects with arbitrary access patterns. It provides a more uniform performance advantage for different types of accesses. Of course, the main disadvantage is that if complex objects need to be reconstructed they will incur joins. But the joins needed will involve only those attributes needed in the retrieval.

■ 4.11 SUMMARY

This chapter has described various approaches for defining, manipulating, and implementing persistent object spaces in object-oriented databases. Six approaches for object-oriented databases have been presented:

Folders

Surrogate	Name	Subject	Creator	. . .
S1	AC525	Account	John Smith	
S200	B898	Invoice		
. . .				

Documents

Surrogate	Name	Subject	. . .
S2	D53	Japanese account	
S3	D89		
. . .			

Folders – Documents

F-Surrogate	D-Surrogate
S1	S2
S1	S3
. . .	

Figure 4.22 Normalized storage model.

1. Novel database data model/data language approach
2. Extending an existing database language with object-oriented capabilities
3. Extending an existing object-oriented programming language with database capabilities
4. Providing extendible object-oriented database management system libraries
5. Embedding object-oriented database language constructs in a host (conventional) language
6. Using application-specific products with an object-oriented model, database capabilities, and an underlying database management system

This chapter has concentrated on approaches 2, 3, and 6. For database languages the chapter demonstrated how SQL standard is being extended with object-oriented features.

The other prominent approach for implementing object-oriented databases that was discussed in the chapter is the extension of object-oriented languages with

Folder – Name

Surrogate	Name
S1	AC525
S200	B898
. . .	

Folder – Subject

Surrogate	Subject
S1	Account
S200	Invoice
. . .	

. . .

Folders – Documents

F-Surrogate	D-Surrogate
S1	S2
S1	S3
. . .	

Document – Name

Surrogate	Name
S2	D53
S3	D89
. . .	

Document – Subject

Surrogate	Subject
S2	Japanese
S3	European
. . .	

. . .

Figure 4.23 Decomposed storage model.

database capabilities. For instance, most object-oriented database companies are providing some sort of extension to C++ to incorporate database capabilities. Similarly, one of the earliest object-oriented languages, Smalltalk, has been extended in Servio's OPAL with database functionality.

This chapter has discussed how application-specific products such as the intelligent office product Office.IQ can incorporate object-oriented database functionality with an external application-specific object-oriented model and an underlying object-oriented database management system that implements it.

Finally, the chapter discussed briefly a number of alternative complex object storage strategies, illustrating the advantages and properties of the direct, normalized, and decomposed storage models.

5

TRANSACTIONS, CONCURRENCY, RECOVERY, AND VERSIONING IN OBJECT-ORIENTED DATABASES

One of the most important features in database management systems is *concurrent sharing*. That is, database management systems, including object-oriented databases, allow the same object space to be used by multiple users at the same time. In order to *control* the concurrent accesses, database management systems use various concurrency control and transaction management techniques. To help the DBMS minimize the overhead of conflicting concurrent accesses, concurrency control, and transaction management techniques, it is highly desirable that a DBMS be flexible in allowing users to "participate" in controlling the concurrency of persistent database. Users know best their application domains and hence the access patterns and conflicts when manipulating the shared object spaces.

Some problems exist with concurrently shared databases. Figure 5.1 illustrates the sources of some of these problems. For example, the persistent object space of a DBMS is stored in complex objects that are concurrently accessed and shared. In Figure 5.1(a) users 1 and 2 need to *cooperate* in updating object *O1*. Users 3 and 4 need to cooperate in updating and manipulating object *O2*. Figure 5.1(b) shows that although users 1 and 2 and users 3 and 4 are working on different object hierarchies, they could conflict because of the *storage organization* of the object space.

Several issues need to be addressed concerning the concurrent access of objects. The first is that sometimes different users might attempt to update the *same*

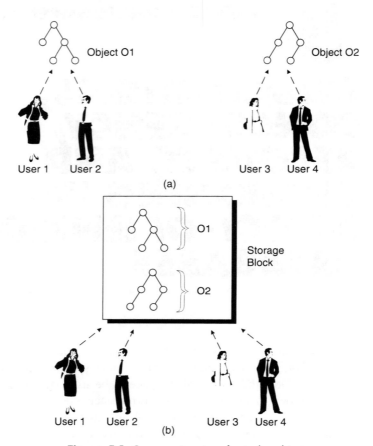

Figure 5.1 Concurrent access of complex objects.

object at the same time. For instance, consider a bank account held jointly by a husband and wife. If both parties attempt to withdraw from the *same* account at the same time the underlying system must deal with the conflict. As another example, consider an intelligent office environment, in which different office workers might attempt to update the *same* folder (e.g., change its subject) at the same time. Again the underlying database management system must take care of the conflict.

Another issue is that in some situations different groups of users (e.g., office workers) might like to *cooperate* in constructing various objects. For instance, in an intelligent office environment the documentation department might be given the task of coming up with the end-user documentation of a product. The various workers in the group need to cooperate in the production of the document.

Given these situations, the underlying database management system must guarantee that the database is maintained in a consistent state in the presence of both conflicting and cooperative object manipulations.

Another issue is that in some cases users want to perform a number of updates to the object space and make the results of the updates visible only after all operations are completed. Furthermore, they would like these execution blocks not to interfere with each other and to maintain the consistency of the database. Also, when something goes wrong (e.g., the system "crashes") they want to restore the database to a consistent state. All of these requirements are achieved in the context of *transactions*.

Traditionally, a transaction has been a program (i.e., sequence of actions) that reads from and/or writes persistent objects and satisfies the *ACID* properties (*atomicity, consistency, isolation,* and *durability*). Briefly, atomicity means that the transaction is either executed entirely or is not executed at all. Consistency means that transactions map a persistent database from one consistent state to another. Isolation means that transactions do not read intermediate results of other noncommitted transactions. Durability deals with resilience; it means that once a transaction is committed its effects (i.e., updates) are guaranteed to endure despite failures. Each of these properties is explained in more detail in the following sections.

The intelligent office environment is used here to illustrate the semantics of transaction processing. Each transaction is carried out by a data entry person at some office in the internetworked environment. The office worker starts a transaction and imports an image, the data corresponding to the image, and indexes based on the content of the image. The worker then inserts the image into the appropriate *folder* and commits the transaction.

Each transaction includes the following sequence of database operations:

1. The worker's record is updated to reflect the work done.
2. The image document and all relevant indexed information concerning the content of the image are entered into the database.
3. The folder of the imported image's subject or category is updated to include the image document.
4. A new record is inserted into the history class.

The key point here is that all of the above steps must be completed for the transaction to be successful. Here the identification of the operations in a transaction is done explicitly.

Several strategies exist for identifying a transaction in object-oriented as well as more conventional database management systems (such as relational). One of the simplest strategies is to make *every database access a transaction*, that is, to treat every database read and every database update (*modify, insert, delete*, etc.) as a transaction. Although this strategy *will* work (and is used in some DBMSs), its overhead is prohibitive. Furthermore, it will not allow users to group together several statements that manipulate the database. Therefore, a better approach is to *delimit* a number of database access and manipulation statements between *Begin Transaction . . . End Transaction* constructs.

Specifically, database languages typically provide language primitives to identify the sections of code that should be run as a transaction. That is, many database management systems support most of the following constructs:

1. *Begin Transaction:* This construct indicates the start of a transaction. The section of code between this statement and *End Transaction* will be executed atomically.

2. *End Transaction:* This construct indicates the end of the transaction. When this statement is executed successfully all of the statements (especially the updates) between *Begin Transaction* and *End Transaction* are committed.

   All updates become committed, and programs that execute afterwards can see the updates performed by the transaction.

3. *Abort Transaction*: Occasionally, the user might decide to *undo* all work and terminate the transaction without committing its updates. To this end database languages provide a transaction abort mechanism. This is also known as transaction *rollback* or transaction *undo*.

For example, consider the following transaction:

```
Begin Transaction
     Give Joe a 10 percent raise.
     Promote Joe to Sales Manager.
End Transaction
```

The atomicity of the transaction guarantees that either Joe gets the raise *and* the promotion *or* he gets neither. That is, since the transaction is atomic we cannot have partial executions. For example, we cannot give Joe a 10 percent raise and then stop, even if there is a power failure or a system crash. When power is restored the database system must ensure that the transaction is continued to the end or that the 10 percent raise is undone when power is restored. Although the actual syntax of the *transaction begin, commit,* and *abort* mechanisms differ in different database systems, the overall intention and semantics are the same.

In a multiuser system, when two or more transactions execute concurrently the database operations (*read* and *write*) can be executed in an interleaved fashion. The interleaving can cause programs to behave incorrectly, or interfere, thereby leading to an inconsistent database. The inconsistency can be in several forms including lost updates or dirty reads. These concepts are discussed in Section 5.2.3.

The rest of this chapter expounds on these ideas and describes the basic concepts of transactions, concurrency control, and resiliency in object-oriented database management systems. In addition, since transaction management in object-oriented databases is an extension of "conventional" transaction management techniques and concepts, this chapter will also, when necessary, explain "traditional" transaction management, concurrency, and recovery issues.

■ 5.1 ORGANIZATION OF THE CHAPTER

This chapter discusses transaction processing in a multiuser, object-oriented database system. The term *multiuser* means that many users are concurrently accessing, updating, querying, and otherwise manipulating the *same persistent object space*. Section 5.2 discusses transaction concepts in object-oriented databases, elucidating the ACID concepts from traditional transaction management. Section 5.3 presents recent object-oriented database concepts such as nested transactions and cooperating transactions. Section 5.4 discusses concurrency control strategies, with special emphasis on locking strategies. Section 5.5 explains recovery concepts in object-oriented databases and discusses how these are implemented in object-oriented databases. Section 5.6 discusses versioning and the concepts related to creating version derivation trees for objects. Section 5.7 provides a summary.

■ 5.2 THE ACID TEST

This section explains in detail the ACID properties: atomicity, consistency, isolation, and durability.

5.2.1 Atomicity

A transaction is a program that is either executed entirely or not executed at all. In other words, either the entire sequence of operations or no operations are applied to the database. This feature is called *atomicity*; transactions are *atomic*.

If the user performs updates to the persistent database within a transaction, then either *all* of the updates must be visible to the outside world or *none* of the updates must be visible. In the former case we say the transaction has *committed*. In the latter case we say the transaction was *aborted*. The database system must ensure that all operations performed by a successfully committed transaction are reflected in the database and that the effects of a failed transaction are completely undone from the database. Thus, a successful image document transaction must update the worker's record, enter the image document into the database, and insert the image document into the appropriate folder. If the transaction fails because of concurrency control or other reasons, any effects on the worker's class, the compound document class, the folder, and the history table must be completely undone.

5.2.2 Consistency

Consistency deals with the preservation of all the semantic constraints on the database. A database is said to be *consistent* if all integrity constraints on the database state are satisfied. The execution of a transaction in the absence of interference from other concurrent transactions is assumed to take the database from one consistent state to another. This is illustrated in Figure 5.2. All of the integrity constraints of the database are satisfied when the database is in state

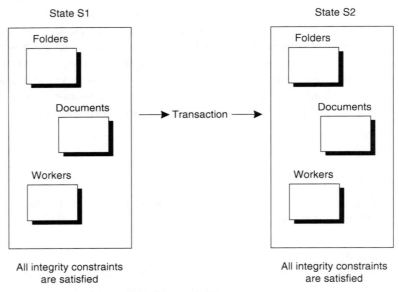

Figure 5.2 Transactions maintain consistency.

S1. When transaction *T* performs updates to the database and terminates, the integrity constraints are still maintained when the transaction is in state *S2*.

Consider the following intelligent office example. In a corporation the total-number-of-workers attribute value should equal the sum of workers in different departments (assuming those departments are disjoint). Similarly, the head count assigned to a department must be greater than or equal to the number of employees working in that department. In the course of executing a transaction the consistency constraint may be momentarily violated. For example, in transferring workers from one department to another and updating the various databases, we can, *within the transaction*, momentarily violate the previously mentioned integrity constraints. The collective logic of the worker transfer transaction taken as whole, however, does not violate the integrity constraints. Thus, if transactions were performed on a database in a strictly serial fashion consistency would be guaranteed. The challenge in implementing an efficient concurrency control scheme is to permit the interleaving of operations from multiple transactions while preserving the database's consistency.

5.2.3 Isolation

The execution of concurrent transactions manipulating the same (concurrently) shared objects can cause anomalies, if the interleaved operations are not protected from one another. Isolation deals with the safeguards provided by the database system against conflicts between concurrent transactions.

Database management systems can provide different levels of isolation between concurrently executing transactions.

There is an inverse relationship between the level of isolation and the throughput of concurrent transactions. More specifically, the more transactions are isolated from one another, the higher the likelihood of conflicts and, hence, transaction aborts. The aborted transactions consume resources; they must be retried. Also, database management systems that attempt to guarantee higher levels of isolation incur more overhead. As will be discussed in the following sections, object-oriented database management system applications (the so-called advanced database applications) have transaction and concurrency requirements that are somewhat different from the well-defined short-duration transactions of more conventional (such as debit/credit) applications. This means that flexibility in isolation levels is even more important in object-oriented databases. Some concepts involved in providing different levels of isolation are discussed below.

Serializability

The greatest level of isolation is *serializability*. Transactions are serializable if the interleaved execution of their operations produces the same effects on the database as their exection in some serial order. This is illustrated in Figure 5.3. Figure 5.3(a) shows transactions *T1* through *T5* executing concurrently. Figure 5.3(b) has a number of serializable executions of the transactions. Note that serialized execution does not imply that the transactions that started first ("clock" time) are necessarily the ones guaranteed to terminate before other transactions in the serial order.

Lost Updates

A less strict level of isolation is just to guarantee that the updates of committed transactions are never lost. Of course, serializability always avoids lost updates. In general, database management systems guarantee that updates will not be lost. The problem of lost updates can be understood through an example.

As illustrated in Figure 5.4, assume that a financial manager sends the scanned image of a financial evaluation of a company and asks two subordinates to send decision-critical comments. The two coworkers simultaneously acquire the document and introduce annotations that describe their evaluations and recommendations.

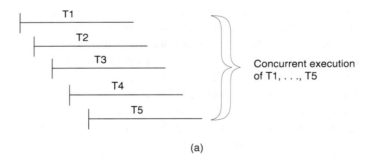

(a)

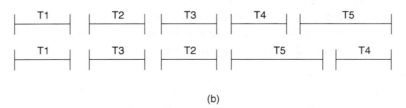

(b)

Figure 5.3 Serializing the execution of transactions.

Now suppose that we have the following sequence of interleaved operations from the two transactions:

1. Worker 1 reads the financial evaluation document and the supervisor's request.
2. Worker 2 reads the *same* financial evaluation document.
3. Worker 1 annotates the document and recommends that the supervisor not invest in the company and gives reasons.
4. Worker 2 also annotates the document but recommends that the supervisor invest in company.

Thus, if two concurrent transactions are not properly synchronized and the above interleaved execution sequence is allowed to occur, the annotations and recommendations performed by one of the workers could be lost.

Numerous methods and strategies exist to avoid these anomalies. For instance, document-imaging products, such as Office.IQ from Portfolio Technologies, allow the users to *check out* the document to perform updates. Since only one worker can check out a document at a time, no document annotations will be lost.

Dirty Reads

A less strict level of isolation than serializabilty is to allow dirty reads. *Dirty reads* can be explained as follows: Transaction $T1$ modifies the state of an object (e.g., changes the value of one of the object's instance variables). Before $T1$

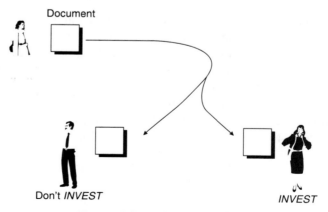

Document

Don't *INVEST*

INVEST

Figure 5.4 Synchronizing updates.

commits, transaction *T2* reads this modified object. If *T1* aborts and its updates get rolled back, *T2* will have read an uncommited state of the object, which should be considered as having never existed.

In many applications, improving the concurrency is more important than guaranteeing an isolation level that avoids dirty reads. This is especially true in object-oriented databases for which long-duration transactions are common. For example, consider a statistical query that is computing an aggregate value over all instances in a huge class extension. It may not be desirable to stop all other transactions from modifying the class extension (by inserting and/or deleting objects from the class treated as a collection) while the time-consuming query is being processed. At the same time the query result may hardly be affected by the additional synchronization because of the sheer number of instances of the class. In such case allowing dirty reads in order to reduce the synchronization overhead may be acceptable.

5.2.4 Durability

Database management systems must guarantee that the updates of committed transactions are never lost. *Durability* means that the updates of committed transaction can be recovered in the case of either system or media failures. Once a user or an application is informed that a transaction is committed, the database system must provide sufficient redundancy to guarantee that the updates will be preserved despite system failures. Durability is primarily a recovery issue (which is discussed in more detail in Section 5.5).

■ 5.3 TRANSACTIONS FOR OODB APPLICATIONS

The previous section discusses the fundamental ACID test for transactions. The ACID properties are applicable to both conventional (e.g., relational) and advanced or object-oriented database applications. Several features are, however, more characteristic of advanced database applications such as CAD, CAM, CASE, and intelligent offices. In fact, a number of object-oriented database management systems provide direct support for managing concurrent transactions in these types of applications. This section describes the fundamental transaction concepts for advanced database applications.

5.3.1 Long Transactions

As stated previously, advanced database applications such as CAD, CAM, CASE, and intelligent offices have different requirements than more traditional database applications such as airline reservations and banking. One reason for the different requirements is that in the more traditional applications transactions are relatively short, retrieving and/or updating few records from the database. Consider, for example, the debit/credit transaction that is often used as a benchmark for relational databases. Each transaction involving a deposit or withdrawal consists of the following actions:

1. An account record is updated to reflect the deposit or withdrawal.
2. A branch total record is updated to reflect the deposit or withdrawal.
3. A teller record is updated to reflect the deposit or withdrawal.
4. A history record describing the transaction is written.

These types of transactions are typical; they are short and update or reference only a few records. Furthermore, the emphasis is on performance measures (in terms of TPS—transactions per second) and robustness (recoverability).

The more recent (or advanced) applications have different requirements and characteristics. This is not to say that advanced database applications do not occasionally allow short-duration transactions while accessing and updating few records. In fact, in applications such as intelligent offices short transactions such as the following are quite common:

- Accessing and updating the instance variables of a worker
- Inserting an element into a folder
- Changing the setting of a scanner
- Updating the resolution of a printer

However, especially in design applications, the notion of a "transaction" is much more complex. Consider, for example, the construction of an electronic document in an office environment. Let's say the document describes the five-year plan of the department and is to be made public. In a sense the "transaction" that builds this document and that could involve many office workers is completed when the document is completed. This is illustrated in Figure 5.5.

The document goes through many intermediate phases, and its preparation could take days. This type of "transaction" presents some interesting challenges and problems for more traditional transaction management strategies. As described by Korth et al. (1990), Gray (1978), Garcia-Molina and Salem (1987), and others, some of these issues are as follows.

When a failure occurs anywhere in the phases or subphases of the transaction the entire transaction has to be rolled back. This is due to the atomicity property of transactions. For instance, say the entire transaction of Figure 5.5 is to be treated as one atomic action and a failure occurs while preparing the second draft; all previous work done on the document needs to be rolled back. Of course, this is unacceptable.

Since the transaction is long-lived it will be accessing many different objects during its lifetime. The larger and more complex a transaction, the greater the likelihood of conflicts with other transactions. For instance, if the research documents are accessed and updated, locks on them are held until the transaction commits. This is due to the isolation property of transactions. The effects of updates to objects such as research documents must not be "released" to the outside world until the transaction commits.

Long-lived transactions usually involve many workers on the path to completion. Computer-supported cooperative work is an important industry trend, and traditional transaction models are ill-suited for such work.

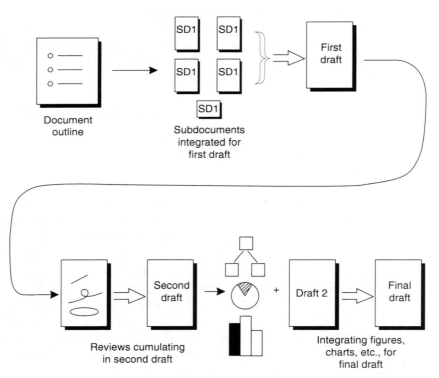

Figure 5.5 The multiple steps to complete a complex document.

Long Transactions in Object-Oriented Databases

A number of object-oriented databases such as ObjectStore, ONTOS, ITASCA, Versant, Statice, and Object/DB provide some support for long-duration transactions and nested transactions. Here, explicit support of long-duration transactions in OODBs such as Versant and ITASCA is discussed. Both of these support the notion of long and short transactions. As illustrated in Figure 5.6, the idea is to have short transactions "nested" within long transactions. (Nested transactions are discussed in more detail in the next section.)

The overall model of long transactions works as follows. The user intends to perform numerous updates to a large complex object, which could take a relatively long period of time (hours or even days). The user starts a long-duration transaction. Only after this transaction is completed will the updates be visible to the outside world. The user can then check out the complex object and its subobjects (the check-out/check-in model is described in Section 5.6.3) from the concurrently shared database and work on these objects in his or her "personal" database. With short transactions the user can perform updates to checked-out objects and commit them. Then, when all of the short transactions are done and all of the operations on the checked-out objects are completed, the user can commit the long-duration transaction and check in all of the checked-out objects.

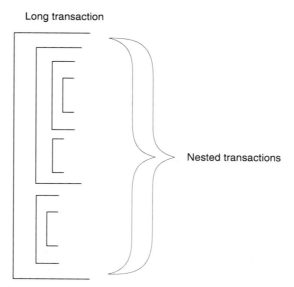

Figure 5.6 Long transaction with nested subtransactions.

5.3.2 Nested Transactions

The long duration of transactions in advanced applications is a characteristic of next-generation database applications. Several strategies related to long durations of transactions have been proposed in database research. Some of these strategies have influenced existing object-oriented database implementations. One of the earliest transaction models proposed to handle the problems of long duration was the nested transaction model introduced by Moss (1981).

As its name suggests, a nested transaction model can contain subtransactions, also called child transactions. For example, see Figure 5.7, where the transaction is a tree structure. There is a root, or top-level, transaction. Nested within the root could be one or more child transactions or subtransactions (*ST1* and *ST2* in the figure). *ST1* and *ST2* are children of the root, or top-level, transaction; *ST11* and *ST12* are children of *ST1*; and so on.

As another example, see the complex document-preparation transaction in Figure 5.8. Here the top-level transaction corresponds to the task of completing the final draft. As for the ACID properties of transactions, top-level transactions satisfy atomicity, consistency, isolation, and durability with respect to other top-level transactions. Subtransactions within a parent transaction are isolated from one another and appear atomic with respect to each other. Their updates are durable.

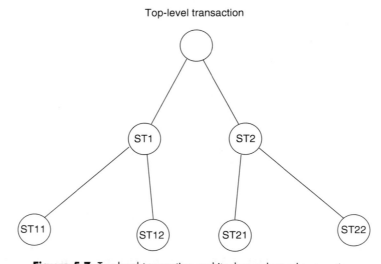

Figure 5.7 Top-level transaction and its descendant subtransactions.

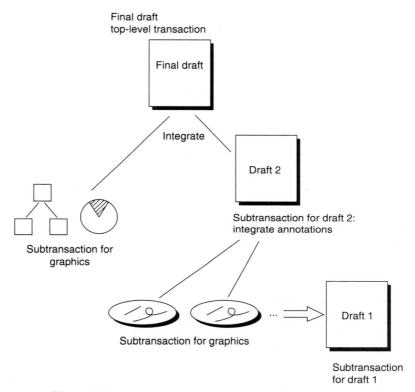

Final draft
top-level transaction

Final draft

Integrate

Draft 2

Subtransaction for draft 2:
integrate annotations

Subtransaction for
graphics

Subtransaction for graphics

Draft 1

Subtransaction
for draft 1

Figure 5.8 Nested transaction in document-preparation example.

In the document-preparation example, if the subtransaction that prepares the second draft fails, the integration transaction (which integrates the second draft and the illustrations) must not see partial results of the second-draft transaction.

In a nested transaction all of the child transactions (subtransactions) must be completed for the top-level transaction to commit. Each subtransaction must be either completed or aborted. For instance, we cannot commit the complex document-preparation top-level transaction of Figure 5.8 if any of the subtransactions are still active.

If one of the subtransactions fails, then the parent of the subtransaction can retry the subtransaction. Alternatively, the parent might decide to take another action and proceed. This alternative action can result in a contingency subtransaction. For instance, if the subtransaction that is preparing the illustrations in Figure 5.8 fails, the parent transaction might decide to retry. Or it might decide to have a contingency subtransaction that prepares a final draft without illustrations and commit. Of course, the parent transaction can always choose to abort if one of its subtransactions fail. If a top-level transaction aborts, the effects of all of its subtransactions will be lost ("undone"), even if the subtransactions were committed.

Nested Transactions in Object-Oriented Databases

Several object-oriented databases, in both research and industry, support nested transactions. These databases include ObjectStore, ONTOS, STATICE, and Objectivity/DB. In ONTOS, for example, users are able to create nested transactions up to 127 levels. In the client server environment of ONTOS the nested transactions do not incur any activity on the screen. The ONTOS model follows the nested transactions quite closely. For example, if any of the ancestors of the nested transactions are aborted, ONTOS undoes any of the changes performed by the nested transactions. When there is already a transaction running, nested transactions are created automatically upon issuing a transaction start call.

5.3.3 Cooperating Transactions

Several advanced applications involving transaction users (e.g., workers) in intelligent offices need to cooperate to perform a task. To this end there have been a number of proposals (e.g., Nodine et al., 1992) for *cooperating transactions*.

In sharp contrast to the isolation levels of traditional transactions, cooperating transactions can see each other's intermediate results. The "correctness" of the transaction model of cooperating transactions is user-defined. This contrasts with the more rigid serializability criteria of the traditional transaction model. For instance, if several office workers are cooperating in the production of illustrations for a document, the illustrations can take alternative forms for screen shots, pie charts, figures, and so on. If each form is assigned to a worker it might be desirable to have the workers see intermediate (noncommitted) updates of each other's work to better coordinate the consistency of the final illustrations. The workers might come up with "rules" that regulate the coordination and synchronize their individual subtransactions. A rule might specify that all of the designers should work on the same version of the product. Although not used extensively, cooperative transactions are powerful.

Note that some commercial object-oriented database systems such as ITASCA and Vbase (the predecessor of ONTOS) have supported the notion of shared transactions, which allow multiple users to cooperate in the completion of a parent transaction.

■ 5.4 CONCURRENCY CONTROL

Strategies are used to synchronize the interleaved access and update operations of concurrent transactions. The transaction isolation levels are captured in the concurrency control mechanism of the database management system.

Traditionally, three main concurrency control strategies have been used: *pessimistic* (Eswaran et al., 1976), *optimistic* (Kung and Robinson, 1981), and *versioning* (Bernstein and Goodman, 1980), or timestamp ordering, algorithms. Pessimistic algorithms assume that concurrent transactions will likely conflict and hence acquire locks before access and update operations. Optimistic algorithms assume that transactions will probably operate without conflict, and only at commit time are checks made to guarantee the isolation of transactions. Version-based schemes create a new version of an object for each update. Since transactions that only read objects can always access a previous consistent snapshot of the database, typical read-only transactions always commit.

There are many variations and hybrids of these three fundamental strategies. Locking-based strategies are by far the most commonly used algorithms in database management systems. Even if one of the other (optimistic and version-based) strategies is used, object-oriented databases typically allow the user or the application program to *explicitly* lock or check out objects. Therefore, the next few sections concentrate primarily on locking strategies, especially as applied to object-oriented databases.

5.4.1 Locking Algorithms and Strategies

Most concurrency control algorithms use locking to synchronize the execution of concurrent transactions. Each persistent object can be locked. This is usually achieved through a lock table, which contains the object identifiers of the locked objects. Before a transaction can access an object it must request a lock. If at least one other transaction is currently holding a lock, the transaction has to wait until the lock is released.

There are many types or "modes" of locking. The two simplest modes are read mode and write mode. The *read (shared) lock* allows multiple transactions to perform read operations on the same object concurrently. The *write (exclusive) lock* reserves access (read and write operations) on an object to the transaction currently holding that lock. Only one write lock can be held on a database object at a time. This restriction includes read locks on the same database object.

The granting of multiple locks, possibly of different modes, against the same database object by the database system is governed by a *compatibility matrix* as illustrated in Figure 5.9. This figure indicates that only shared locks are compatible with one another. This means that if a transaction *T1* holds a shared lock on

	Shared	Exclusive
Shared	Y	N
Exclusive	N	N

Figure 5.9 Compatibility matrix.

an object O, and another transaction $T2$ requests a lock on O, the lock will be granted if and only if it is a shared lock request. If a transaction is holding an exclusive lock on an object O, no lock (shared or exclusive) can be held on O by another transaction.

Two-Phase Locking

To guarantee that transactions are serializable, concurrency control mechanisms often conform to the *two-phase locking* protocol. This protocol clearly separates a transaction into a growing phase and a shrinking phase. During the growing phase all locks must be acquired, possibly incrementally. During the shrinking phase all locks are released, possibly incrementally.

The following lock protocol satisfies the two-phase locking protocol:

1. Before performing any read operation on an object the transaction must acquire a share lock mode on that object.
2. Before performing any write operation on an object the transaction must acquire an exclusive lock mode on that object.
3. After releasing a lock the transaction must never acquire any more locks.

It has been proven that all transactions are serializable if they obey the two-phase lock protocol. Consequently, the database consistency is preserved.

Multigranularity Locking

In an object-oriented database there are objects of different "granules." For instance, there are instances of classes such as a folder, a worker, and a compound document. Then there are collections of these instances, such as a set of workers. There are also larger collections, such as the extension of a class. Furthermore, in the physical-implementation level, the persistent objects are stored in secondary-storage disk pages. These pages are arranged in clusters, or areas. Furthermore, different operating system files are used to contain the pages and storage areas.

Hence, at both the conceptual (class–collection–instance) and physical (database–file–area–page) levels, there are various "granules" of objects.

A lock manager can lock a "coarser" object (such as a class and its extension; or a storage area and all the objects contained in it), implicitly locking all the objects it contains. Different transactions have different requirements. Some transactions need to access few individual object instances. Others need to access more complex objects or aggregates. In general, the coarser the granule, the less the locking overhead. However, locking objects of a larger granularity has the side effect of reducing concurrency, since conflicts become more likely. Multi-granularity locking allows different transactions to set locks at different levels. Thus, long transactions that access large portions of the database can use coarser granules than short transactions that touch only small portions of the database.

The fundamental motivation for multigranule locking protocol is therefore to minimize the number of locks to be set in accessing the database. For example, when most of the instances in the class are to be accessed it is wiser to lock the entire class rather than lock on each instance of the class. When only a few of the instances need to be accessed, however, it is wiser to lock the instances individually. This allows other concurrent transactions to access other instances.

As mentioned earlier, the selection of the locking granule is a tradeoff between overhead and concurrency. When the lock granule is at a finer level—for instance, at the individual instance level—there is more overhead. Concurrency, however, is increased because several transactions want to update different instances of the same class concurrently. When the lockable unit is at a coarser level—for instance, at the class level—there is less overhead. The concurrency, however, is decreased because all instances of the class are locked, thus forbidding other transactions to access any instances of the same class.

Conceptually, object-oriented databases have (at least) two granules for locking: classes and instances. Each class or instance can be locked either in share mode or in exclusive mode. Locking at a class level in either share or exclusive mode implicitly locks all instances of that class in the same mode. These are the instances that are instantiated directly from the class. These instances are included in the class extent.

Besides the class instances, the requester has access right to the class definition when a class is locked in either share or exclusive mode. The class definition includes the external interface, internal structure, implementation of methods, and class extent. A share mode is required on a class to read the class definition. An exclusive mode is required on a class to update the class definition.

Class Hierarchy Locking

The classes in object-oriented databases are organized into inheritance hierarchies, where some classes in the hierarchy can have extensions or existing instances. It is therefore important to provide granularity locking along these structures. For instance, locking a superclass would implicitly lock all of its subclasses in the same lock mode. The subclasses include the direct descendants of the superclass and their subclasses' descendants.

Locking along the class hierarchy structure provides a coarser unit compared to the single class locking described in the previous section. It incorporates locking the "deep" extension that was discussed in Chapter 3.

To understand concurrency consider the two node types in Figure 5.10. Classes are represented by rectangles and instances by circles. The instances that pertain to a class are represented by links incident to the class. The term *descendant* will be used here to denote both subclasses and instances of a class. Thus, the immediate descendants of a superclass node include the subclass nodes and the instances of the superclass node. The descendants of a subclass node at level i include subclass nodes at level $i + 1$ and the instances of subclass node i. A node at the lowest subclass level in the hierarchy corresponds to the class without any derived class. Thus, the descendants of the lowest subclass are the instances of that class.

An example of the lock hierarchy structure is shown in Figure 5.11. In this example, the OfficeWorker class is a superclass. Both the SalesManager

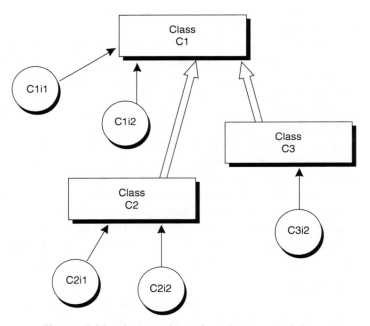

Figure 5.10 Inheritance hierarchy with instances of classes.

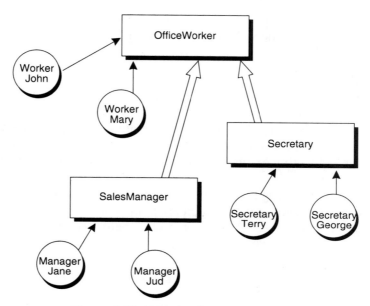

Figure 5.11 Hierarchy of OfficeWorkers.

and Secretary classes are subclasses of the OfficeWorker class. The immediate descendants of the OfficeWorker class include the Office-Worker instances, SalesManager class, and Secretary class. The descendants of the SalesManager class and the Secretary class are their class instances. Note that the instances in the OfficeWorker class's instances do not include the instances of the SalesManager class or the Secretary class. The instances of the subclasses are found directly under each subclass's descendants.

Under the extended lock hierarchy structure each node in the hierarchy structure can be locked. If a transaction requests for an exclusive mode lock on a node and the lock is granted, then the transaction will have exclusive access to that node and implicitly to each of its descendants. Similarly, if a transaction requests a share mode lock to a node and the lock is granted, then the transaction will have shared access to that node and implicitly to each of its descendants. Therefore, when the lock request is granted the transaction has an explicit access right to the locked node and an implicit access right to all nodes of the subtree rooted at that locked node.

Since the exclusive mode lock has exclusive rights to all locked nodes, it is incompatible with a share mode lock request. Conversely, share mode locks can share access with other share mode locks; thus, they are compatible with each other. As mentioned previously, the entire subtree of a locked node X can be locked implicitly.

Intention Locks

With multigranularity locking objects in a database can be organized hierarchically; nodes can be instances or classes. The ancestors of a class are its superclasses. The ancestors of an instance are its class and superclasses. (In the next section we discuss complex object locking, where the "ancestor" of an object can be a complex object.) To lock a fine-granule object a transaction must first lock one or more of its ancestors in some less restrictive lock mode. The objective is to propagate the effect of fine-granule locking activities to a containing coarser granule using an appropriate *intention lock*. Thus, a transaction must set an intention-read (IR) lock on a class before setting read locks on instances of the class. Similarly, a transaction must set an intention-write (IW) lock on a class before setting write locks on the instances of the class.

Sometimes, a transaction might want to read many instances of a class and modify only a small number of those instances. This can be accomplished by setting a read-intention-write (RIW) lock on the class and then setting write locks on instances that need to be modified. The RIW lock on the class implicitly locks all instances within the class for reading. Thus, it is not necessary to lock individual instances for reading. A compatibility matrix for different lock types in a multigranularity locking scheme is illustrated in Figure 5.12.

As the name suggests, intention locks are used as "intentions" or "tags" on ancestors of the locked nodes. The implication is that locking is being done on the descendants of the node. Intention locks enhance throughput by preventing any explicit or implicit lock request on the ancestor node that can lead to incompatibility with the locked node and its descendants.

	R	W	IR	IW	RIW
R	Y	N	Y	N	N
W	N	N	N	N	N
IR	Y	N	Y	Y	Y
IW	N	N	Y	Y	N
RIW	N	N	Y	N	N

Figure 5.12 Compatibility matrix for multigranularity locking.

The use of intention locks can be illustrated through an example. To lock the SalesManager class in Figure 5.11 in a share lock mode the intention lock should be obtained on the OfficeWorker class from which the SalesManager class is derived before the transaction locks the SalesManager class itself. The granting of share access of the SalesManager class would implicitly lock all instances of the SalesManager class, its subclasses (none in this case), and the subclasses' instances. In the same example, to lock a particular instance of SalesManager, intention locks are obtained on the OfficeWorker class and SalesManager class, before the instance itself is locked.

The Intention lock is used only on nodes that are not leaf nodes. Thus, the Intention lock is available only at the class node and not at the instance node (of course, we are not considering complex object locking here; complex object locking is discussed in the next section). When locking a node in an intention lock on a class the requester may not access, read, or update the class definition directly without obtaining the appropriate lock on the class itself. However, a new instance can be added, or an existing instance can be deleted from the class extent. This is possible because the instance itself is further locked in exclusive mode, thus avoiding the deletion of the same object from two distinct transactions.

Locking along class structure is useful in many applications, including schema changes and database queries. These applications usually involve not the one specific class but a chain of classes along the class hierarchy. For instance, in the schema change new attributes are added to a class. This will cause the class definition to be changed. In addition, the existing instances in the database must be modified to make room for newly defined fields. The instances of the modified class include the instances of its class as well as all instances of all subclasses.

Complex Object Locking

As discussed earlier, in object-oriented databases that support locking, objects can be locked in either a share or an exclusive mode. Given an object $O1$, its instance variables $Iv1, \ldots, Ivn$ can be as follows:

- *Values*, such as base values (e.g., integers or character strings) or tuples that are values (e.g., [LastName, FirstName]). Values do not have identities. They are totally "embedded" in or dependent on the object.
- Existentially constrained objects. As discussed in Chapter 3, some instance variables could be existentially constrained on the object.
- "Independent" objects that, although referenced by an instance variable of the object, are neither values nor existentially constrained on the object.

Note that values and existentially constrained objects are also instances of classes. With the locking scheme described so far these objects must be locked separately. This method is rather inconvenient because a large number of locks must be set. In a large complex object containing several dependent subobjects, each subobject must be locked separately in the same lock mode as the parent object.

To solve this problem several "composite object" or "dependent object" locking schemes for complex objects have been introduced (e.g., the locking scheme in ORION—Kim et al., 1987; or the locking scheme in GDM—Thaweethai, 1990).

Here the Intention Component lock scheme of Thaweethai (1990), which is actually a generalization of the ORION strategy, is briefly described. The *intention component* lock is used as a "tag" on the component class of a complex object. When the component class is locked in intention component mode the instances of that class require no further explicit locking. The instances that exist as the dependent objects of a parent (complex) object are implicitly locked in the same lock mode (exclusive or share) as its parent object. Other instances of the component class that are owned by a different parent object are not locked. They can be implicitly locked in the same manner by other transactions.

Before locking a component class in the intention component mode the transaction must acquire either share or exclusive lock mode on the parent object. Once the locks are granted the transaction will have the same access right to the dependent objects in the component class as the parent object.

Any class node along the lock hierarchy structure can be locked in intention component mode. Before locking a class node in intention component mode all ancestors must be locked in the intention lock in the same manner as the shared and exclusive mode. The intention component mode implicitly locks not only the instances of the class but also the instances of its subclasses that are owned by a parent object. Once a class node in the lock hierarchy structure is locked in the intention component mode, the partial subtree rooted at the locked node is implicitly locked in the same mode as the parent object.

For complex object models that support existentially constrained values and other types of "dependent" objects in complex objects, this locking scheme provides a mechanism to lock embedded and dependent objects without having to lock each individual component object. The dependent objects that are existentially constrained are implicitly locked when the complex object is locked in the share or exclusive mode and the dependent object's class is locked in the intention component mode. For independent objects that are referenced from the complex object the referenced objects must be locked separately.

To illustrate locking a complex object consider a "floor" or department in an intelligent office, as illustrated in Figure 5.13. The department has a `Name`, a reference to the company or subsidiary to which it belongs, and a manager. The manager is an instance of class `DepartmentManager`, which inherits from `OfficeWorker`. The manager of the department is a dependent object.

To lock the `Department`, instance X, and all attributes in exclusive mode the transaction acquires the following locks:

1. Lock the `Department` class in *Intention* lock.
2. Lock `Department` instance X in exclusive mode.
3. Lock the `OfficeWorker` class in *Intention* lock.
4. Lock the `DepartmentManager` class in intention component mode.
5. Lock the `Company` class in *Intention* lock.
6. Lock `Company` instance Y in exclusive mode.

Before locking `Department` instance X in exclusive mode in step 2, the `Department` class is locked in intention exclusive mode in step 1. As a result, the department name is implicitly locked by step 2. To lock the dependent objects found in the department manager attribute, the `Department-Manager` class must be locked in intention component mode. Before locking

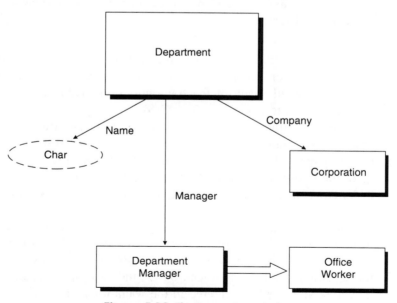

Figure 5.13 The `Department` class.

the DepartmentManager class in step 4, however, the OfficeWorker class, which is the superclass of the DepartmentManager class, is locked in *Intention* lock. For the reference object, Company instance Y, it is locked separately. Before locking the Company instance Y in exclusive mode in step 6, the Company class is locked in *Intention* lock. After all locks are granted, the transaction has an exclusive access right to all attributes of Department instance X.

In the above example, suppose that the locking scheme does not support the intention component class lock in step 4. The transaction must either (1) request an exclusive lock on the DepartmentManager class in step 4 or (2) request an intention exclusive lock on the DepartmentManager class in step 4 and request an exclusive lock on each DepartmentManager instance found in the department manager attributes. None of these choices is very efficient. The first choice implicitly locks all instances of the DepartmentManager class in exclusive mode. Other transactions that wish to access other instances of the DepartmentManager class must wait until the current transaction releases the lock. Thus, the number of concurrent operations is reduced. On the other hand, the second choice introduces more overhead since each DepartmentManager instance owned by Department instance X must be explicitly locked. With the intention component lock there is less overhead because each individual dependent object requires no further locking. More importantly, multiple transactions can access different dependent objects of the same class as long as the complex objects are different.

Deadlocks

The main problem of locking-based concurrency control schemes is the *deadlock*. A deadlock occurs when two or more transactions are waiting for a lock that will never be granted. Each of the transactions involved in the deadlock is waiting for the other(s) to release the lock before it can proceed. A situation of deadlock involving two transactions is shown in Figure 5.14. Transaction 1 is waiting for object *A*, and transaction 2 is waiting for object *B*. At the same time, object *B* is currently granted to transaction 1, and object *A* is currently granted to transaction 2. In the two-phase lock protocol a transaction cannot release any lock until all locks are granted. Thus, neither transaction 1 nor transaction 2 can release the lock, and so both will wait forever.

The main technique for detecting deadlocks is through the construction of a *waits-for* graph. This structure shows the relationships of transactions waiting for each other. For instance, if transaction *T1* attempts to lock object *O* and transaction *T2* is holding a lock on *O*, then a new arc emanating from *T1* with its vertex at *T2* will be entered in the waits-for graph. The arc indicates that *T1* is waiting for *T2*.

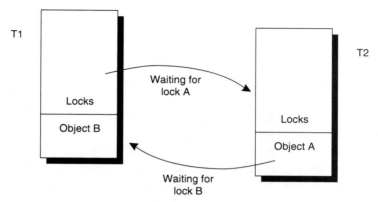

Figure 5.14 Deadlock.

A deadlock results if the waits-for graph has a cycle. There are at least two strategies for resolving deadlocks:

1. Abort the transaction causing the cycle. A less drastic approach would be to inform the transaction that the lock cannot be granted.

2. Detecting cycles incurs substantial overhead on the concurrency controller. A more efficient scheme is to time-out the locks. With time-outs an attempt is made to obtain the lock on behalf of a transaction. If the lock cannot be obtained (i.e., it is granted to another transaction), the lock request will be timed out and the requestor will be informed that the lock cannot be granted. If the lock wait (or time-out) time can be set to an appropriate parameter, time-outs provide an efficient solution for deadlocks.

5.4.2 Concurrency Control Mechanisms in Object-Oriented Databases

Object-oriented databases have incorporated most of the concurrency control mechanisms and concepts discussed in the previous sections. Servio's Gem-Stone, for instance, supports both optimistic and pessimistic (locking) concurrency control mechanisms. With the optimistic approach the system allows the user to continue updating a committed copy of the database in his or her own workspace. When the user attempts to commit his or her transaction the system might refuse the commit due to conflicts. A conflict would arise if, for example, an object that was read and updated was already modified and committed by another transaction.

The pessimistic concurrency mechanism in GemStone is an add-on to the optimistic scheme. Users are given the option to lock individual objects. A transaction can lock some objects while accessing others optimistically (i.e., without locking). There are three types of locks:

1. Read (shared) locks
2. Write locks
3. Exclusive locks

Multiple transactions can hold read locks on the same object, but only one transaction can hold a write lock or an exclusive lock on an object. If a transaction holds a read lock on an object it prevents other transactions from updating or writing the object. For example, if $T1$ gets a read lock on Joe's personnel record no other transaction can update an attribute of Joe (e.g., his age or salary) and commit. With a read or a write lock other transactions can still read the object. With an *exclusive* lock, however, other transactions cannot even read the object and commit. With the GemStone strategy locking is done at the individual object level.

More elaborate locking schemes are supported by object-oriented database management systems such as Versant, ITASCA, ONTOS, and Objectivity/DB. For instance, in Versant users can specify *write locks, intention-write locks, update locks, read locks, intention-read locks, and null locks.* The latter is not a lock at all and lets the user read an object immaterial of other locks held on the object.

In Objectivity/DB, processes (user application programs) can have either *read* or *update* locks. Update locks are like write locks that prevent other processes from reading or writing the locked object. Objectivity/DB also provides support for multiple granularity locking through the container object, database, and *federated* database (which corresponds to one or more database objects) levels. It also supports the checking out of objects, which is a useful feature in advanced applications. This allows locking for more extended periods of time. The lock *persists* on behalf of the user. The *Checkin* function removes the persistent locks on the object.

ONTOS supports both optimistic and pessimistic concurrency control mechanisms. It provides a pessimistic concurrency control mechanism to support applications for which short-duration transactions are dominant. It provides an optimistic transaction mechanism that, together with explicit locking by the user, supports better transactions that are of long duration. Different types of locks are supported, including read lock, write lock, and write-intent lock. Users specify the lock types when "get"-ting or activating an object. Users who obtain locks on objects explicitly can also set the conflict resolution policy.

■ 5.5 RECOVERY MANAGEMENT

As mentioned earlier, transactions are atomic. This means that the database management system must guarantee that *partial* results or partial updates of transactions that fail are not propagated to the persistent database. There are three types of failure from which a system must recover. To discuss the implications of each failure type, assume an underlying two-level memory system: a volatile main memory and a stable secondary memory (e.g., a magnetic or optical disk). The persistent data are always propagated to the secondary storage.

The three failure types are as follows (Gray, 1978).

Transaction failures: A transaction failure occurs if a transaction fails to commit. This could be due to concurrency control conflicts (e.g., deadlocks) or user aborts, or because the transaction violates an integrity constraint.

Systems failures: A system failure can occur because of hardware or software problems. The general assumption is that after a system failure the contents of volatile memory are lost. System failures are usually caused by software errors in the operating system or the database management system or by power failure. This corresponds to a system crash in an operating system. When a system failure occurs the contents of the main memory are lost. As a result, all database cache buffers are also lost. The secondary disk storage, however, remains intact.

Media failures: Media failures are usually caused by hard disk crashes or other nonrecoverable errors on the hard disk. A portion (possibly all) of the data on the hard disk is lost. Media failures are the most difficult failures from which to recover. If care is not taken to replicate the data in either logs or mirrored databases, mission-critical data could be lost due to media failures.

5.5.1 Recovery Manager

Reliability and the graceful recovery from these types of failure is an important feature of a database management system. The *recovery manager* is the module that handles the techniques for recovering from these failures. There are several different data structures and strategies that are used to implement the recovery manager.

One of the most commonly used data structures for recovery management is the *log*. The log is used to record and store the *before* and *after* images of updated objects. The before image is the state of the object before the transaction update, and the after image is the state of the object after the transaction update. Depending on the particular recovery algorithms used, one or both types of images must be stored on the log.

The before and/or after images are recorded on the log during the normal execution of transactions. When a failure occurs and the system is restarted the recovery manager is invoked to reconstruct a consistent database from the log and the data on the secondary storage (the hard disk, assuming the failure was not a media failure).

5.5.2 Recovery Strategies

The updates of a committed transaction must be written to a durable storage—typically a magnetic or optical disk medium. There are two main strategies for propagating transaction updates to stable storage:

1. *Updating in place:* Each object is stored in one or more disk pages. With updating in place, the old object value is replaced by the new value through overwriting the old value. The modification of the old value implies that *undo logs* must be used to restore the old values, in case the transaction that performed the updating in place aborts.

2. *Out-of-place-updating:* The alternative to updating in place is to store the new values in a different (in many cases, a *shadow*) page (or pages). Then, at commit time, the pages containing the older values are replaced by the pages containing the new, updated values. If shadow pages are used, the page tables are updated to reflect the swapping of the pages containing the values before the committed transaction's updates with the pages containing the new committed values.

In addition to the update strategy, there are other dimensions and issues involved in recovery. These include *commit processing*, which deals with the strategy used at commit time for propagating the updates in primary storage to secondary storage; *replication strategies*, to allow recovery from media errors; and others.

The recovery manager is one of the most complicated modules in a database management system. Different object-oriented (as well as "traditional") databases have alternative solutions and strategies for enhancing the resilience of the database system. However, most of the strategies, algorithms, and implementations of recovery are hidden from the users or application developers.

5.5.3 Recovery In Object-Oriented Databases

Almost all object-oriented databases provide some support for recovery. Most OODBMSs use logging for recovering the database to a consistent state. Some use data replication or mirroring. For example, Servio's GemStone object-oriented database management system allows the user (actually, the system administrator) to create replicas, or mirrors, of the persistent database. The replica is created through a system command such as

```
SystemRepository replicateWith: < file name >
```

where <file name> specifies the location of the replica. The replica can reside on the same disk as the original persistent database or on an entirely different disk volume. A different disk volume must be used if we want protection from media failures.

When a transaction performs an update, *all* replicas are updated *before* the transaction commits. Maintaining these replicas incurs execution time and storage overhead. However, many critical applications, such as medical, military, and real-time transaction systems, require fault tolerance from any kind of failure. In these situations, users are willing to live with the extra overhead as long as they are guaranteed very fast recovery and access to their databases.

ONTOS, on the other hand, provides a utility called DBRecover that lets users recover the databases to a consistent state. There is a special storage area called the Journal that basically stores all of the activities (updates and modifications) on the database. When a failure, such as a disk crash, occurs the system administrator can use the DBRecover utility to recover the database to a consistent state as before the failure. Thus, the journal is basically a redo/undo log.

In Versant recovery and logging can be turned *ON* or *OFF.* Turning the recovery mechanism *ON* will affect the performance. If recovery and logging were on, however, the system would be able to roll the database back to a consistent state. Versant provides *startdb* and *stopdb* utilities that, respectively, restart the database to a consistent state or stop all database operations in case of an abnormal condition.

■ 5.6 VERSIONING

Access to previous states or alternate states of objects is an inherent part of many applications. Application domains that require access to the evolution of object states include engineering design applications (such as computer-aided design, computer-aided manufacturing, or computer-aided software engineering), intelligent offices (for heterogeneous office object management), as well as more traditional financial or accounting applications.

In these applications the same object undergoes multiple changes, or state transitions, and it is desirable to access or investigate previous states, or *versions,* of the object. For example, consider the chapters in this book. Each chapter underwent an evolution. For some chapters various versions, which differed in organization and at times in content and emphasis, were kept. For some chapters, the final *version* was an integration of different components of previous versions. It proved extremely useful to keep the previous versions and to use parts of them in subsequent versions. This happens often in document management and for complex document systems.

Version management in an object-oriented database consists of tools and constructs to automate or simplify the construction and organization of versions, or configurations. Without these tools it would be up to the user to organize and maintain the versions. The user would have to create and maintain his or her own versions. One way to do so would be to use a naming convention to keep track of the different versions of the same object and the *relationship* (the derivation tree) of the versions to one another. This procedure is quite laborious and error-prone. Thus, in complex design applications automatic version management is an extremely useful and powerful utility.

Many engineering and design applications use versioning to create progressively more enhanced versions of the design object. In design engineering applications the design objects are typically stored in a central (persistent) repository. Designers *check out* a persistent object from the database, work on it, and, when satisfied that they have a better implementation, *check in* their object as a different version.

After a versioned object is created the root of a *version set* contains all of the versions of the object. Designers then create new versions of existing versions of objects. The main property that is common to all versions of the *same* object is the *identity* of the object. Throughout its versioned history an object may undergo multiple state and even structural modifications.

If all of the versions of an object are created sequentially we get a *linear* version set. In general versioning, however, multiple designers can create *alternative* versions of an object. This is illustrated in Figure 5.15 for the object O1. The version set of O1 is { V1, V2, V3, V4, V5, V6, V7}. The version V1 was the original version and V7 the final released version. V2 and V3 are alternatives of V1. V4 and V5 are alternatives of V2. The path V1 to V3 to V6 to V7 is a

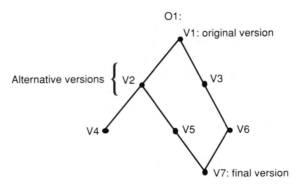

Figure 5.15 Version set of O1.

linear versioning path from V1 to V7. As the figure illustrates, the versions are partially ordered. Each version has *successors* and *predecessors.*

Some object-oriented languages that support versioning provide language constructs to do the following:

- Check out and check in object versions
- Retrieve successors or predecessors of versions

For example, to create a version in Iris (which is the basis of HP's commercial OODBMS called OpenODB) a user must first name and check out a successor version of an existing version, that is, predecessors, immediate predecessors, all successors, and immediate successors of a version. For example, using the versions in Figure 5.15,

```
Successor(V2)
```

will return all the successors of V2:{V4, V5, V7}. Similarly,

```
Predecessor(V6)
```

will return all the predecessors of V6: { V3, V1 }.

Alternative approaches for creating versioned objects are as follows:

1. *Inheritance:* One approach is to inherit from a "history bearing," or a *Version*, class. With this approach classes that need to have versioned instances can inherit from the versioning class. Then methods such as *Predecessor, Successor,* and *Merge* become applicable to the instances of the class. For example, in Figure 5.16 VersionedFolder inherits from both Folder and Version. As the figure illustrates, the versioning methods of Version are now part of the protocol of instances of Versioned Folder.

2. *Explicit property:* A similar but slightly alternative approach is to explicitly declare a class or an instance to be *versioned.* This property makes the versioning methods and the check-out/check-in mechanism for creating versions available and applicable to objects that have the versioned property set (e.g., when the object is created).

5.6.1 Configurations

In many applications that involve complex objects references between objects need to be consistently maintained. Moreover, as objects undergo modifications

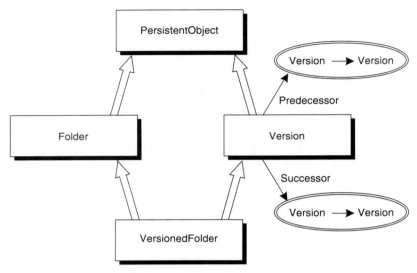

Figure 5.16 Versioned objects through multiple inheritance.

and states of referenced (or mutually referenced) objects get modified a mechanism is needed to identify mutually consistent (Cattell, 1991) states of aggregate objects. These collections of objects that must be maintained mutually consistent are called *configurations*. A configuration can be thought of as a collection of objects that is to be treated as a unit for locking and versioning purposes. Individual objects within the configuration can undergo modifications, so each object can have a "history" of versions. Different objects within the configuration are updated at different times and not necessarily with the same frequency. Consider, for example, a compound document in an intelligent office. Some *pages* in the compound document might be updated more frequently than others. In other situations hyperlinks between pages must be maintained consistent (e.g., when the referencing each other with bidirectional links) with the correct versions.

In Figure 5.17(a) the horizontal axis has versions of the same objects. The figure also shows versions of the various configurations, which represent consistent relationships between the objects in them. Figure 5.17(b) illustrates the evolution of the configurations temporally. Here the horizontal axis represents time. Note that each time any object within the configuration is modified and a new version is created the versioning *percolates* to the configuration and creates a version of the configuration. Also note that in some cases mutually dependent objects are updated together. For instance, the text object describing a graph or an image in a compound document and the image itself must be updated together.

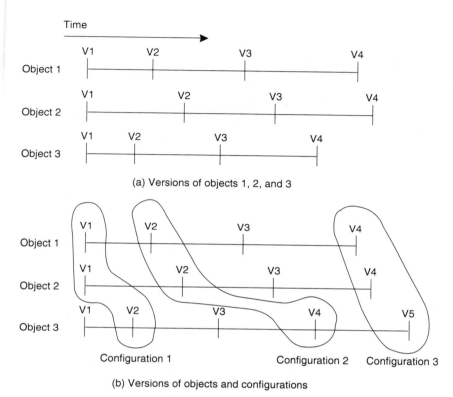

(a) Versions of objects 1, 2, and 3

(b) Versions of objects and configurations

Figure 5.17 Versions of objects and configurations.

5.6.2 Historic Versions

As discussed by Copeland and Khoshafian (1987), some applications use the concepts of generations of data based on historic versions. A temporal model that incorporates historic versions can be used for keeping track of the evolution of objects during their lifetime. The main disadvantage of versioning based on a temporal model is that the versioning is basically *linear*, as illustrated in Figure 5.18(a). *Alternatives*, or *branching*, as illustrated in Figure 5.18(b), is not supported directly. If the OODB supports historic versioning, however, it can be easily augmented or extended with support for named versions and alternatives.

5.6.3 Check-Out/Check-In Model and Versioning

The intelligent offices example is used here to illustrate the relationship between the check-out/check-in model and versioning. Concurrently shared objects must be "checked out" from common areas or libraries, operated upon, then checked

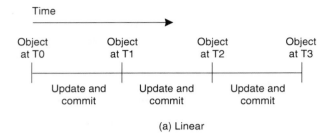

(a) Linear

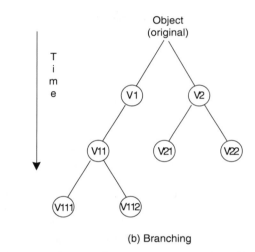

(b) Branching

Figure 5.18 Linear historic versions versus branching.

in. The overall algorithm for accessing objects concurrently in client/server architectures is as follows:

Step 1: Begin the transaction.

Step 2: Navigate or locate the object(s) to be manipulated.

Step 3: Check out the objects with either read or write lock, depending upon the intent.

Step 4: Manipulate and possibly update the object(s).

Step 5: Check in object(s) back to the common area (repository), possibly creating a new version.

Step 6: Commit the transaction.

If the process goes smoothly and the object is updated a new version of the object is created. If anything goes wrong (either because of transaction, system, or user conflicts) the transaction can be aborted, the locks released, and any updates on the checked-out objects undone.

Figure 5.19 illustrates how client/server architecture corresponds to an object repository and the office worker's workspace. Objects can be checked out by the following techniques:

1. Providing its unique identifier (its object number or key value)

2. Providing various selection criteria

The first strategy involves having the office worker check out the object using a "handle." The second strategy involves performing searches, then checking out an object according to its attribute values or its relationship with other objects. For instance, documents in a folder whose type is WordPerfect can be checked out using the following pseudocode:

```
Check-Out Documents D In Folder Fl
    WHERE D.Type = "WordPerfect"
```

Another important issue with respect to object check-out/check-in is the granule and levels of the objects. For example, when a folder is checked out, what objects have been checked out? When the office worker checks out folder *F1*, is he or she checking out all objects in *F1*? When a compound hypermedia document is checked out, are all of the documents linked to the hypermedia document also checked out?

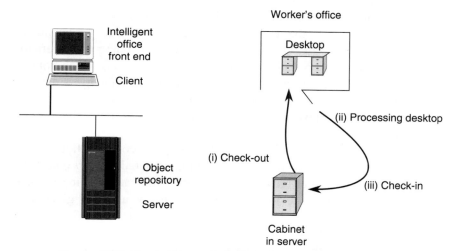

Figure 5.19 The check-out and check-in of objects from the repository.

We see that the process of checking out a document can imply a substantial amount of locking. In client/server architectures the step of locking large objects reduces the concurrency and has diverse effects on the throughput of the system. The process of checking in or checking out large numbers of objects can incur a substantial overhead in locks and could even prohibit the office worker from accessing all of the objects that he or she needs.

Since the office worker has the most knowledge about what he or she needs to access, the office repository can provide the following alternatives:

1. Given an object handle O, check out only O. Other office workers or applications cannot access or update the attributes of O, and if O contains other objects they cannot insert or delete objects in O. They *can*, however, access or even check out objects that are contained in O or are reachable from O.

2. Given an object handle O, check out O and *all of its immediate children*. For instance, if O is a folder, this option will involve checking out O and all documents and/or folders immediately contained in O. The advantage is that the office worker has access to all of the objects in the folder without locking the entire "universe" reachable from the folder.

3. Check out all objects that are directly or transitively linked or reachable from the object handle. This option can be useful for accessing self-contained hypermedia documents.

5.6.4 Versioning in Object-Oriented Databases

Several object-oriented databases support versioning. For example, ITASCA allows automatic versioning of objects tagged as versioned. When programs reference an object the default is to access the most recent version of the object (as expected). In ONTOS, which provides a versioning and alternatives mechanism for objects, users can create *configuration* objects, which contain all of the objects of the same version. The configuration hierarchy is actually a tree. Thus, ONTOS supports both linear versions and alternatives of the same version. Only the configurations at the leaves of the tree are updateable. Inner configurations can only be deleted.

ObjectStore from Object Design supports configurations and versioning with alternatives. The configurations are manipulated in *workspaces*, which are themselves objects that provide the "context" for manipulating configurations. Given a parent workspace that is shared by many users, a given user can create a "child" workspace. The user can then check out a configuration from the parent workspace to the child workspace. After performing the necessary modifications the user can check the object back into the shared workspace, creating a new version.

■ 5.7 SUMMARY

This chapter has presented the main transaction management concepts and approaches of object-oriented databases. A transaction is a program that is executed either entirely or not at all. Transactions must map databases from one consistent state to another. In order to maintain consistency transactions must pass the ACID test: atomicity, consistency, isolation, and durability.

Transactions in object-oriented database applications are typically longer than those in more conventional business applications. Nested transactions are used to resolve some of the problems associated with long-duration transactions. Also, in advanced applications tasks typically involve multiple users; cooperative transactions are used to support such cooperative tasks.

Transactions map databases from one consistent state to another. Several concurrency control algorithms can be used to guarantee serializability of transactions and consistency of the database. The most notable of these is *locking*. In object-oriented databases locking can be associated with various granules that are manipulated by users, including classes, instances, and complex objects.

In order to support durability of transactions object-oriented databases provide recovery managers to bring the database back to a consistent state, making sure that all of the effects of failed transactions are undone and that those for committed transactions are consistently reflected in the database. Typically, redo/undo logs are used to recover the database, although to guarantee against media recovery (e.g., disk crash) disk mirroring or mirrored databases are also used.

Finally, reflecting the need for various versions of an object as it undergoes modifications in the database, this chapter has discussed versions and alternatives in object-oriented databases. It has presented configurations that are used to maintain mutually consistent versions of objects. The chapter also discussed the check-out/check-in model and its relationship to versioning.

6

CLIENT/SERVER ARCHITECTURES AND OBJECT-ORIENTED DATABASES

Chapters 1 through 5 have discussed the object-oriented and database features of object-oriented databases. This chapter discusses the emerging client/server architectures and their relationship to object-oriented databases.

As mentioned in Chapter 1, in the 1960s almost all computers were mainframes, and interaction with them took place through input/output devices such as card readers and printers or dumb terminals. Using these devices programmers input programs in assembly or higher-level languages such as COBOL, PL/I, C, or Pascal and received output on interactive terminals or line-printer printouts. The computers were large, difficult-to-use mainframes such as the IBM 360/370 series.

In the 1970s minicomputers (especially the VAX family of systems from DEC) were introduced. At this time, especially in universities, the UNIX operating system became popular and provided multitasking and concurrent access capabilities. Although interaction still took place primarily through dumb terminals, client/server ideas and models were experimented with and implemented.

Personal computers were introduced in the early 1980s. Although Apple pioneered and launched the personal computer era, it was only after the adoption of the Intel-chip-based personal computer by IBM that PC systems started to be used in serious business applications. It is estimated that about 60 million personal computers are in use today, with this number steadily increasing. It is also estimated that about 50 percent of these PCs are on local area networks (LANS). It is ironic that the personal computer, which was supposed to *isolate* and personalize computation, has, after less than a decade, become the backbone of distributed computation.

Soon after the introduction of the personal computer in the early 1980s *file servers* on local area networks enabled the sharing of files and resources such as printers. One of the most popular file servers and network operating systems is Novell's NetWare. Novell dominates the market, having provided nearly 70 percent of all installed file servers.

The late 1980s and early 1990s saw the emergence of *database servers* such as the SQL Server from Microsoft and Oracle's OS/2 Server (Khoshafian et al., 1992a; 1992b). In the early stages these were *single-database servers*; that is, the DB servers had no mechanism for executing transactions involving multiple servers and multiple databases.

The next evolutionary step, supported by relational and object-oriented database vendors, was *distributed databases*. The earlier distributed databases allowed the execution of transactions spanning various databases and servers involving DBMSs from the *same vendor*. These are sometimes called *homogeneous* distributed databases. The next step has been to support distributed databases involving DBMSs from *various* vendors involving *various* database models (relational *and* object-oriented). In other words, the next step has been the support of *heterogeneous distributed databases*.

The distributed database trend is expected to continue. In one sense, object-oriented databases will "objectify" the distributed database trends of relational databases. As discussed throughout this book, this is especially true of OODB solutions that are extensions of relational database management systems. More recently, however, *object-oriented approaches* for client/server and distributed computing have emerged. In a sense, object orientation is best suited for client/server computing and distributed computing since, taken to its logical extreme, in the object-oriented model of computation each object is a *server providing a number of services* (namely, its *protocol*). In fact, there are a number of *concurrent* object-oriented models for which the method execution and operation of the objects are done concurrently.

As far as the industry is concerned, the emergence of the OMG group and the participation of a large number of companies in its standardization effort resulted in a number of interesting ideas and implementations, the most notable of which was the Object Request Broker standard (X/Open and OMG, 1992). The Common Object Request Broker Architecture (or CORBA, for short) allows a wide variety of "objects" to interact in a distributed environment. The architecture allows a client object to perform a request from a "server" object, and the system is responsible for locating the object's implementation and satisfying the request. Since objects can span networks CORBA has the potential of providing a very powerful and general distributed object management capability.

The rest of this chapter expounds on these client/server and distributed database concepts and illustrates how they are or could be applied to object-oriented databases.

■ 6.1 CHAPTER ORGANIZATION

This chapter is organized as follows. Section 6.2 discusses the backbone of client/server architectures and distributed computing, namely local area networks. Sections 6.3 and 6.4 discuss file servers and database servers, respectively. They explain the main features of file and database server architectures and illustrate the differences between the two types of servers. Section 6.5 presents the main features of distributed databases. Section 6.6 shows how some of these distributed database and client/server concepts are implemented in existing object-oriented databases. Section 6.7 gives a summary of the chapter.

■ 6.2 LOCAL AREA NETWORKS

The emergence of local area networks during the latter half of the 1980s has brought about major changes in the way business computing is conducted. Business computing used to be the exclusive domain of centralized mainframe/minicomputers, powered by expensive centralized MIS departments. The advent of LANs, combined with phenomenal increases in PC computing horsepower, has brought about the decentralization of corporate information management.

A LAN is a group of computers connected together covering a limited geographical area. Each computer, or node, can communicate with any other computer, or node, and each node contains its own processor. Basically, a LAN enables a variety of independent devices to communicate with one another to share data and services.

A LAN typically connects from one to several hundred workstations, as shown in Figure 6.1. Though the use of bridges and gateways LANs can be internetworked, providing access to an almost unlimited number of nodes. Each LAN can contain several nodes that provide various *services* to the client nodes on the network.

The concept of a server is basic to the network. Services on the local area network are provided by servers. The server, which contains the hardware and software needed to provide services, offers a centralized and shared location for

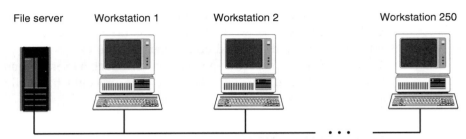

File server   Workstation 1   Workstation 2   Workstation 250

Figure 6.1 A typical LAN.

that service. It sits at a location remote from the user, providing both multiuser and multitasking access to the shared network objects.

The types of resources or devices placed on a server are complicated to set up and maintain, are expensive, and by definition require concurrent, multiuser access. An example of such a device is an optical jukebox. The jukebox, with a potential capacity of a terabyte or more, requires the dedicated hardware horsepower that only a server can provide. Given the fact that the price of a large jukebox can reach six figures, it is not cost-effective to place the jukebox on a single user's workstation.

Servers range in functionality from generalized servers, such as file servers that provide a variety of services, to specialized and dedicated servers, such as print servers, database servers, or asynchronous communication servers, that provide a specific service.

6.2.1 Networking Topologies

A LAN can be configured and organized in a number of ways. Network configurations range from centralized, in which a single network mainframe computer performs all of the processing for users connected at a remote site, to fully distributed, in which the processing is distributed among multiple remote sites. Typically, the LAN of the 1990s uses a distributed topology.

The major network topologies are grouped into the six types illustrated in Figure 6.2: star, ring-based, bus, point-to-point, multipoint, and hierarchical; the bus and ring configurations are most commonly used for LAN topologies. These topologies may be described as follows:

1. The star is an example of a centralized architecture. The main computing site acts as the hub of the network. Each remote site gains access to the main site via a single communications line.

2. Ring structure topologies, also distributed in nature, use a closed-loop, or ring, methodology. Each node in the ring is connected to the node on either side. The main advantage of this topology is the speed of transmission;

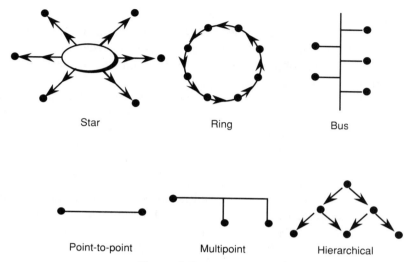

Star Ring Bus

Point-to-point Multipoint Hierarchical

Figure 6.2 LAN topologies.

the algorithms for avoiding and detecting data collision and garbling are simple.

3. Bus-structure topologies are also a distributed architecture. The bus structure uses the concept of a central backbone communications line with arms or nodes connected off the backbone. As the signal traverses the backbone via a coaxial, fiber-optic, or twisted-pair cable all nodes on the system listen to the signal to determine whether it is intended for them. This topology is flexible, allowing each node to attach into the network anywhere along the backbone.

4. Point-to-point networks are simple in design. A single client node is attached to a single server processing computer via a communication line. The client node may be used in an on-line or batch-processing mode.

5. Multipoint networks are an extension of the point-to-point configuration. Instead of a single client node attached to the server, multiple nodes may be attached. Each node may be directly connected to the server via its own communications line or may be multiplexed together via a single communications line.

6. A hierarchical network is an example of a fully distributed topology. Hierarchical configurations employ the notion of having one or more mainframes at the top of the hierarchy, with midrange computers tied into them; these computers in turn have mini- or microcomputers tied into them. Each node has its own processing power and may access the resources of those nodes higher or lower on the hierarchy.

6.2.2 Networking Protocols and Standards

In 1977 the International Standards Organization (ISO) organized a committee to investigate the compatibility among various pieces of network equipment. The work of this committee led to the development of the Open Systems Interconnection reference model (OSI).

The OSI model defines seven layers of network functionality whose purpose is to provide a concise network model, thereby allowing equipment from competing companies to coexist in the network. Figure 6.3 illustrates the OSI model.

The layers of OSI are as follows:

1. **The physical link (layer 1)** is the hardware base of the network. It includes such items as cabling and network cards. Whereas the other six layers are implemented via software, this layer is strictly hardware-based. This layer controls the mechanical and electrical behavior of the hardware and is mandatory for conformance with the OSI model.

2. **The data link (layer 2)** defines the protocol for accessing and sharing the hardware of layer 1. The concept of token passing and signal collision detection belong to this layer.

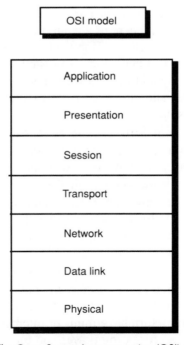

Figure 6.3 The Open System Interconnection (OSI) reference model.

3. **The network layer (layer 3)** is defined for networks that require routing mechanisms to pass packets among the nodes.

4. **The transport layer (layer 4)** provides the low-level connection functions for the network. This level is involved with the sending and receiving of packets, error detection and correction for packet transmissions, and packet flow control.

5. **The session layer (layer 5)** provides for the establishment and termination of data stream connections between two or more nodes on the LAN. The main purpose of a LAN is to allow two or more nodes to connect together for communication purposes. This linking process is known as starting a session and is the purpose of this layer. Network address mapping to node connections is a function of the session layer.

6. **The presentation layer (layer 6)** provides information translation services for the application layer. Data unpacking, character set conversion, protocol translation, encryption, and decryption are provided by this layer.

7. **The application layer (layer 7)** provides network services to users of the LAN. This protocol layer is responsible for the initiation and reliability of data transfers. Items such as error recovery, handshaking, and network access are all part of this layer.

Another widely used network model is System Network Architecture (SNA). SNA was developed by IBM in 1974 to provide an overriding structure for the increasingly complex world of networks. The OSI model was proposed three years later by the ISO committee and is very similar to the SNA approach.

6.2.3 Data Transport Protocols

Data transport protocols provide a means of passing data from one network note to another. To see where these higher-level protocols fit into the network model this section discusses IPX, SPX, NETBIOS, APPC, and TCP/IP protocols.

Internetwork Packet Exchange

Internetwork Packet Exchange (IPX) is the underlying protocol for Novell's network software. It is a close adaptation of the Xerox network standard (XNS) packet protocol.

IPX supports only datagram-style messages (it is said to be "connectionless"). A datagram message is one that is never acknowledged by the receiver. This means that IPX does not guarantee the delivery of a packet or that packets will be delivered in any particular sequence. IPX corresponds to the network layer of the OSI model.

Sequenced Packet Exchange

Sequenced Packet Exchange (SPX) is a session-level, connection-oriented protocol. A session-level protocol is a logical connection between two workstations in which delivery of a message is guaranteed. A connection must be established between two nodes before information may be exchanged. This protocol is part of the transport layer of the OSI model, one layer higher than IPX. Both IPX and SPX were developed by Novell.

Network Basic Input/Output System

The Network Basic Input/Output System, more commonly referred to as NETBIOS, was originally developed by IBM for their PC-LAN product. NETBIOS supports both datagram and session-level connections. NETBIOS corresponds to the network layer, the transport layer, and the session layer of the ISO model. This is a higher-level protocol than either IPX or SPX.

Advanced Program to Program Communications

Advanced Program to Program Communications, or APPC, is also a session-level protocol developed by IBM. APPC provides a high-level mechanism for two programs to communicate with one another on a peer-to-peer basis. It is based on the use of IBM's Logical Unit 6.2, or LU6.2, which provides a mechanism for creating logical connections between workstations. APPC corresponds to the session level of the OSI model.

Transmission Control Protocol/Internet Protocol

Transmission Control Protocol/Internet Protocol, or TCP/IP, was designed by the Department of Defense (DoD) for their ARPANET wide area network. TCP/IP is a layer of protocols. TCP is similar to NET BIOS and APPC in that it provides point-to-point guaranteed delivery communications between workstations. The IP is a datagram-based protocol whose functionality is similar to Novell's IPX. In regards to the OSI model TCP/IP is entirely different. TCP/IP defines its own layers and is not compatible with the OSI model.

6.2.4 Network Operating Systems

Network operating systems (NOSs) are the software packages that operate the network, providing a host of services to network users. File storage and retrieval, file sharing, network administration, user and resource security, network management, name space resolution, resource accounting, and electronic mail are all functions of the NOS. Other advanced features such as transactions and location transparency may also be part of the NOS. Of course, network operating systems differ in the way they support these various network administration capabilities. The NOS should not be confused with such communications protocols as TCP/IP.

An NOS provides functionality far beyond a particular communications protocol; it can provide support for several different communications protocols.

Three methodologies are currently used in the creation of network operating systems:

1. The first methodology relies on building the NOS from scratch, tailoring it to the task at hand. The most popular network operating system, Novell's NetWare, has taken this approach.

2. The second methodology retrofits an existing operating system with the required functionality so that it may act as an NOS. Banyan has adopted this approach. The Vines network operating system supports and complements the UNIX operating system.

3. The third method creates a separate software component that is responsible for the network functionality and is loosely tied to an underlying existing operating system that provides the NOS layer with access to the resources of the machine. Microsoft's LAN Manager was developed in accordance with this third methodology.

The key point to remember is that network operating systems provide a number of useful features for administering and managing the network resources. This is in addition to the basic information and resource sharing provided in the LAN. In some cases the functionality of an NOS is complemented by product offerings from third-party venders.

Databases (including object-oriented databases) often provide features and functionalities similar to those offered by a network operating system or a network administration utility. Some of these features are fundamental database features discussed in earlier chapters: locking, security, transactions, and backup. In most cases, the database management system provides its own implementation of multi-user administration functions. Users who are logged in to the network might be asked to "log-in" to the database and provide a password for the database access. The network operating system and the database management system are de-coupled. The database management system typically uses the communication protocol of the NOS to allow clients access to the server. The DBMS itself organizes the database objects utilizing a number of (network) operating system files. However, the concurrency, security, and overall administration of these objects are (typically) performed by the database management system (instead of "calling" the NOS functions or utilities). It is expected that next generation NOS will provide more powerful "database" capabilities, providing the DBMS with the opportunity for tighter integration with the networking environment. Software that "bundles" a DBMS with the NOS is already available.

6.2.5 Client/Server and Peer-to-Peer Models

There are two basic models of computing in the network environment: client/server and peer-to-peer. The client/server model dictates that one or more centralized servers are responsible for all of the shared resources on the network. Individual workstations must acquire access to and use the shared resources via the appropriate central server. If the workstation wishes to share information with any other workstation it must first upload that information so that others may use it. Any physical device that resides only on the workstation, such as a printer, hard drive, or fax board, can never be shared or used by other workstations.

The advantage of this model is that security and management of the client/server network resources can be centralized and tightly controlled. The centralized server is also dedicated and optimized to perform workstation requests quickly and efficiently. The disadvantage is that a major portion of the resources connected to the network via the workstation are not accessible to the network and are therefore underutilized. A great deal of replication, with the associated expense, is inherent in the client/server model.

The peer-to-peer model does not need a centralized server. Every workstation on the network is capable of acting as a server to every other workstation. Information stored on the workstation is directly accessible by other workstations (provided the "client" on the other workstation has the appropriate access rights). Sharing of information and devices is easily accomplished in the peer-to-peer model.

The advantages of the peer-to-peer model are that the use of resources on the network is far greater and the sharing of information is easier to accomplish. There is a great deal more flexibility in this model. The disadvantage of such systems is that they are hard to manage. Security is also a problem, and performance cannot compete with the client server model. Figure 6.4 illustrates a peer-to-peer architecture.

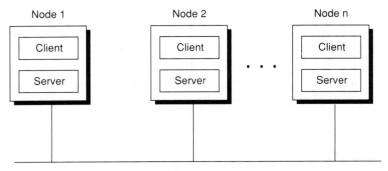

Figure 6.4 Peer-to-peer architecture.

6.2.6 Security and Authorization

One of the drawbacks of new technologies is that they have a tendency to create new problems. Before the era of LANs security for information stored on single personal computers was relatively easy to achieve. The emergence of LANs has opened up critical data to hundreds and thousands of users, making the task of security a monumental chore.

The basic motivation driving the growth of the local area network is the need to increase productivity by facilitating access to a growing body of information. The ability of a LAN to provide for a growing user group greater amounts of information with greater ease is what networking is all about, but herein lies the great paradox: One goal is to provide easy access to vital information to a large user group; another goal is to prevent users from gaining access to information without proper privileges or authorization.

Authorization defines the access rights of the users on the network. It determines what resources users have access to and what operations they may perform on those resources. Security authorization and security go hand in hand.

Local area networks present a unique set of problems when it comes to security. First of all, the level of information distribution presents more avenues by which that information may be accessed. Any user sitting at a workstation can gain access to information, and unless that user's access is carefully monitored he or she can gain unauthorized access to sensitive data. This possibility, along with the ability of remote terminals to gain dial-in access to a network, makes for a difficult security situation.

Security and authorization start with the concepts of users and passwords. The network administrator defines every new user for the system, gives the user an account, and assigns to that user the rights to various network objects. To gain access to the system the user must log on to the system, specifying both user name and password.

There are various methods of ensuring password protection. The first is to require a password of minimum acceptable length. Another is to make sure that all passwords are encrypted and are always sent across the network in encrypted form. A third way to ensure password protection is to be sure that all passwords are unique. One final way is to require the periodic changing of passwords.

In conventional network environments, files, directories, and devices can be protected by access rights. The user can be given specific privileges (such as read, write, update, delete, modify attributes, perform directory searches, execute, create) at the file level or the directory level or both. Files themselves may be further protected by attributes such as a read-only status, which prevents a file from being modified.

Some systems support the notion of a security database responsible for assigning and tracking the privileges of objects on the network. All objects, such as users and files, must be registered in the security database. The database then determines who is allowed to access what object. Novell supports this notion by using a "database" called *the bindery*, which, among other things, binds network objects with a list of authorization rights.

All network operating systems support a form of security. Many people feel that security is sufficient. Others have added third-party security software to add security measures such as enveloping the workstation in a protective shell or encrypting all information, including filenames, on the network.

Object-oriented databases often build their security mechanism on top of the security and authorization of the underlying NOS. More advanced and "object-oriented" notions of security are sometimes incorporated in the object-oriented database.

6.2.7 Backup and Archiving

To prevent a catastrophic loss of data, backing up network data is vital. Backing up information, however, has been made complicated by the LAN model: Not only do multiple servers need to be backed up, but so do numerous workstations, all with local hard disk storage and all containing valuable information.

There are two types of information backup. In the first, called backup, the daily changes to the information base are temporarily stored on an alternate device in case the primary storage devices fail. The information on the alternate device is frequently overwritten by subsequent backups and is not saved for a long period of time. The second type of backup, called archiving, provides long-term off-line storage of critical data for historical and statistical processing. This type of information is never overwritten.

Backup is performed by a combination of hardware and software. Previously, tape drives were the only backup hardware devices. However, tape drives are difficult to maintain, tapes break easily, and tapes cannot provide random access to the information that is saved. Optical storage has significantly changed the ability to back up information by providing unsurpassed capacity, random access, and freedom from the failures of magnetic tape. Optical storage is also the only technology that can effectively handle both backup and archiving. Erasable disks are used for daily backup, and WORM disks are used for archiving.

Most network operating systems provide some type of backup software, but this software is often not up to the task and should not be used unless the LAN is simple and small. Third-party companies offer more suitable software. A conspicuous missing feature in network backup software, however, is the ability to back up all nodes on the network automatically. Object-oriented databases also provide backup utilities, but usually the backup is for backing up the persistent database objects (not the entire object space on the network).

Whether performed through network operating system utilities or through object-oriented database services, in many cases the backup process uses three sets of backup media. The first time a backup is performed three identical backup sets are made and then stored off site. After that the sets are rotated in a round-robin fashion. The set of backup media that is the oldest (most out-of-date) is used to perform the backup. If the system should fail, during either normal use or the backup process, the most recent backup is used to restore the system. If that backup set should fail the final set may be employed to prevent total data loss.

A standard backup is done on a set time basis—daily, weekly, monthly, etc. Its primary purpose is to prevent the catastrophic loss of information. Erasable optical drives are the medium of choice for this operation.

Archiving, which is concerned with the long-term preservation of information, is performed whenever the current state of critical data must be saved. Write Once optical media is preferred for this operation.

The devices used for the backup/archive are determined by the backup rules. The office administrator selects the default device(s) for backup and the default device(s) for archiving. These devices may be overridden based on the backup rule and the object being saved. For example, all folders that deal with employee records may be sent to a backup device located in the human resources department.

■ 6.3 CLIENT/SERVER ARCHITECTURES: FILE SERVERS

The file server was the original enticement that inspired the LAN revolution. As more personal computers entered the office the need to exchange information between those computers grew. The original method of transfer, used even to this day, is known as "sneaker net." Bob needs a file that is on Anne's PC, so he runs over to Anne's desk, copies the file onto a floppy disk, runs back to his desk, and loads the file.

File servers were, as the name indicates, designed to provide file services to multiple users. Through file servers users can concurrently share resources, the most prominent of which are the data and commonly used resources such as printers.

As the complexity and the needs of LANs have grown the responsibilities of the file server have increased. The network operating system, with all of its features, resides on the file server. Services such as electronic mail, message handling services, security, and printing services (there are also dedicated print servers) are the domain of the file server.

The file server can be dedicated or nondedicated. A dedicated file server takes over all of the resources and cannot be used as a workstation. A nondedicated file server acts as both a file server and a workstation, providing a less expensive

LAN solution but also suffering in terms of performance. With the falling prices of PCs nondedicated file servers are being used less and less.

The computers that house file servers have undergone significant change in recent years. The first computers were simple PCs that were undifferentiated from the workstation. As the complexity of the network operating system and the number of users grew the need for specialized hardware has become evident.

Companies such as Compaq now make PCs designed to house powerful file servers, or "super" servers. These computers can have gigabytes of storage, contain multiple CPUs to increase the computing horsepower, and can incorporate new bus architectures for improved disk performance.

6.3.1 Other Services

A specialized type of file server often used in imaging, document processing, and intelligent office applications is an *optical file server*. An optical file server is dedicated to providing mass archival storage to each workstation on the network. It is especially relevant in data-intensive applications, which are actually advanced object-oriented database applications. Typically, an optical server using a dedicated PC with a large Winchester drive for caching will provide access to one or more daisy-chained jukeboxes and optical drives.

In addition to optical disks other types of servers or services are supported on a file server. One service that is becoming increasingly important is faxing and fax servers.

Figure 6.5 illustrates how many servers and services could be available on the same local area network for which logic and resources are managed by a file server. The figure illustrates optical disk servers for supporting data-intensive applications such as imaging, fax server, and printer server all on the same network.

6.3.2 Partitioning Functions in a Client/Server Architecture

Figure 6.6 illustrates how in a typical file server environment the functionality is partitioned between the file server and the clients. The file server performs the file- and block-, or page-, level, I/O. It typically contains and manages multiple disk *volumes* that are concurrently shared by the clients. It also provides primitives for controlling concurrent access in order to maintain the consistency of the concurrently shared information.

Semaphores (which are data structures used for synchronizing access between concurrent client requests), for instance, are provided by the network operating system to control the concurrent activities. *Logical semaphores* are used to lock various logical (as opposed to physical) objects on the network. Client

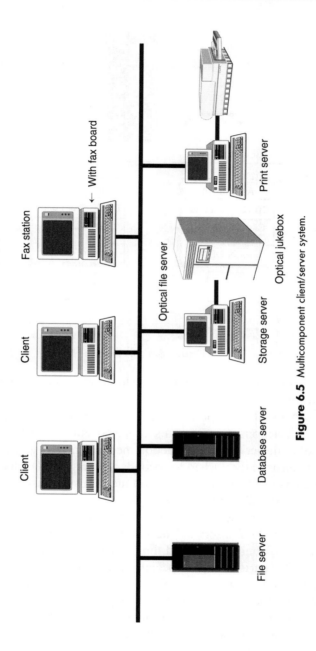

Figure 6.5 Multicomponent client/server system.

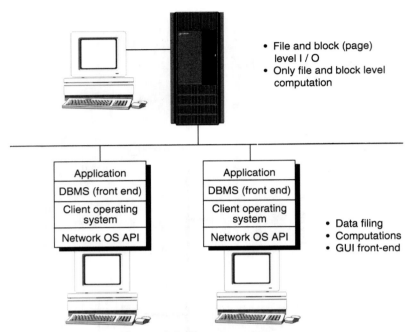

- File and block (page) level I / O
- Only file and block level computation

- Data filing
- Computations
- GUI front-end

Figure 6.6 File server architecture.

software can use logical semaphores to control access to various concurrently shared resources on the network.

File servers also support *transactions*, which were discussed in Chapter 5. Briefly, transactions are programs executed either entirely or not at all. In the context of a file server the transaction mechanism will guarantee that the pages of a file are consistently flushed to secondary storage. File servers deal with block-, or page-, level I/O and the transaction mechanism is used to guarantee the ACID properties at the file and page level.

File servers provide caching or buffering mechanisms to allow faster response of disk I/Os by the file server. The file server system can preload some additional data when performing reads and thus make the data available for subsequent requests. Buffering is useful, especially for data that is accessed very frequently, because the concurrent users making requests will often have their requests satisfied through the cache without incurring disk I/Os.

The *execution* of the application is typically done on the client side. For instance, if three clients are attempting to execute, say, a database management system software, then the execution of the DBMS software is done on the clients' CPUs and not the server's. This is true for any application executing on client nodes. In fact, in most cases the file server appears as a disk drive or volume. Therefore, the application's data is stored on the server whereas the executable is executed on the client (the executable's files could be stored on either a local client disk or server). As indicated earlier, there is actually server software that executes on the file server, but the server software provides file I/O, buffering, locking (i.e., through semaphores), concurrent access, backup, and authorization functionality.

An interesting trend is to have *executable modules* on the server side. Novell has introduced *NLMs* (NetWare Loadable Modules), which are executables on the server side. Oracle and Sybase are providing NLMs for their database server systems to execute on the file server. Other relational and object-oriented databases, such as ObjectStore from Object Design, are also expected to follow suit.

Figure 6.7 illustrates an architecture that incorporates a database server *and* file server on the same LAN. Database servers will be discussed in the next section. If the database management system functionality is not incorporated in the file server (e.g., through an NLM in Novell) we have two physically separate nodes, as illustrated in Figure 6.7(a)—one for the file server and the other for the database server. However, if the database functionality *is* incorporated into the

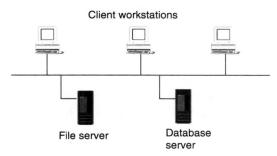

(a) Separate database and file server nodes

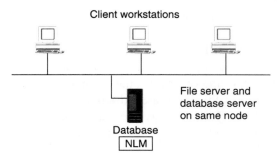

(b) Database server as an NLM

Figure 6.7 Alternative file/database server architectures.

file server we have just one file/database server node, and we incorporate both functions through a single server, as illustrated in Figure 6.7(b). This tight integration of database engine and operating system has the advantages of improved security and efficiency.

In fact, this approach of having various NLMs for different services, all provided through the same file server node, is applicable to other types of services as well. For instance, rather than having a separate fax server node for the network we can incorporate server faxing as an NLM on the file server. Similarly, rather than having a separate node to manage the optical jukeboxes or drives optical disk management functionality can be incorporated on the file server as an NLM.

6.3.3 File Servers and Object-Oriented Databases

Most object-oriented databases will be operating in environments incorporating not only the OODB servers but also other servers and services. Database servers will be discussed in the next section.

Internetworked computing environments are expected to incorporate multiple database servers and file servers, as well as other servers and services on the network. There are a number of ways that the file and database (object-oriented or otherwise) server functionalities can be integrated. Here are a few examples of how database servers, file servers, and network operating systems can operate in the same environment:

1. **OODB Storing Server and Services Information**: The object-oriented database can be used to store detailed information about the various object on the network. These objects include

   - Users
   - Groups
   - Devices such as FAX, printer, and scanner
   - Storage media and services

   Thus extensive information about server resources can be stored in the object-oriented database. For instance, the addresses of users, their FAX numbers, and other attributes of network users can be stored in the OODB. Users can then be searched based on their attribute values. Office.IQ from Portfolio Technologies provides additional attributes (FAX number, employee number, addresses, etc.) to Novell users (according to the Novell binderies).

   Therefore one approach in the integration of the file and database server functionality is to use the OODB as an extensive repository of information about network resources.

2. **Tighter Integration of Concurrency, Authorization, and Recovery Mechanisms:** Most object-oriented database management systems provide their own concurrency control, transaction, security, and recovery mechanisms. As stated earlier, many network operating systems provide concurrency (e.g., semaphores), transaction, authorization, and recovery support. It is conceivable that in next-generation product offerings the object-oriented database will rely more on the NOS for supporting these functionalities. There is the problem of granules, as database granules can be much smaller ("object" level) than NOS granules ("block" or "file" level). Nevertheless, there is much room for improved efficiency in incorporating the NOS support of these functionalities in the OODBMS.

3. **OODBs as clients of NOSs:** Object-oriented databases can become (and in most cases are) *clients* of network operating systems. For instance, an OODB can rely on the communication protocol supported by the NOS. More specifically, an OODB operating on Windows clients and UNIX servers can rely on the TCP/IP modules (TSRs) supported by the NOS vendor.

   The OODB can use other services and servers on the network, supported by the NOS. Some of these include storage devices that appear as volumes, or drives, on the network; various services such as FAXing and printing, which could be accessed through the OODBMS; and others.

   Another aspect of an OODBMS behaving as clients of the NOS are the users of the NOS. In most cases the NOS users log-in to the network and are certified through a password. Object-oriented databases can either "inherit" these network users or, alternatively, provide an additional log-in to the database. In the former case the database users will be a subset of the network users, with the same IDs and passwords.

▪ 6.4 CLIENT/SERVER ARCHITECTURES: DATABASE SERVERS

With the growth of client/server computing database servers have become an important part of the LAN environment. Database servers maintain the information base of the network, provide concurrent access to the information base, and maintain the consistency and validity of the data. Transaction control of database accesses is another key feature of the database server, although, as mentioned earlier, files servers also provide transaction and locking support at the file and I/O block levels.

The differences between file servers and database servers, including the additional functions provided by database servers, are illustrated in Figure 6.8. In the most straightforward implementation a database server is a separate node on the network that provides an interface to client nodes. The interface, which is often in the form a library of functions, allows clients to submit their requests to the database server and get back from the server the results of their queries.

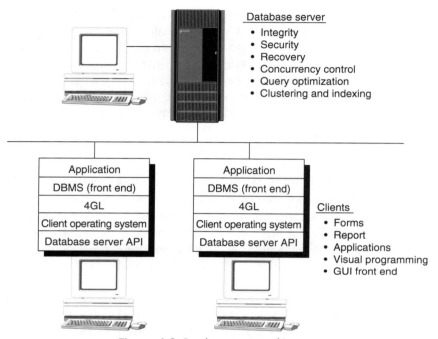

Figure 6.8 Database server architecture.

A fundamental difference between a file server architecture and a database server architecture is the fact that with a database server the client workstation passes a "high-level" request in message form to the server. This is in contrast to the block I/O and file access requests in the case of a file server. The database server processes the request and then returns only the results. This is illustrated in Figure 6.9. Since the database request can be a complex query this saves great

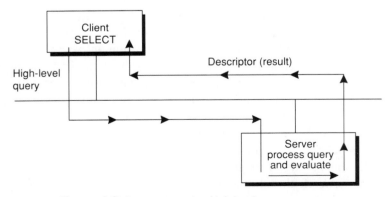

Figure 6.9 Server processing high-level query statements.

deal of network traffic, since the code that processes the query and the data both reside at the same location.

6.4.1 Functions Performed on the Database Server Nodes

Unlike the file server approach, in which all DBMS executables are executed on the client side, with the database server approach the database management system's engine is executed on the server side. More specifically, the following functions might be performed by the database server node:

1. *Integrity:*As discussed in Chapters 2 and 3, database management systems allow the definition of various integrity constraints. The database server approach is *object-oriented* when it comes to integrity constraints. Rather than performing the integrity checking in the application programs that execute on the client side, the database server approach allows the database designer to define integrity constraints *with the data* or as a constraint on the objects. The constraint itself, whether in the form of an explicit constraint (such as a range constraint, a *NOT NULL* constraint, or an existential constraint) or through triggers, is verified and executed on the server. It is associated with the persistent objects, and its verification resides and is executed with the objects.

2. *Security:*File servers *do* have security but only at the file and directory levels. This means that various groups and users can be given or denied access to particular files and/or directories. Some directories might not be "visible" to certain users. Database servers, on the other hand, have the potential to provide security at the *object* level. Users can be granted various privileges on logical objects and collections of objects. These privileges might include read or update operations, create operations, or execution of methods associated with persistent objects. With a file server architecture the file server software checks and imposes the file-and-directory-level security, executing on the file server node. With the database server architecture the software that stores and executes the database server security resides and is executed on the database server node.

3. *Recovery:* Some file servers, such as Novell, have transaction support at the file I/O level, and so the file server can return to a consistent state if, for example, a client's I/O is interrupted (e.g., the client crashes—which is quite common with PCs). Database servers and database management have much more sophisticated operations. In a database server architecture, as with the security mechanism, the maintenance and support of recovery for logging and backing up the database is performed by the database node.

4. *Concurrency control:* File servers provide very basic concurrency control mechanisms. One of the most often used techniques is to provide read or write privileges on files and/or directories for different users. With database servers complex concurrency control algorithms can be implemented on the

server side. As discussed in Chapter 5, both optimistic and pessimistic algorithms can be supported. Furthermore, since the server recognizes the object structures, much finer granularity "object"-level concurrency control can be supported. This could greatly enhance the performance of concurrently executing transactions.

5. *Method/query execution and optimization:* Perhaps the most important functionality (or at least the most "visible") is the execution of various queries, accesses, and update operations or methods on the client side. Object-oriented and relational database management systems that utilize a database object server approach have software on the database server side, which executes queries. If the query is a declarative statement expressed in, say, an object-oriented extension of SQL, then the database node might even perform query optimization to determine the most efficient access plan for executing the query. In some object-oriented and relational database servers the system allows the storing of precompiled and optimized procedures so that clients who request stored procedures need only provide parameters and get the results evaluated very quickly without incurring the overhead of compilation and optimization. Stored procedures are similar to methods, and, in fact, object-oriented databases that support the object-server approach allow methods to be executed on the database server node (as opposed to client nodes with file servers).

6. *Clustering and indexing:* The database server also incorporates the storage manager module of a DBMS. The storage manager supports the clustering and indexing of persistent object collections. As discussed earlier, clustering stores objects or records that are frequently accessed together in the same storage extent. In particular, the "children" of a compound or complex object are stored in some specified (depth-first or breadth-first) order. The software that performs the clustering executes on the database server, although clustering can be supported (and often is) with file server architectures. The same is true for indexing. With file servers the indexing is performed on the client side (although some file servers do provide executables on the server side to perform indexing of records). With a database server the software to perform the indexed searches and updates executes on the server nodes.

Other functionalities and features of the DBMS that execute on the database server nodes as opposed to the client nodes with file server architectures include buffer management, data verification, multimedia object management, and metadata (schema) management.

The features above demonstrate that *engine* features of the database management system can be executed on the database server node. However, a DBMS in general and an object-oriented DBMS in particular has other components as well. In addition to the DBMS engine the following are typically found:

1. The application programming interface to the engine
2. Various libraries and tools, such as graphical user interface tools, for application development

Figure 6.10 illustrates an architecture for which all of the "engine"-specific database functionality, including query processing, is performed on the server node.

The database server API stands for "application programming interface" to the server. APIs are callable libraries that applications on the client side use to communicate with the server. Thus to manipulate persistent objects, application programs just need to call the methods, or functions, of the database server API. APIs are discussed further in the following section.

6.4.2 Programming Interfaces to Database Servers

Programming interfaces to database servers (or any server, for that matter) are the tools or programs used to interact with the server. They constitute the client side of the software that is used to interact with the database. Typically, a database server vendor will provide the following software (illustrated in Figure 6.11):

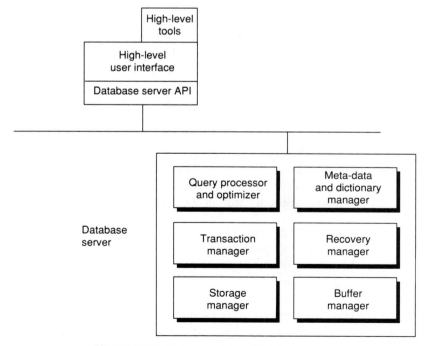

Figure 6.10 Various modules of database servers.

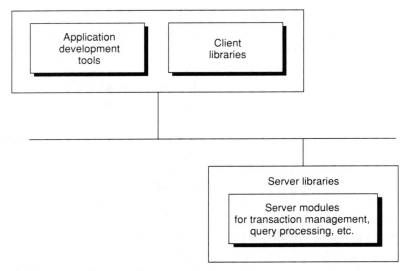

Figure 6.11 Client and server components provided by an OODBMS vendor.

- Software to install and run on a database server node
- Software that is installed on client nodes and is used to interface with the database server

In object-oriented databases the "programming interface" could be in the form of C++ classes whose member functions are used to make requests and get results from the database server. There are a great many differences between database servers when it comes to the partitioning of functionality between the server component of the system and the client modules that reside on the client nodes. Almost every object-oriented database implementation has a different approach to partitioning the database functionality between the clients and the server.

6.4.3 Partitioning the Functions between Clients and Server
The same functionality is often replicated on both the client nodes and the server node. This is especially true in the following situations:

1. Peer-to-peer architecture: In a distributed peer-to-peer architecture each node has the potential of becoming both a client and a server (as illustrated in Figure 6.4, although there could be many variations). The client components can "request" services from either the servers on their nodes or remote servers. Databases could be distributed (as discussed in the next section), and requests or queries could span several nodes. This would require distributed database transaction management, which is discussed in Section 6.5.

2. Local and personal databases: Many "advanced" database applications have a check-out/check-in model of application development. The user checks out an object and then checks it back in. The processing of the checked-out objects can be performed on the client nodes. In fact, most of the time the user will be working on checked-out objects.

It is therefore conceivable to have a fully functional OODBMS on the client node to provide querying and navigating capabilities. The OODBMS modules for manipulating the local or personal databases can also perform other database functions such as buffering, indexing, and clustering.

As for the "splitting," or partitioning, of the functionality between the client and server components of an OODBMS, several strategies can be identified (although, as stated earlier, there are many variations and extensions to these strategies—each OODB vendor and relational vendor with object extension provides its own particular solution).

Consider Figure 6.12, which depicts a possible layered architecture of an OODBMS. This figure does not illustrate all of the modules of a database engine. It gives the various layers and mappings from the top-level objects manipulated by application programs to low-level physical I/O blocks. Typically, the storage and index manager and server buffer manager reside on the server node.

The top "conceptual" object layer represents the objects as "seen" and manipulated by an application. The application layer manipulates the persistent object

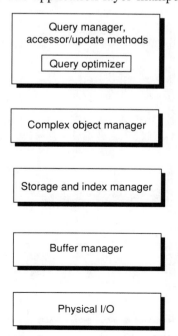

Figure 6.12 A (possible) layered architecture of an OODBMS.

space through accessor/update methods or queries. Object-oriented databases typically have two types of object accesses:

1. *Navigational:*In this type of access various "reachable" objects are accessed through attribute values or elements of referencing or parent objects. For instance, in intelligent office applications users can access a folder and then navigate to the elements of the folder. If a folder contains, say, another folder, the navigation can proceed with the elements of this folder and so on.

2. *Query (or declarative) access:* An alternate mechanism is a *search* mechanism through a query. With this approach the user specifies a query to qualify the object he or she is searching for. For instance, the user might be interested in the folder(s) whose name is "Portfolio." Figure 6.13 illustrates the query depiction and expression in Office.IQ.

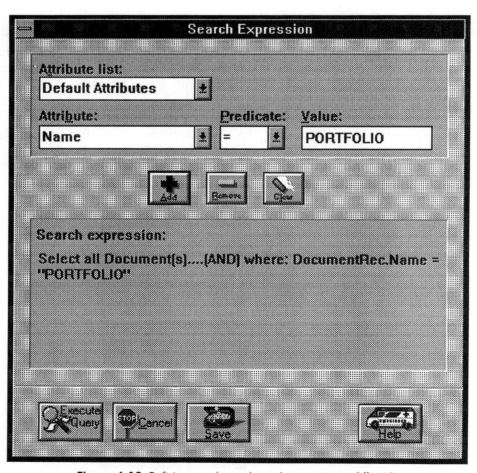

Figure 6.13 Defining an advanced search expression in Office.IQ.

The various strategies for partitioning the functionality between clients and servers will have different performance characteristics for these two alternative object access strategies. Each layer can be used to partition functions between client and server nodes. Furthermore, the same function can sometimes be replicated in the client and server nodes. For instance, both the client and server software of an OODBMS can have buffering. This is also true for the other modules, such as transaction management, which could exist on both client and server nodes.

The following are some alternative strategies for the layers included in the server:

1. *Query and accessor/update/method interface:* This is the highest level that could be supported by the server. With this alternative the server executes methods, including accessor and update methods, and queries. For the latter the query is submitted to the server, which compiles and optimizes it prior to execution. Most relational database servers provide a SQL interface and execute the SQL statement on the server node. Besides queries, object-oriented databases for which servers execute the highest-level interface allow the execution of methods on the database servers. There are many advantages to this approach. For one thing, it is more "object-oriented"; the operations are stored with the data and provide the highest-level protocols to the data. This is definitely a trend of future "object-manager" architectures. With this approach the processing requirement for optimizing and executing queries and methods is on the server and not the clients. This greatly simplifies the software that needs to execute on client nodes. The resource requirements for clients are less. Figure 6.9 illustrated the dynamics of such systems. The client submits a query or method to be executed on the server. The client and server have a data exchange convention that serves as a self-describing structure descriptor such as the SQLDA in a SQL-based system. There can also be arbitrary "objects" for which instance variables are "loaded" by the handshaking between the client and server components of the system.

2. *Complex Object Interface:* With this option the server provides a slightly lower-level interface than the query or method access option. Here, basically, the server provides the ability to create, navigate, and update objects. The server model does incorporate ("understand") complex objects, but it is less sophisticated than the first strategy above in that query processing is not performed on the server. Instead, after the query is processed its requests are satisfied by accessing and navigating the complex object interface of the database server. Therefore, with this alternative the complex object model is "visible" in the server—the server can cluster, access, navigate, and update elements of complex objects. However, the method execution and query processing are performed on client nodes. Thus the server can be thought of as

an "object" server: the term object refers here to the structural (as opposed to operational or behavioral) aspect of objects. This is very reasonable since the main purpose of databases is the efficient storage and retrieval of (complex) objects.

3. *Storage and index manager layer interface:* The previous two approaches have interfaces that reflect the complex object model. In fact, it is conceivable that both of these interfaces could be "exported" to the application problems. With either of the previous two approaches the database system vendor could provide, say, C++ class libraries, which are basically the client-side interfaces of the server's functionality. The mapping from the client side to the server is then "direct" through either messaging or remote procedure calls. However, in this approach (the storage layer interface) and the next (physical I/O) approaches, the interfaces are "physical" and not higher-level application-programming interfaces. In other words, the client-side software of the OODBMs provides a "higher"-level programming interface to the application programs. The calls to these interfaces are subsequently mapped onto lower-level calls to the server. With the storage and index manager layer approach the server software does include the modules that maintain various indexes (i.e., B-trees) and storage management functionality. This could include, for instance, the management of very large objects (or blobs) to store multimedia data such as images or voice. Thus, with this architecture, although the server does not recognize the complex object model, it is nevertheless more sophisticated than a file- or page- (block-) level server in that it incorporates storage and indexing modules of the DBMS.

4. *Physical file and block I/O:* This architecture is similar to file server architectures with the exception that the management and concurrency control of the I/O blocks are performed by modules provided by the database management system vendor (as opposed to the network operating system executing on the file server). In other words, the software that controls the concurrent accesses to the blocks and provides various locking and/or other transaction control is actually performed by OODBMS modules and not services provided by a file server or network operating system.

■ 6.5 DISTRIBUTED DATABASES

So far file servers and database servers have been discussed in the context of a single LAN with either a single file server or a file server and a database server. There can, however, be more than one file server or database server on the network. Furthermore, the LANs could be internetworked through bridges and gateways so that data stored on remote networks can be accessed from local

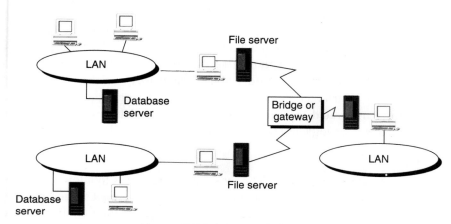

Figure 6.14 Internetworked LANS.

clients. It is conceivable that users might wish to have either a combination of data on different servers or a distribution of a large database to various nodes in an internetworked architecture of LANs. Such an architecture is illustrated in Figure 6.14.

With architectures in which multiple databases exist on different nodes in a LAN or different LANs, there is a constant need to combine information from various databases. Furthermore, due to performance or locality concerns it is also desirable to distribute the data of large databases onto various nodes and sites, hence the need for distributed databases.

With distributed databases the client sees one logical database that can consist of many physical databases distributed across server nodes of LANs. This is illustrated in Figure 6.15.

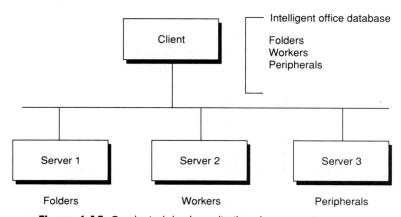

Figure 6.15 One logical database distributed across various servers.

6.5.1 Distributed Database Strategies

There are various strategies for incorporating "distributed database" support in an internetworked architecture of databases. This section provides an overview of these strategies. The next section discusses the bottom-up and top-down approaches for developing distributed databases.

The distributed database strategies range from requests to remote databases to fully integrated logical views of distributed databases. Here is a brief overview of these strategies. The taxonomy here follows IBM's SAA distributed database strategy:

1. *Remote Request:* The most basic strategy is to allow a local client to open a session with a remote database, submit a request, and get the results of the request. For instance, in an intelligent office environment one database, say DB1, might contain identifiers of objects in a remote database, say DB2. Then if the distributed database support in the OODBMS supports remote requests, the remote objects in DB2 could be accessed from the DB1 environments.

2. *Remote Updates:* Extending the remote request support, an OODBMS can perform *updates* of remote database objects. Thus one database can execute an update transaction on behalf of another (remote) database or request. In IBM's SAA terminology, remote requests incorporate both reads and updates, performed as transactions.

3. *Remote Unit-of-Work:* Further extending the remote request and update strategies, a remote unit-of-work involves both read and update requests to a remote database within a transaction. In other words, a local client submits a transaction to a remote database, involving both reads and updates within the same transaction. For instance, from a local client a user can submit a transaction that reads the contents of a remote folder and updates the contents of a remote compound document in the same transaction.

4. *Distributed Request:* If the OODBMS supports distributed requests, users will be able to execute distributed transactions involving reads and updates from multiple distributed databases. For example, again using intelligent office databases, a user will be able to remove a document D contained in folder F1 in database DB1 and place it in folder F2 in database DB2 in one transaction. Since transactions are atomic, this request (deleting D from F1 and inserting in F2) either completed or not performed at all (e.g., we cannot have D removed from F1 without inserting it in F2).

6.5.2 Approaches for Developing Distributed Databases

As discussed in Khoshafian et al. (1992a), there are at least two fundamental approaches for developing a distributed database:

1. a bottom-up integration approach for providing a global view of existing databases; and
2. a top-down approach for partitioning a logical database and distributing the fragments in distributed sites.

As discussed in the subsequent paragraphs, the most elegant paradigm for the bottom-up integration of existing databases is generalization. Similarly, specialization provides a powerful mechanism for fragmenting logical databases in distributed sites.

Bottom-Up Integration

Bottom-up integration is very suitable for enterprises that have various distributed sites and departments. For instance, as discussed in Chapter 10 of Khoshafian et al. (1992b), the top level of an intelligent office environment contains a building representing the corporation as a whole. The corporation node in the hierarchy could contain an integrated view of all the databases contained in distributed departments. The integration of these various distributed databases is bottom-up.

An elegant and efficient way for integrating existing databases is through *generalization*. Generalization is a bottom-up approach of software construction. For instance, if one site contains all of the information about `SalesPeople` and another site all the information about `Developers`, the two classes and their extensions could be integrated from the bottom up by generalizing them to, say, an `OfficeWorker` class.

Note that in many enterprises the databases used in various departments and sites are *heterogeneous*. This means they have different hardware, software, and database models. Many (if not most) of these databases will be relational. As discussed in Chapters 2 and 3 of this book, generalization can be integrated in the relational language SQL to easily allow the bottom-up integration of distributed tables of the enterprise.

Top-Down Distribution

Top-down distribution is applicable in environments developing distributed databases from scratch. Here, unlike in the bottom-up approach, there is first a global view and model of the databases. Once this global enterprise database is designed, the next step is to fragment the database and distribute the fragments to various departments, or sites, of the enterprise.

Top-down distribution is especially suitable for homogeneous environments where there is more uniformity in the model and platforms of the distributed sites. Since the same global view and model is maintained with top-down distribution, and based on various access patterns or workloads, the fragments could be reassigned to different sites, without changing the application programs manipulating the global view.

Just as generalization is suitable for bottom-up integration, specialization can be used for top-down distribution. One useful application for top-down distribution is specialization through predicates, or restrictions. For instance, we can create a class OfficeWorker and subclasses SanJoseWorkers and LA-Workers. SanJoseWorkers are specified as those workers in the Office-Worker class whose Location = San Jose. Similarly, LAWorkers are those whose Location = LA. Then, if we have a SanJose site and an LA site we can specify that the storage location of SanJoseWorker is the San-Jose site and that of LAWorker is LA. Then, every time an OfficeWorker is inserted in the (distributed) database, depending upon the value of Location, the actual object will be stored in either the LA site or the SanJose site (or the "default" site if neither).

6.5.3 Characteristics of Distributed Database Systems

As presented in Khoshafian et al. (1992a), Sheth and Larson (1990), and Ozsu and Valduriez (1991), there are three fundamental dimensions that can be used to characterize distributed databases. These three aspects are *autonomy*, *distribution transparency*, and *heterogeneity*.

Autonomy

As defined in Kohshafian et al. (1992a):

> Autonomy . . . represents the degree to which sites within the distributed database system may operate independently.

There are two extremes of the autonomy dimension. With *tight-coupling* all users and applications of the different sites always have the view of the integrated database. The mapping to individual site or department requests is performed by the distributed database system.

The other extreme is *total isolation*. Here each site is aware only of its own local database. The bottom-up integrated database view is layered on top of the local sites. The "older" local applications manipulate the local databases. After the bottom-up integration of the local databases, new applications can manipulate the integrated view of the distributed databases.

Distribution Transparency

In a distributed database, the different sites of the enterprise will store and maintain various fragments of the enterprise database. There will be various applications manipulating the distributed database. *Distribution transparency* indicates the extent to which the fragmentation of the data is transparent to the users and applications of the distributed database. If the distribution is very transparent, the database designer has the freedom to move and replicate the fragments without affecting existing application programs or users.

Heterogeneity

Consider a large enterprise system with geographically distributed sites and internetworked LANs. If the sites have evolved their computing environments independently, there could be (and often is) formidable *heterogeneity* in the various environments. Here are some of the sources of heterogeneity:

1. Different hardware platforms and systems
2. Different client operating systems: UNIX vs. Windows vs. Macs, etc.
3. Different network operating systems
4. Different server operating systems
5. Different client and server software
6. Different database management systems, and/or models

The integration of these heterogeneous environments to provide one homogeneous distributed database view could be a formidable task.

Currently, relational databases dominate, especially in business and office applications. Relational databases with object-oriented features or "purer" object-oriented databases are starting to appear. The integration of various heterogeneous relational *and* object-oriented databases possesses formidable technical challenges for the next decade.

6.5.4 Distributed Transaction Management

To guarantee consistency, DBMSs employ concurrency control strategies to coordinate the concurrent execution of transactions. Various concurrency control and transaction management strategies were discussed in Chapter 5. With distributed databases, concurrency control is more complex than in a centralized environment. If an integrated enterprise view incorporating various distributed databases is to be supported, transactions on the integrated enterprise database could involve updates to local databases in various sites. To maintain the ACID properties of transactions (as discussed in Chapter 5), the local, or site, transactions participating in the distributed transaction must be coordinated.

Section 6.5.1 discussed various distributed database strategies. Distributed requests involve reads and updates from various databases within the same transaction. The distributed transaction support of a distributed request must guarantee that not only each transaction participating in the distributed transaction supports the ACID test, but also the distributed transactions must satisfy the ACID properties.

The most frequently used algorithm for distributed transaction management is the two-phase commit protocol, discussed in the next section.

6.5.5 Two-Phase Commit

The two-phase commit algorithm is explained in the context of Figure 6.16(a) and (b). Figure 6.16(a) shows a successful commit of a distributed transaction. Figure 6.16(b) shows the abortion of a distributed transaction. There are two types of transactions in the two-phase commit protocol:

1. *Transaction Coordinator*, which coordinates the participating transactions at the various sites

2. *Participants or Participating Transactions*, which include the various transactions at different sites

Now consider Figure 6.16(a). During Phase I the coordinator asks each participant to prepare to commit and waits for responses. If each participant votes OK, then Phase II commences and the coordinator tells all the participants to commit.

Figure 16.6(b) illustrates the abort scenario for distributed transactions. After the prepare to commit, if one of the participants votes Failed or times out, then the coordinator instructs all the participants to abort in Phase II.

■ 6.6 CLIENT/SERVER ARCHITECTURES IN OBJECT-ORIENTED DATABASES

The previous section describes the various client/server and object-oriented database concepts. As mentioned earlier, these concepts are applicable to both relational and object-oriented databases. The market share of relational DBMSs is steadily increasing and is expected to continue to increase as corporations downsize from larger hierarchical and network-based systems to client/server systems that use relational DBMS servers. What this means for commercial OODBMSs and relational DBMSs with object-oriented capabilities is the ability to access and integrate with existing DBMSs in a corporation.

As discussed previously, the dual concepts of bottom-up integration and top-down distribution can be handled elegantly by the complementary concepts of generalization and specialization, provided that these two concepts are handled adequately by the OODB and that the OODB allows these constructs to be used for the integration of heterogeneous or homogeneous databases.

Although there have been some attempts and prototypes, as of the writing of this book there are no commercial OODBs that fully utilize specialization and generalization to integrate various databases.

This is not to say that existing OODBs (or relational databases) do not provide some features of distributed databases. Several of them do. More importantly at this stage, most of them provide elegant client/server solutions to their users.

There have been numerous discussions of the client/server capabilities in commercial relational databases (see, for example, the work by Khoshafian et al.,

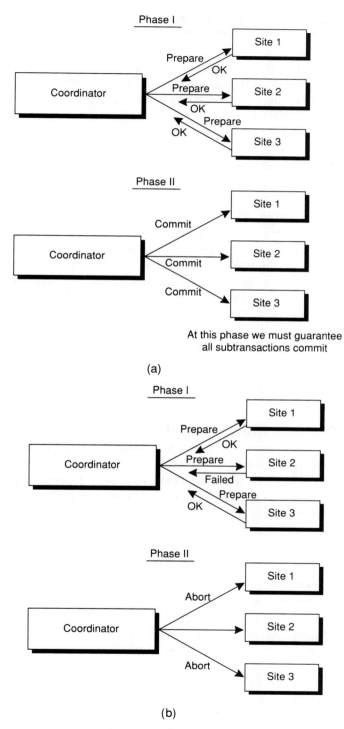

Figure 6.16 Two-phase commit protocol for distributed transactions (a) Commit; (b) Abort.

1992a). Here a brief discussion of the client/server and distributed database capabilities of a number of existing "pure" OODB products is provided. A description of some products in the market today is also included, with an understanding that all OODB products are moving toward more enhanced client/server and distributed database capabilities.

6.6.1 ONTOS Object Database

ONTOS Object Database is a powerful object-oriented database system that employs a distributed client/server architecture. Among other "tools" ONTOS Object Database allows the client software to access distributed databases either through the C++ *client* library or through ONTOS Object SQL—which like OSQL in OpenODB is an object-oriented extension of SQL.

Although multiple clients can be attached to and access data from the same database, the content of the database might be *physically* distributed to many servers. A client in ONTOS is created by linking an application code to the ONTOS C++ library. A server is a process that manages functions of the physical database accessed by a client. Also with ONTOS, application developers can access *logical databases* that can be composed of multiple physical databases. Since these multiple databases are managed by many servers, ONTOS utilizes a distributed two-phase commit protocol to commit transactions involving multiple databases on a network.

6.6.2 OpenODB from Hewlett-Packard

OpenODB is an object-oriented database product that offers a number of interesting client/server and "distributed" database features. Architecturally, OpenODB incorporates a client component and a server component. As is the case with most client/server database products, with OpenODB the user or application developer does not need to be concerned about the functionality provided by the server. The client interface and components supports:

- An OSQL (object-oriented SQL) utility
- A graphical browser to browse the data depiction or schema on the server
- A programming interface (or application programming interface) to provide application developers an interface to the server through C, C++, COBOL, FORTRAN, or Pascal. Similar in approach to relational databases, the API uses OSQL-embedded statements.

The server incorporates an Object-Manager and an underlying Relational Storage Manager. In fact, the server incorporates a run-time version of the ALL-BASE/SQL relational database product of HP. In its approach and its operation of the client/server architecture OpenODB is closer to relational client/server systems than perhaps most other OODB products. The OpenODB server component processes and executes the OSQL calls of the OpenODB clients. For its execution it utilizes the underlying ALLBASE/SQL Relational Engine.

OpenODB also allows its application developers to create and execute external functions. These are functions that are written in a general-purpose language such as C or C++ by the application program developer but are called by OSQL statements.

6.6.3   ITASCA

ITASCA also supports distributed databases. It allows a shared database to be distributed on multiple nodes or sites in a network. The client code provides transparent access (location independence) to various partitions of the database. A persistent object is stored on one of the sites and can be moved from one site to another without affecting the application program that accesses the object. ITASCA does not rely on a central node to coordinate various activities and functionality of the DBMS. ITASCA uses the two-phase commit protocol for distributed transactions. The ITASCA system also performs distributed query optimization.

6.6.4   VERSANT

The VERSANT object-oriented database also supports client/server and distributed database capabilities. The client component of VERSANT (the Object Manager) maintains its own object cache in order to minimize the communication needed with the server component (the Object Server). The Object Manager sends modified objects at transaction commit time to the Object Server. The Object server provides access to collections of objects to the Object Manager through a RPC (Remote Procedure Call) mechanism that allows for streaming of objects between the two components. The Object Server incorporates query processing capabilities and only sends objects requested by the Object Manager.

As mentioned earlier, VERSANT supports nested transactions. The subtransactions of a nested transaction can execute at different (distributed) database sites. The Object Manager takes care of the necessary two-phase commit protocol to ensure that each top-level transaction (along with its nested subtransactions) are committed atomically.

6.6.5   ObjectStore

ObjectStore from Object Design supports a flexible client/server architecture. Each server can support many clients; there could be many databases on several servers, and all these databases could be accessed simultaneously from the same client.

The servers manage the physical databases and are responsible for the concurrent access and control of physical data. Servers have "callback" mechanisms to handle contentions of locked pages and free pages locked by clients.

The servers support both *conventional* transactions and *long* transactions. Conventional transactions can be *update* transactions or *read-only* transactions. The ObjectStore client/server system also manages nested transactions, allowing users abort or commit sub transactions within a longer transaction. ObjectStore uses a two-phase commit protocol to commit transaction updates in servers. The persistent storage management by the servers include Files, Database, Segments, and pages. Segments consist of pages, databases contain multiple segments, and databases are stored in operating system files.

The ObjectStore memory mapping architecture for persistent data allows applications to access and update persistent objects easily, transparently. ObjectStore is able to "detect" accesses to persistent data and if the object is not already in main memory, transfer the page conferring the data to the applications (virtual) memory. The pointers to persistent ObjectStore objects are regular virtual memory addresses. When the application or the client site attempts to access the object referenced by the pointer the underlying operating system will "signal" ObjectStore to transfer the data and perform the virtual memory mapping. This makes the accesses and updates of persistent objects easy to use and efficient.

■ 6.7 SUMMARY

This chapter has discussed the client/server architectures in object-oriented databases. Local area networks are the backbone of client/server architectures. The past few years have witnessed the proliferation of LANs. Internetworked local area networks are fast replacing "archaic" mainframe systems. Similarly, smaller businesses are interconnecting their stand-alone PCs with LANs to share various resources. In these architectures and networked environments client/server computation is the norm.

Networks can contain different types of servers, including files servers, database servers, optical disk servers, fax servers, and so on. In the case of database servers there are different types of functionalities that could be provided by the database server, ranging from high-level database programming language processing (such as the processing of SQL or object-oriented extensions of SQL) to database servers that provide concurrent accesses to I/O blocks or objects. Various object-oriented databases fall in different categories.

Since databases can be large and accessed frequently at various locations, in enterprises this raises the need for *distributed databases* and various distributed database concurrency control strategies to keep transaction semantics consistent when transactions involve multiple databases.

Besides having provided an overview of the file server, database server, and distributed database technologies, this chapter has also provided a brief summary of the client/server and distributed database capabilities of a number of existing object-oriented databases.

7

SUMMARY

■ 7.1 INTRODUCTION

The preceding six chapters have described the main concepts of object-oriented databases. This emerging technology integrates object-oriented features with database capabilities. It draws from the strengths and advantages of object orientation and database management systems. Because of their object-oriented attributes object-oriented databases provide direct and intuitive models for application development. In addition, through their database capabilities object-oriented databases allow users to concurrently share persistent information. Although object-oriented databases are usually identified as the ideal repositories for a number of "advanced" database applications, the modeling capability and the object-oriented primitives supported by these next-generation OODBs are useful for almost any application domain.

Whether through "novel" solutions or extensions of relational databases, the main goal of object-oriented databases is to provide better models and tools for application development. Inevitably, the main bottleneck of automation for information processing in the next decade will be the "software" bottleneck. The application environments of the late 1990s will be fast-paced and complex. There will be great diversity in the way information is accessed, manipulated, and presented. Object orientation is proving to be an enabling technology that makes it easy to construct and maintain complex systems from individual components.

Despite any initial skepticism, object orientation has been incorporated into the mainstream of software development and is starting to provide solutions to the tremendous software engineering problems of the 1990s.

An equally important trend in the computer industry is the emergence of the *downsized* client/server architecture as *the* architecture of choice in internetworked environments. Large mainframe systems are being replaced by internetworked LANs at a much lower cost—yielding much greater efficiency. It is becoming increasingly evident that the backbone of these client/server systems is the *database server*, which serves as the repository of all concurrently shared information on the network.

7.1.1 Combining Object Orientation and Database Capabilities

Object-oriented databases *combine* and *integrate* the concepts of object orientation and databases to satisfy the computation needs of not only "advanced" database applications but also general corporate computing. The purpose of this book was to elucidate both the object-oriented and database capabilities of this emerging object-oriented database technology.

An object-oriented database was defined as follows:

$$\text{Object-oriented database} = \text{object orientation} + \text{database capabilities}$$

where object orientation was defined as

$$\text{Object orientation} = \text{abstract data types} + \text{inheritance} + \text{object identity}$$

and database capabilities were defined as

$$\begin{aligned}
\text{Database capabilities} = &\text{ persistence} + \text{concurrency} + \text{transactions} \\
&+ \text{recovery} + \text{querying} + \text{versioning} \\
&+ \text{integrity} + \text{security} + \text{performance}
\end{aligned}$$

7.1.2 Two Major Trends: Extending Existing DBMSs versus Novel Concepts

In terms of the evolution of database data models, object-oriented databases extend the relational and other traditional database models with object-oriented features. Object-oriented databases integrate powerful modeling features of complex object models, semantic data models, and object-oriented systems.

There are many approaches to developing an object-oriented database system (six were identified in this book, but there could be more). However, there are actually two main trends in integrating object orientation into the development of object-oriented databases:

1. *Extension:* The first, more conservative trend is to incorporate object-oriented features into existing (mostly relational) database management systems. The most notable attempt in this category has been to extend the most popular Structured Query Language (SQL) of a relational DBMS to include object-oriented concepts. The champions of this approach are, of course, relational DBMS vendors (although as discussed throughout the book a number of OODB products incorporate object-oriented subsets of SQL as query languages). These companies do not need to develop either entirely new engines or entirely new systems for object orientation in databases. Rather, they can incrementally extend their existing engines and systems with object-oriented features.

2. *Construction of novel DBMSs from the bottom up:* The second trend is exemplified by the handful (now more than 10!) of new companies that since 1986 have developed and marketed database management systems identified as *object-oriented*. Of course, there are numerous approaches: completely novel languages, C++ class extensions, embedded solutions, etc. These have been summarized throughout this book.

Both of these two trends are expected to continue, with the former being endorsed by relational database management system vendors and the latter by the emerging "startup" object-oriented database vendors.

7.1.3 Six Approaches

At least six approaches can be identified for the incorporation of object-oriented capabilities into databases. This list is not at all comprehensive. There can be solutions or approaches that are hybrids of these. Furthermore, the same OODB vendor can provide various approaches within the same product. The following is a summary of the six approaches:

1. *Using a novel database data model/data language approach:* The most aggressive approach for incorporating object-oriented capabilities into databases is to develop an entirely new database language and database management system with object-oriented capabilities.

2. *Extending an existing database language with object-oriented capabilities:* Programming languages such as C++, Flavors (an extension of Lisp) and Object Pascal have been extended with object-oriented constructs. It is conceivable to follow a similar strategy with database languages. Since SQL is a standard, and by far the most popular database language, the most reasonable solution is to extend this language with object-oriented constructs, reflecting the object-oriented capabilities of the underlying database management system. As mentioned in the previous section, this approach

is being pursued by vendors of relational systems as they develop their next-generation products. However, as mentioned earlier, it is also interesting to note that some object-oriented database vendors who follow the "novel" DBMS approach also provide declarative database management system interfaces through their own object-oriented extension of SQL.

3. *Extending an existing object-oriented programming language with database capabilities:* Another approach is to introduce database capabilities into an existing object-oriented language. The object-oriented features (abstract data typing, inheritance, object identity) will already be supported by the object-oriented language, and the extensions will incorporate database features (querying, transaction support, persistence, etc.). This is the approach in Servio's OPAL database language, which extends Smalltalk with database capabilities.

4. *Providing extendible object-oriented database management system libraries:* A number of database companies have introduced C++ libraries for database management. In fact, especially in the case of C++, the distinction between a language extension that needs to be preprocessed and a library is often blurred, and more often *both* mechanisms are used to "embed" or incorporate database capabilities within the object-oriented language (C++). The libraries include classes for aggregates (sets, lists, arrays) and types. There are classes with methods for *start/commit/abort* transactions, recovery, versioning, exception handling, and object clustering.

5. *Embedding object-oriented database language constructs in a host (conventional) language:* Database languages can be embedded into host programming languages. For example, SQL statements can be embedded into PL/I, C, FORTRAN, and Ada. The types found in SQL (i.e., relations and rows in relations) are different from the types in systems of these host languages. Some object-oriented databases take a similar approach with a host language and an object-oriented database language. This is similar to the previous approach, except that the host language does not need to be object-oriented.

6. *Using application-specific products with an underlying object-oriented database management system:* Another interesting approach is the development of application/domain-specific tools and environments that either use object-oriented database technologies or provide an object-oriented database view for the application domain. The intention in application/domain-specific solutions is not to provide a general-purpose object-oriented environment. Rather, only useful or application-specific constructs, with object-oriented and database features, are made visible to the user. This book has concentrated on one exciting application-specific area, namely *intelligent offices.*

▪ 7.2 OBJECT-ORIENTED CONCEPTS

Object orientation can be loosely defined as *the software modeling and development (engineering) disciplines that make it easy to construct complex systems out of individual components*. The three fundamental concepts of object orientation are abstract data typing, inheritance, and object identity.

7.2.1 Abstract Data Typing

Abstract data typing models various *classes* in object-oriented database applications, where each class instance has a *protocol:* a set of messages to which it can respond. With abstract data types there is a clear separation between the *external* interface of a data type and its *internal* implementation. The implementation of an abstract data type is *hidden*. Hence, alternative implementations could be used for the same abstract data type without changing its interface.

A class is like a factory that produces *instances*, each with the same structure and behavior. A class has a name, a collection of operations for manipulating its instances, and a representation. The operations that manipulate the instances of a class are called *methods*. The state or representation of an instance is stored in *instance variables*. The methods are invoked by sending *messages* to the instances. Sending messages to objects (instances) is similar to calling procedures in conventional programming languages. However, message sending is more dynamic.

Abstract data typing allows the construction of complex software systems through reusable components—the classes. Thus, through abstract data typing programming becomes modularized and extendible. Abstract data typing supports a much more natural representation of real-world problems; the dominant components are the *objects* rather than the procedures. Abstract data typing allows objects of the same structure and behavior to *share* representation (instance variables) and code (methods).

7.2.2 Inheritance

Inheritance allows a class to inherit the behavior (operations, methods, etc.) and the representation (instance variables, attributes, etc.) from existing classes. Inheriting behavior enables *code sharing* (and hence reusability) among software modules. Inheriting representation enables *structure sharing* among data objects. The combination of these two types of inheritance provides a most powerful modeling and software development strategy.

Inheritance is achieved by *specializing* existing classes. Classes can be specialized by extending their representation (instance variables) or behavior (operations). Alternatively, classes can be specialized by *restricting* the representation or operations of existing classes. When a class $C2$ inherits from class $C1$ then the instance variables *and* the methods of $C2$ are a superset of the instance variables and methods of $C1$. The subclass $C2$ can *override* the implementation of an inherited method or instance variable by providing an alternative definition or implementation.

Most existing object-oriented systems allow developers to extend an application by *specializing* existing components (in most cases, *classes*) of their application. Specialization is a top-down approach to the development of object-oriented database applications. Generalization is the complement of specialization. It uses a *bottom-up* approach by creating classes that are *generalizations* (or superclasses) of existing subclasses. Generalization is a bottom-up approach for object-oriented database development.

7.2.3 Object Identity

The third fundamental concept of object orientation is *object identity*. The inheritance hierarchies organize the object-oriented *code* and support extendibility and code reusability. Object identity organizes the *objects* or instances of an application in arbitrary graph-structured object spaces.

Identity is a property of an object that distinguishes the object from all other objects in the application. In programming languages identity is realized through memory addresses. In databases identity is realized through identifier keys. User-specified names are used in both languages and databases to give unique names to objects. Each of these schemes compromises identity.

In a complete object-oriented system each object is given an identity that will be permanently associated with the object immaterial of the object's *structural* or *state* transitions. The identity of an object is also independent of the *location*, or address, of the object. Object identity provides the most natural modeling primitive to allow the same object to be a subobject of multiple parent objects.

With object identity, objects can contain or refer to other objects. Object identity clarifies, enhances, and extends the notions of pointers in conventional programming languages, foreign keys in databases, and file names in operating systems. Using object identity, programmers can dynamically construct arbitrary graph-structured composite or complex objects, objects that are constructed from subobjects. Objects can be created and disposed of at run time. In some cases objects can even become persistent and be reaccessed in subsequent programs.

■ 7.3 MODELING AND DESIGN FOR OBJECT-ORIENTED DATABASES

Before solving any problems using an object-oriented database we must have a *high-level requirement specification*. Among other things, the high-level requirement specification is used to specify the following:

The functionality: What capabilities do the different components of the system provide for the user?

The paradigm: What type of interaction or execution model does the system provide for the user?

The environment: Where or on what systems and platforms is the system supported?

The interfaces: What are the graphical user-interface paradigms used for the system?

Once the high-level requirement specification is complete the next step is to perform an *object-oriented analysis* (OOA) of the system. The analysis provides a detailed description, which is complete, consistent, readable, and reviewable by different interested people and can be tested against reality.

The object-oriented analysis will be incorporated in the object-oriented design (OOD) of the software. The object-oriented design phase provides detailed specifications for the classes of the problem/product domain *and specifies additional support classes for the implementation.*

Thus, object-oriented design, which is perhaps the most important phase of development in object orientation, allows the *classification* (definition of classes) of the project. This is especially true for object-oriented databases. Chapter 3 introduced strategies for designing databases and discussed a node-and-link object-oriented design mechanism for object-oriented databases, which explicitly captures persistence and object identity.

The top-down design of object-oriented databases involves the following steps:

1. Specifying end-user views and models
2. Merging external end-user views and models to generate the conceptual model
3. Mapping the conceptual model onto the persistent classes of the object-oriented databases
4. Implementing the physical design

7.3.1 Implementation of Various Database Data Models

The design and implementation steps of a database management system application are performed vis-à-vis a particular database model. The database model can be *networked, hierarchical, relational,* or *object-oriented.*

Hierarchical model: The hierarchical data model represents the structure of the persistent database as a collection (forest) of trees such that each node of the tree represents a set of objects (records) of the same type.

Network model: The network model is more general than the hierarchical model. Although the only type of relationship supported by the network model is one-to-many, it is possible for the same record type to be a child, or a *member*, with multiple parent, or *owner*, record types.

Relational model: In the relational world a database structure is a collection of *relations*, or tables. The relational model imposes the *first-normal-form constraint* on databases. In both the *network* and *hierarchical* models it is possible for an attribute to reference a *set*, or collection, of objects, capturing the one-to-many (in the case of hierarchical models) or many-to-many (in the case of network models) relationships between "child" and "parent" entities. In relational databases each "cell" is an atomic value. The relational model defines a relational algebra with commutative, associative, and distributive properties. The relational model has a clean semantics and a solid theoretical foundation.

Object-oriented database data models: It has sometimes been erroneously stated that OODBMSs do not have rigorous data models. Actually, there have been many calculi and algebras proposed for object-oriented data models. (However, it is true that unlike the relational model and its algebra, which is very well understood and implemented, there is no single agreed-upon model of an OODBMS.) Many of these models are set-and-tuple models that, like their relational counterparts, define algebraic operations for object-oriented databases that incorporate arbitrary containment (set) or referencing relationships (through object identity).

Object-oriented database models are complex object models that can be

- *Value-based.* These models do not incorporate object identity, and the uniqueness of an object is based on its state.
- *Identity-based.* These models associate an object identity with each object in the system.
- *Hybrid.* These models allow the designer to specify whether an attribute should be a value or an object with identity.

Object Algebras

The first step in defining an object model is to define the object spaces. The second step is to define the operations, that is, the algebra that applies to the object spaces. Typically, these operations are the basis of a query language for the underlying object-oriented database language. Queries expressed through algebraic operators tend to be procedural in the sense that the query indicates the order of execution of the operators. A *calculus* provides a set-forming notation for the algebraic operations, as is typically done for relational databases.

Typically, query languages in database systems (object-oriented or relational) tend to be based on the calculus. For instance, relational database query languages, such as SQL or QUEL, define syntax and semantics based on the relational calculus. Query languages such as SQL are "declarative." They allow users to specify *what* they need to retrieve from the database without specifying how the results of the queries must be evaluated. In most relational database management systems the SQL query (or the query expressed in a language based on relational calculus) is "translated" onto a relational algebra query tree. The underlying query optimizer of the relational database management system then decides on an "optimal" query execution plan using optimization rules and cost estimates for the query.

Some object-oriented databases also perform query optimizations. At the very least, if a query specifies a select criteria and an index is available on the selected attribute of a collection the underlying system will attempt to use the index in its optimizer.

Unlike relational systems, the calculus and algebra for object-oriented databases is not so clear. Many proposals and operations are needed in such a model. Some of the algebraic operations that are used in set-and-tuple object models include

Set operations	Other operations
Union	*General Selection*
Intersection	*Nest*
Difference	*UnNest*
Cartesian Product	*Flatten*

Classification and Design of Object-Oriented Databases

The design of an object-oriented database includes the definition of the classes, the relationships (containment, referencing, etc.) between classes, and the inheritance of classes. The OOD can be represented with *node-and-link* diagrams, in which nodes represent classes, sets, and other relationship types and links connect the nodes (classes) of the diagram, capturing the specific design of an OOD. Nodes can also represent operations or member functions (methods). Object-oriented design must not only capture the static representation but must also incorporate the representation of the dynamic behavior of the system. Dynamic behavior can be captured in state transition diagrams. Alternatively, *object instance diagrams* can be used to represent the behavior of object instances and their dynamic relationships.

Integrity Constraints in Object-Oriented Databases

Through transactions database management systems map one *consistent* (correct) database data onto another (transactions were discussed in Chapter 5). The consistency of the database is typically expressible through *predicates*, or conditions, on the current state of the database. Predicates can also apply to objects or attribute values in the database. The predicates that capture the consistency of a database are called *integrity constraints*. Generally, a number of integrity constraints must be enforced on a database state to guarantee its consistency.

The integrity constraints for object-oriented databases include the following:

1. Unique/primary key constraints
2. Referential and existential constraints
3. *NOT NULL* constraints
4. Integrity rules
5. Triggers
6. Pre- and postconditions for methods
7. Specialization constraints
8. Disjointness constraints
9. Covering constraints

■ 7.4 PERSISTENCE

The main philosophy behind persistent programming languages is to make persistence orthogonal to the type of objects. In other words, *any* type of object should be allowed to persist. Several strategies indicate which objects should become persistent. The following are three strategies used to create and identify persistent objects:

1. *Persistent extensions:* The notion of a *persistent* extension has always been a fundamental assumption in database management systems. In conventional DBMSs (such as relational), when the user defines a schema using a data definition language (such as the DML of SQL), persistent extensions define both a structure and an extension. In object-oriented languages users define the structure of objects through the class construct.

2. *Persistence through reachability:* The second strategy is to have one or more persistent database roots and to make every object *reachable* from these roots persistent.

3. *Persistence instances:* Another strategy is to render particular instances of a class persistent either by explicitly declaring them to be persistent

or by making an existing object persistent through a function call. With this approach persistence is not a property of classes. Rather, the user can construct databases and "place" objects in various databases.

Therefore, the main steps for implementing an application using an OODBMS that supports persistent C++ extensions or class libraries are as follows:

> *Step 1*: data definition. Either through a specific data definition language defined by the object-oriented database vendor or through a C++ header file, the user first defines the specific persistent classes.
>
> *Step 2*: implementation of the persistent classes. After defining the persistent classes the application developer must implement the member functions of the persistent classes. Some of these member functions are *accessor* functions, which access the "hidden" member variables or instance variables of the persistent classes. Other member functions are *update* functions, which modify the state or values of the instance variables of instances of the persistent class. Still other member functions perform more sophisticated operations.
>
> *Step 3*: implementation of the GUI classes. Although conceivably it is possible to perform input/output through the persistent class implementations, a more reasonable approach is to have separate classes to deal with the end-user graphical user interface (GUI) interactions. The GUI objects include various types of *windows, menus* (pop-up, pull-down, etc.), *forms, dialogs, tool bars, buttons, list boxes,* and semantics of mouse movements. The *values* of the various items are in many cases retrieved from the underlying databases; therefore, in many cases the GUI objects reference and access instances of persistent classes.
>
> *Step 4*: compiling and linking. Once the persistent classes and the front-end GUI classes are implemented the next step is to compile and link these classes.

7.4.1 Alternative Storage Strategies

There are several alternative storage strategies for complex objects. The main goal of complex object storage strategies is to provide efficient retrieval and update performance for complex objects. The following are three possible complex object storage strategies:

> **Direct storage model:** With the direct storage model an attempt is made to store complex objects as "directly" as possible, reflecting the

way in which the complex objects are either defined or populated in the database. Thus, *subobjects* are stored close to their parent objects whenever possible.

Normalized storage model: The approach in the normalized storage model is similar to the approach of mapping a complex object model onto a relational database.

Decomposed storage model: The approach in the decomposed storage model is to pair each attribute value of an object with the surrogate of the object.

■ 7.5 TRANSACTIONS, CONCURRENCY, RECOVERY, AND VERSIONING

7.5.1 Transactions

A transaction is a program that is executed either entirely or not at all. Transactions must map databases from one consistent state to another. In order to maintain consistency, transactions must pass the ACID test: atomicity, consistency, isolation, and durability.

Atomicity

Since a transaction is either executed entirely or not at all, either the entire sequence of operations or no operations are applied to the database. This feature is called *atomicity*; transactions are *atomic*.

Consistency

A database state is said to be *consistent* if all its integrity constraints are satisfied. The execution of a transaction, in the absence of interference from other concurrent transactions, is assumed to take the database from one consistent state to another.

Isolation

Since transactions execute concurrently against the same database, they must be *isolated* from each other's operations. Otherwise the interleaved operation of concurrent transactions can give rise to anomalies. Thus, database management systems support isolation, which provides safeguards against interference between concurrent transactions.

Durability

Durability refers to the ability of the database system to recover from system and media failures. The updates of a committed transaction must be preserved and recorded on some durable medium. Enough redundancy must be maintained in order to reconstruct a consistent database.

Nested Transactions

Transactions in object-oriented database applications are typically longer than those in more conventional business applications. The long duration of transactions in advanced applications is a characteristic of next-generation database applications. Several strategies related to the long duration of transactions have been proposed in database research. Some of these strategies have influenced existing object-oriented database implementations.

Nested transactions are used to resolve some of the problems associated with long-duration transactions. A nested transaction model can contain subtransactions, also called child transactions. In a nested transaction all of the child transactions (subtransactions) must be committed in order for the top-level transaction to commit. Each subtransaction must be either completed or aborted. Also, in advanced applications tasks typically involve multiple users. Cooperative transactions are used to support such cooperative tasks.

7.5.2 Concurrency

Several concurrency control algorithms can be used to guarantee serializability of transactions and consistency of the database. The most notable of these is *locking*. In object-oriented databases locking can be associated with various granules that are manipulated by users, including classes, instances, and complex objects.

In object-oriented databases there are two aspects of locking that are relevant to the concurrent sharing of objects:

> **Class hierarchy locking:** The classes in object-oriented databases are organized into inheritance hierarchies such that each class in the hierarchy has an extension or existing instance. It is therefore important to provide granularity locking along these structures. For instance, locking a superclass would implicitly lock all of its subclasses in the same lock mode. The subclasses include the direct descendants of the superclass and its subclasses' descendants.
>
> **Complex object locking:** Object-oriented databases contain objects that can reference or embed other objects. Furthermore, some objects are "values," whereas others have identity. To optimize the concurrency in the presence of models involving complex objects several "composite object" or "dependent object" locking schemes for complex objects have been discussed.

7.5.3 Recovery

Reliability and the graceful recovery from failure are important features of a database management system. The *recovery manager* is the module that handles the techniques for recovering from these failures. The three failure types that must be taken care of by a recovery manager are *transaction failures, systems failures,* and *media failures.*

One of the most commonly used data structures for recovery management is the *log*. The log is used to record and store the *before* and *after* images of updated objects. The before image is the state of the object before the transaction update, and the after image is the state of the object after the transaction update.

Almost all object-oriented databases provide some support for recovery. Most OODBMSs use logging for recovering the database to a consistent state. Some use data replication or mirroring.

7.5.4 Versioning

Access to previous states or alternate states of objects is an inherent part of many applications. This is achieved by having multiple *versions* of the same object. Version management in an object-oriented database consists of tools and constructs to automate or simplify the construction and organization of versions, or configurations. Without these tools it would be up to the user to organize and maintain the versions.

We can think of a configuration as a collection of objects that is to be treated as a single unit for locking and versioning purposes. Individual objects within the configuration can undergo modifications, so each object can have a "history" of versions. Different objects within the configuration are updated at different times and not necessarily with the same frequency.

▪ 7.6 CLIENT/SERVER ARCHITECTURES

The past few years have witnessed the proliferation of LANs. Internetworked local area networks are fast replacing "archaic" mainframe systems. Similarly, smaller businesses are interconnecting their stand-alone PCs with LANs in order to share various resources. In these architectures and networked environments client/server computation is the norm.

Networks can contain different types of servers, including file servers, database servers, optical disk servers, fax servers, and so on. In the case of database servers there are different types of functionalities that could be provided by the database server, ranging from high-level database programming language processing (such as the processing of SQL or object-oriented extensions of SQL) to database servers that provide concurrent accesses to I/O blocks or objects. Various object-oriented databases fall in different categories.

7.6.1 File Servers

File servers are, as the name indicates, designed to provide file services to multiple users. By means of file servers users can concurrently share resources, the most prominent of which are the data and commonly used resources such as printers.

The file server performs the file- and block-, or page-level I/O. It typically contains and manages multiple disk *volumes* that are concurrently shared by the clients. It also provides primitives for controlling the concurrent access in order to maintain the consistency of the concurrently shared information.

7.6.2 Database Servers

Database servers maintain the information base of the network, provide concurrent access to the information base, and maintain the consistency and validity of the data. Transaction control of database accesses is another key feature of the database server, although file servers can also provide transaction and locking support at the file and I/O block level.

Unlike the file server approach, in which all of the DBMS executables are executed on the client side, with the database server approach the database management system's engine is executed on the server side. More specifically, the following can be performed by the database server node:

1. *Integrity*
2. *Security*
3. *Recovery*
4. *Concurrency control*
5. *Method/query execution and optimization*
6. *Clustering and indexing*
7. *Buffering*

7.6.3 Distributed Databases

With distributed databases the client sees one logical database that can consist of many physical databases distributed across server nodes of LANs. There are at least two approaches for developing a distributed database:

1. A *bottom-up* approach of integrating existing databases that run on heterogeneous systems into a virtual, distributed database for global applications, while at the same time preserving existing applications that run against individual single-site databases. Generalization provides a powerful object-oriented model for the bottom-up integration of existing databases

2. A *top-down* approach of decomposing a logically centralized database schema (against which all applications run) into fragments and allocating those fragments to sites of a distributed system. Specialization provides a powerful object-oriented model for the top-down distribution of a logically integrated database

In enterprise-wide computing distributed databases allow both the autonomous operation of individual sites *and* the ability for various nodes that are internet-worked through local or wide area networks to share and access remote databases. Some powerful distributed database management systems also allow transactions to span various databases, guaranteeing atomicity of transactions involving reads and even updates from various distributed databases.

■ 7.7 CONCLUSION

Object-oriented database started appearing in the marketplace in the mid-1980s. There are currently more than 10 object-oriented database companies selling more than 25 object-oriented database products. Furthermore, relational databases are incorporating object-oriented features into their next-generation products. Both trends ("novel" companies and relational DBMS vendors with object-oriented features) are expected to continue. Both provide powerful object-oriented modeling capabilities to application developers.

This book has identified six approaches to object-oriented databases. In fact, there can be more approaches as well as hybrids of those described in this book. The key point is that object-oriented databases constitute an important step in the evolution of database management systems. Furthermore, although object-oriented databases are typically characterized as those whose features satisfy the requirements of "advanced" database applications, *all* database applications can benefit from the powerful modeling concepts of object-oriented databases.

In the foreseeable future many users will benefit from products that provide an object-oriented model with persistence and other database capabilities. The emphasis will be on the benefits of object orientation and object-oriented databases to the end user. Thus, as mentioned earlier in this book, both application developers and end users stand to benefit from object-oriented databases. Nevertheless, there are still some challenges and open issues, especially in the area of agreed-upon standards and models.

In a world whose problems seem to be compounded by the hour some simplification of its "models" will perhaps be welcome. Databases and database servers will definitely be the backbone of computation as we move into the twenty-first century. Whether as extensions of relational databases or as "novel" OODBMS products and companies, a substantial percentage of DBMS technologies is expected to be object-oriented.

REFERENCES

Abiteboul, S., and Bidoit, N. (1984). "An Algebra for Non Normalized Relations," *ACM International Symposium on PODS,* March.

Abiteboul, S., Beeri, C., Gyssens, M., and Van Gucht, D. (1990). "An Introduction to the Completeness of Languages for Complex Objects and Nested Relations." In S. Abiteboul, P. C. Fischer, and H. J. Schek, (eds.) *Lecture Notes in Computer Science: Nested Relations and Complex Objects in Databases.* Berlin: Springer-Verlag.

Abiteboul, S., Fischer, P. C., and Schek, H. J. (eds.) (1990). *Lecture Notes in Computer Science: Nested Relations and Complex Objects in Databases.* Berlin: Springer-Verlag.

Abrial, J. R. (1974). "Data Semantics." In J. W. Klimbie and K. L. Koffeman (eds.), *Data Base Management.* New York: North-Holland.

Agha, G., and Hewitt, C. (1987). "Concurrent Programming Using Actors." In A. Yonezawa and M. Tokoro (eds.), *Object-Oriented Concurrent Programming.* Cambridge, MA: The MIT Press.

AIA/ATA (1990). "SFQL: Structured Full-Text Query Language," AIT/ATA Subcommittee 89-9C Specification, December 1989, revised February 1990.

Ait-Kaci, H., and Nasr, R. (1986). "Logic and Inheritance," *ACM Symposium on Principles of Programming Languages,* January.

Albano, A., Cardelli, L., and Orsini, R. (1985). "Galileo: A Strongly-Typed Interactive Conceptual Language," *ACM Transactions on Database Systems,* 10(2).

Anderson, L., Echland, E., and Maier, D. (1986). "Proteus: Objectifying the DBMS User Interface." In K. Dittrich and U. Dayal (eds.), *Proceedings of 1986 International Workshop on Object-Oriented Database Systems.* IEEE Computer Society.

Andrews, T., and Harris, C. (1987). "Combining Language and Database Advances in an Object-Oriented Environment," *Proceedings of OOPSLA-87.*

ANSI (1991). *ISA-ANSI Working Draft Database Language SQL2 and SQL3*, X3H2-90-309, August.

Astrahan, M. M., et al. (1976). "System R: A Relational Approach to Data Management," *ACM Transactions on Database Systems, Vol. 1.*

Atkinson, M., Bancilhon, F., DeWitt, D., Dittrich, K., Maier, D., and Zdonik, S. (1992). "The Object-Oriented Database System Manifesto." In Bancilhon et. al. (eds.), *Building an Object-Oriented Database System: The Story of O2.* Morgan Kaufmann.

Atkinson, M., Buneman, P., and Morrison, R. (eds.) (1985). *Persistence and Data Types Papers from the Appin Workshop.* Glasgow, Scotland: University of Glasgow.

Atkinson, M. P., Bailey, P. J., Cockshott, W. P., Chisholm, K. J., and Morrison, R. (1983). "An Approach to Persistent Programming." *Computer Journal*, 26, November.

Backus, J. (1978). "The History of FORTRAN I, II and III." *ACM Sigplan Notices*, 13(8).

Ballard, S. and Shirron, S. (1983). "The Design and Implementation of VAX/Smalltalk-80." In G. Krasner (ed.), *Smalltalk-80: Bits of History, Words of Advice.* Reading, MA: Addison-Wesley.

Bancilhon, F., Delobel, C., and Manellakis, P. (eds.) (1992). *Building an Object-Oriented Database System: The Story Of O2.* San Mateo, CA: Morgan Kaufmann.

Bancilhon, F., Thanos, C., and Tsichritzis, D. (eds.) (1990). *Lecture Notes in Computer Science: Advances in Database Technology—EDBT90.* International Conference on Extending Database Technology. Berlin: Springer-Verlag.

Bancilhon, F., Briggs, T., Khoshafian, S., and Valduriez, P. (1987). "FAD—a Simple and Powerful Database Language," *Proceedings of VLDB 1987.*

Bancilhon, F., et al. (1983). "VERSO: A Relation Back End Data Base Machine," *Proceedings of 2nd International Workshop on Database Machines.*

Bancilhon, F., and Khoshafian, S. (1989). "A Calculus for Complex Objects." *Journal of Computer and System Sciences*, 38(2). Originally appeared in *ACM International Symposium on PODS*, March 1986.

Banerjee, J., et al. (1987). "Data Model Issues for Object-Oriented Applications." *ACM Transactions on Office Information Systems*, 5(1).

Barker, R. (1989). *Case*Method™ Entity Relationship Modeling.* Workingham, England: Addison-Wesley.

Barth, P. S. (1986). "An Object-Oriented Approach to Graphical Interfaces." *ACM Transactions on Graphics*, 5(2), 142–172.

Beech, D. (1988). "A Foundation for Evolution from Relational to Object Databases." In J. W. Schmidt, S. Ceri, and M. Missikiff (eds.), *Lecture Notes in Computer Science: Advances in Database Technology—EDBT 1988*, Springer-Verlag.

Bernstein, P. A., and Goodman, N. (1980). "Timestamp-based Algorithms for Concurrency Control in Distributed Database Systems." *Proceedings of VLDB.*

Bernstein, P. A., Hadzilacos V., and Goodman N. (1987). *Concurrency Control and Recovery in Database Systems.* Reading, MA: Addison-Wesley.

Black, A., Hutchinson, N., Jul, E., Levy, H., and Carter, L. (1987). "Distribution and Abstract Types in Emerald." *IEEE Transactions on Software Engineering,* 13(1).

Blum, R. L. (1982). "Discovery and Representations of Casual Relationships from a Large Time-Oriented Clinical Database: The RX Project," *Lecture Notes in Medical Informatics,* Vol. 19. New York: Springer-Verlag.

Bobrow, D. G., et al. (1988). *Common LISP Object Systems Specification.* X3J13 Document 88-002R, June.

Bobrow, D. G., et al. (1986). "Common Loops Merging Lisp and Object-Oriented Programming," *Proceedings of OOPSIA-86.*

Booch, G. (1991). *Object-Oriented Design with Applications.* Redwood City, CA: Benjamin Cummings.

Booch, G. (1986). *Software Engineering with Ada* (2nd ed.). Menlo Park, CA: Benjamin Cummings.

Borning, A., and O'Shea, T. (1987). "DeltaTalk: An Empirically and Aesthetically Motivated Simplification of the Smalltalk-80 Language," *ECOOP '87,* June, Paris.

Brachman, R. J. (1985). "I Lied about the Trees—or, Defaults and Definitions in Knowledge Representation." *AI Magazine,* 6(3), 80–93.

Brown, A. W. (1991). *Object-Oriented Databases, Applications in Software Engineering.* New York: McGraw-Hill.

Bruce, K. B., and Wagner, P. (1986). "An Algebraic Model of Subtypes in Object-Oriented Languages." *ACM Sigplan Notices,* 21 (10).

Burstall, R. M., and Goguen, J. A. (1977). "Putting Theories Together to Make Specifications," *Proceedings of IJCAI-77.*

Buzzard, G. D., and Mudge, T. N. (1985). "Object-based Computing and the Ada Programming Language." *Computer,* March.

Cardelli L., (1984a). "Amber." AT&T Bell Labs Technical Memorandum 11271-840924-10TM.

Cardelli, L. (1984b). "A Semantics of Multiple Inheritance." In K. Gills, D. B. McQueen and G. Plotkin (eds.), *Lecture Notes in Computer Science* (173). New York: Springer-Verlag.

Cardelli, L., and Wegner, P. (1985). "On Understanding Types, Data Abstraction, and Polymorphism." *Computing Surveys,* 17(4).

Carey M. J., et al. (1990). "The EXODUS DBMS Project: An Overview. In S. T. Zdonik and D. Maier (eds.), *Readings in Object Oriented Databases.* San Mateo, CA: Morgan Kaufmann.

Carey, M., DeWitt, D., and Vanderberg, S. (1988). "A Data Model and Query Language for EXODUS," *Proceedings of the 1988 SIGMOD Conference.* Chicago, IL.

Cattell, R. G. G., (1991). *Object Data Management, Object-Oriented and Extended Relational Database Systems.* Reading, MA: Addison-Wesley.

Caudill, P. J., and Wirfs-Brock, A. (1986). "A Third Generation Smalltalk-80 implementation," *Proceedings of OOPSLA-86*, Portland, OR.

Ceri, S., Pernici, B., and Wiederhold G. (1987). "Distributed Database Design Methodologies." *IEEE Proceedings Special Issue on Distributed Database Systems*, 75(5).

Ceri, S. and Pelagatti, G. (1984). *Distributed Databases: Principles and Systems*. New York: McGraw-Hill.

Chamberlin, D. D., Astrahan, M. M., Eswaran, Griffiths, Lorie, Mehl, Reisner, and Wade. (1976). "SEQUEL 2: A Unified Approach to Data Definition, Manipulation, and Control." *IBM Journal of Research and Development*, 20, 560–575.

Chan, A., Khoshafian, S., Abnous, R., and Blumer, R. (1991). "Intelligent Object Oriented Features in Distributed Databases," *IEEE COMPCON Conference Proceedings*.

Chang, C. L., and Walker, A. (1986). "PROSQL: A Prolog Programming Interface with SQL/DS." In L. Kerschberg (ed.), *Proceedings of the First International Workshop on Expert Data Systems*. Menlo Park, CA: Benjamin Cummings.

Chen, P. P. (1976). "The Entity-Relationship Model—Toward a Unified View of Data." *ACM Transactions on Database Systems*, 1(1).

Cleaveland, C. (1986). *An Introduction to Data Types*. Reading, MA: Addison-Wesley.

Clifford, J., and Warren, D. S. (1983). "Formal Semantics for Time in Databases." *ACM Transactions on Database Systems*, 8(2).

Coad, P., and Yordon, E. (1990). *Object-Oriented Analysis*. Englewood Cliffs, NJ: Prentice-Hall.

Codd, E. F. (1988). "Fatal Flaws in SQL," *Datamation* 34 (16–17).

Codd, E. F. (1985). "Is Your DBMS Really Relational?" *Computer World*, October 14.

Codd, E. F. (1979). "Extending the Database Relational Model to Capture More Meaning." *ACM Transactions on Database Systems*, 4, 397–434.

Codd, E. F. (1970). "A Relational Model for Large Shared Data Banks." *Communications of the ACM*, 13, 377–387.

Cointe, P. (1987). "Metaclasses Are First Class: The ObjVLisp Model," *Proceedings of OOPSLA-87*. December.

Collard, P. (1989). "Object-Oriented Programming Techniques with Ada: An Example." *ACM Ada LETTERS*, (6), September/October, 119–126.

Conklin, J. (1987). "Hypertext: A Survey and Introduction." *IEEE Computer*, 20(9), 17–41.

Copeland, G. P., and Khoshafian, S. (1985). "A Decomposition Storage Model," *Proceedings of the ACM/SIGMOD International Conference on the Management of Data*.

Copeland, G. P., and Maier, D. (1984). "Making Smalltalk a Database System." *Proceedings of the SIGMOD Conference*. Boston, ACM.

Copeland, G., Franklin, M., and Weikum, G. (1990). "Uniform Object Management." In F. Banchihon, C. Thanos, and D. Tsichritzis, (eds.), *Advances in Database Technology—EDBT 1990*. Lecture Notes in Computer Science. Springer-Verlag.

Copeland, G. P., and Khoshafian, S. (1987). "Identity and Versions for Complex Objects," *Proceedings of Persistent Object Systems: Their Design, Implementation, and Use*. Research Report No. 44. University of St. Andrews, Scotland.

Cox, B. (1986). *Object-Oriented Programming: An Evolutionary Approach*. Reading, MA: Addison-Wesley.

Cox, B. (1984). "Message/Object Programming: An Evolutionary Change in Programming Technology. *IEEE Software*, January, 50–61.

Cox, B., and Hunt, B. (1986). "Objects, Icons, and Software ICs." *BYTE*, August.

Dahl, O.-J., and Nygaard, K. (1966). "Simula—An ALGOL-based Simulation Language." *Communications of the ACM*, 9, 671–678.

Dahl, O.-J., Myhrhaug, B., and Nygaard, K. (1970). *The SIMULA 67 Common Base Language*. Publication S22. Oslo, Norway: Norwegian Computing Centre.

Date, C. J., (1990). *An Introduction to Database Systems*, Volume I, Fifth Edition. Reading, MA: Addison-Wesley.

Dayal, U., Goodman, N., and Katz, R. (1982). "An Extended Relational Algebra with Control Over Duplicate Elimination," *Proceedings of PODS*.

Deppsich, U., Paul, H. B., Schek, H.-J. (1986). "A Storage System for Complex Objects." *Proceedings of 1986 International Workshop on Object-Oriented Database Systems*, September, Pacifica Grove, CA.

Deutsch, L. P., and Bobrow, D. G. (1976). "An Efficient Incremental Automatic Garbage Collector. *Communications of the ACM*, 19(9).

Deux, O., et al. (1990). "The story of O2." *IEEE Transactions on Knowledge and Data Engineering*, 2(1).

Dewhurst, S. C., and Start, K. T. (1989). *Programming in C++*. Englewood Cliffs, NJ: Prentice-Hall.

Dion, J. (1980). "The Cambridge File Server." *Operating Systems Review*, ACM SIGOPS, 14(4).

Dittrich, K. (1986). "Object-Oriented Database Systems: The Notion and the Issues." *Proceedings of the International Workshop on Object-Oriented Database Systems*, September, Pacific Grove, CA.

Dittrich, K., and Dayal, U. (eds.) (1986). *Proceedings of 1986 International Workshop on Object-Oriented Database Systems*. Pacific Grove, CA.

Dittrich, K., Dayal, U., and Buchmann, A. P. (eds.) (1991). *On Object-Oriented Database Systems*. Berlin: Springer-Verlag.

Elmagarmid, A. K. (ed.) (1992). *Database Transaction Models for Advanced Applications*. San Mateo, CA: Morgan Kaufmann.

Ehrig, H., Kreowski, H., and Padawiz, P. (1978). "Stepwise Specification and Implementation of Abstract Data Types." *Proceedings of the 5th ICALP*.

Eswaran, K. P., Gray, J. N., Lorie, R. A., and Traiger, I. L. (1976). "The Notions of Consistency and Predicate Locks in a Database System." *Communications of the ACM*, 19, 624–633.

Everest, G. C. (1986). *Database Management: Objectives, System Functions, and Administration.* New York: McGraw-Hill.

Fagin, R. (1980). "Horn Clauses as Relational Dependencies," *Proceedings of the ACM Conference on Foundations of Computer Science.* April, Los Angeles.

Fisher, A. S. (1988). *CASE Using Software Development Tools.* New York: Wiley.

Fishman, D., et al. (1989). "Overview of the Iris DBMS." Hewlett-Packard Technical Report HPL-SAL-89-15. Hewlett-Packard.

Fishman, D., et al. (1987). "Iris: An Object Oriented Database Management System." *ACM Transactions on Database Systems,* 5(1).

Garcia-Molina, H., and Salem, K. (1987). "SAGAS," *Proceedings of ACM SIGMOD.* San Francisco, CA.

Goguen, J. A., Thatcher, J. W., Wegner, E. G., and Wright, J. B. (1975). "Abstract Data Types as Initial Algebras and Correctness of Data Representation," *Proceedings of the Conference on Computer Graphics, Pattern Recognition and Data Structures.*

Goldberg, A. (ed.) (1988). *A History of Personal Workstations.* New York: ACM.

Goldberg, A., and Robson, D. (1983). *Smalltalk-80: The Language and its Implementation.* Reading, MA: Addison-Wesley.

Goldstein, I.P., and Bobrow, D.G. (1984). "A Layered Approach to Software Design." In D. Barstow, H. Shrobe, and E. Sandewall (eds.), *Interactive Programming Environments* (pp. 387-413). New York: McGraw-Hill.

Graham, I. (1991). *Object-Oriented Methods.* Wokingham, England: Addison-Wesley.

Gray, J. N. (1981). "The Transaction Concept: Virtues and Limitations." *Proceedings of the 7th International Conference on Very Large Data Bases,* September.

Gray, J. N. (1978). "Notes on Database Operating Systems." IBM Research Report RJ2188. IBM Research Center, San Jose, CA.

Guiting, R. H. (1988). "Geo-Relational Algebra: A Model and Query Language for Geometric Database Systems." Springer Verlag 303, Extending Database Technology. Venice: Springer-Verlag.

Gupta, R. and Horowitz, E. (eds). *Object-Oriented Databases with Applications to CASE, Networks, and VLSI CAD.* Prentice-Hall Series in Data and Knowledge Base Systems. Englewood Cliffs, NJ: Prentice-Hall.

Guthrey, S. (1989). "Are the Emperor's New Clothes Object Oriented?" *Dr. Dobb's Journal,* December.

Guttag, J. (1977). "Abstract Data Types and the Development of Data Structures." *Communications of the ACM,* 20.

Hall, P. A. V., Owlett, J., and Todd, S. J. P. (1976). "Relations and Entities." In G. M. Nijssen (ed.), *Modeling In Data Base Management Systems.* New York: North-Holland.

Hammer, M., and McLeod, D. (1981). "Database Description with SDM: A Semantic Database Model." *ACM Transactions on Database Systems,* 6(3).

Harper, R., MacQueen, D., and Milner, R. (1986). "Standard ML." ECS-LFCS-86-2. Department of Computer Science, University of Edinburgh.

Hayes-Roth, B. (1985). "A Blackboard Architecture for Control." *Artificial Intelligence,* 26.

Hayes-Roth, B. (1984). *BB1: An Architecture for Black Board Systems that Control, Explain, and Learn about Their Own Behavior.* Technical Report HPP-84-16. Stanford University.

Hayes-Roth, F., Waterman, D. A., and Lenat, D. B. (1983). *Building Expert Systems.* Reading, MA: Addison-Wesley.

Herot, C. F. (1980). "Spatial Management of Data." *ACM Transactions on Database Systems,* 5.

Hewitt, C. (1977). "Viewing Control Structures as Patterns of Passing Messages." *Artificial Intelligence,* 8(3).

Hewitt, C., Bishop, P., and Steiger, R. (1973). "A Universal, Modular Actor Formalism for Artificial Intelligence," *Proceedings of IJCAI,* August.

Howe, G. R., and Lindsay, J. (1981). "A Generalized Iterative Record Linkage Computer System for Use in Medical Follow-up Studies." *Computers and Biomedical Research,* 14.

Hughes, J. G. (1991). *Object-Oriented Databases.* New York: Prentice-Hall.

Hull, R. (1990). "Four Views of Complex Objects: A Sophisticate's Introduction." In S. Abiteboul, P. C. Fischer, and H. J. Schek (eds.), *Nested Relations and Complex Objects in Databases.* Lecture Notes in Computer Science. Berlin: Springer-Verlag.

Hull, R., and King, R. (1987). "Semantic Database Modeling: Survey, Application, and Research Issues." *ACM Computing Surveys,* 19(3).

Hull, R., and Yap, C. K. (1984). "The Format Model: A Theory of Database Organization." *Journal of the ACM,* 31(3).

Jacobs, B. E. (1982). "On Database Logic." *Journal of the ACM,* 29(2).

Jaeschke, G., and Schek, H. (1982). "Remarks on the Algebra of Non First Normal Form Relations," *Proceedings of the ACM International Symposium on PODS,* Los Angeles.

Jagannathan, D., Guck, R. L., Fritchman, B. L., Thompson, J. P., and Tolbert, D. M. (1988). "SIM: A Database System Based on the Semantic Data Model," *Proceedings of ACM SIGMOD.*

Jeffcoate, J., Hales, K., and Downes, V. (1989). *Object-Oriented Systems: The Commercial Benefits.* Ovum Report. London: Dudley.

Johnson, J., Roberts, T., Verpiank, W., Smith, D.C., Irby, C.H., Beard, M., and Mackey, K. (1989). "The Xerox Star: A Retrospective." *IEEE Computer,* September, 11–26.

Kaehler, T., and Krasner, G. (1983). "LOOM—Large Object-Oriented Memory for Smalltalk-80 systems," In G. Krasner (ed.), *Smalltalk-80: Bits of History, Words of Advice.* Reading, MA: Addison-Wesley.

Katz, R. H. (1987). *Information Management for Engineering Design.* Berlin: Springer-Verlag.

Katz, R. H., and Lehman, T. J. (1984). "Database Support for Versions and Alternatives for Large Design Files." *IEEE Transactions on Software Engineering*. SE-101, No. 2.

Kerschberg, L., and Pacheco, J. E. S. (1976). *A Functional Data Base Model*. Tech. Rep. Pontificia Univ. Catolica do Rio de Janerio, Rio de Janeiro, Brazil.

Ketabchi, M. A. (1985). *On the Management of Computer Aided Design Databases*. Ph.D. Dissertation, University of Minnesota.

Ketabchi, M. et al. (1989). "Object-Oriented Database Management Support for Software Maintenance and Reverse Engineering," *Digest of Papers COMPCON*.

Khoshafian, S. (1991a). "Intelligent SQL." *Computer Standards and Interfaces* 12(1–3). Presented at the X3/SPARC/DBSG OODB Task Group Workshop, Atlantic City, N.J., 1990.

Khoshafian, S. (1991b). "Modeling With Object-Oriented Databases." *AI EXPERT*, October.

Khoshafian, S. (1990). "Insight Into Object-Oriented Databases." *Information and Software Technology*, 32(4).

Khoshafian, S. (1989). "A Persistent Complex Object Database Language." *Data and Knowledge Engineering*, 3 (1988/89).

Khoshafian, S., and Thieme, L. (1991). "Declarative Reasoning Extensions to Commercial SQL Database Management Systems," *COMCON 91*. San Francisco.

Khoshafian, S., and Abnous, R. (1990). *Object Orientation: Concepts, Languages, Databases, User Interfaces*. New York: Wiley.

Khoshafian, S., and Valduriez P. (1990). "Persistence, Sharing, and Object Orientation: A Database Perspective." In F. Bancilhon and P. Buneman (eds.), *Advances in Database Programming Languages*. Reading, MA: Addison Wesley.

Khoshafian, S., and Valduriez, P. (1989) "A Parallel Container Model for Data Intensive Applications," *Proceedings of IWDM*. June, France.

Khoshafian, S., and Briggs, T. (1988). "Schema Design and Mapping Strategies for Persistent Object Models." *Information and Software Technology*, December.

Khoshafian, S., and Frank, D. (1988). "Implementation Techniques for Object Oriented Databases," *Proceedings of the Second International Workshop on Object-Oriented Database Systems*. September, Germany.

Khoshafian, S., and Valduriez, P. (1987). "Parallel Execution Strategies for Declustered Databases," *Proceedings of IWDM '87*.

Khoshafian, S., and Copeland, G. (1986). "Object Identity," *Proceedings of OOPSLA-86*. Portland, OR. Also appeared in S. Zdonik and D. Maier (eds.), *Readings in Object-Oriented Database Systems*. 1990, San Mateo, CA: Morgan Kaufmann.

Khoshafian, S., Chan, A., Wong, A., and Wong, H. K. T. (1992a). *A Guide to Developing Client/Server SQL Applications*. San Mateo, CA: Morgan Kaufmann.

Khoshafian S., Baker, B., Abnous, R., and Shepherd, K. (1992b). *Intelligent Offices*. New York: Wiley.

Khoshafian, S., Blumer, R., and Abnous, R. (1991). "Inheritance and Generalization in Intelligent SQL." *Computer Standards and Interfaces* 13(1–3).

Khoshafian, S., Franklin, M. J., and Carey, M. J. (1990a). "Storage Management for Persistent Complex Objects." *Information Systems*, 15(3).

Khoshafian, S., Parsaye, K., and Wong, H. (1990b). "Intelligent Database Engines." *Database Programming and Design*, July.

Khoshafian, S., Valduriez, P., and Copeland, G. (1988). "Parallel Processing for Complex Objects," *Proceedings of the Fourth International Conference on Data Engineering*, February.

Kim, W. (1991). *Introduction to Object-Oriented Databases*. Cambridge, MA: The MIT Press.

Kim, W., and Lochovsky F. H., (eds.) (1989). *Object-Oriented Concepts, Databases, and Applications*. Reading, MA: Addison-Wesley.

Kim, W., et al. (1987). "Composite Object Support in an Object-Oriented Database System," *Proceedings of OOPSLA-87*.

King, R., and McLeod, D. (1985). "Semantic Database Models." In S. B. Yao (ed.), *Database Design*. New York: Springer-Verlag.

King, R., and McLeod, D. (1984). "A Unified Model and Methodology for Conceptual Database Design." In M. L. Brodie, J. Mylopoulos, and J. W. Schmidt (eds.), *On Conceptual Modelling: Perspectives from Artificial Intelligence, Databases, and Programming Languages*. New York: Springer-Verlag.

Klausner, A., and Goodman, N. (1985). "Multi-relations—Semantics and Languages." *Proceedings of VLDB 1985*.

Korth, H. F., Kim, W., and Bancilhon, F. (1990). "On Long-Duration CAD Transactions." In S. T. Zdonik and D. Maier (eds.), *Readings in Object-Oriented Databases*. San Mateo, CA: Morgan Kaufmann.

Kowalski, R. (1979). *Logic for Problem Solving*. New York: North-Holland.

Krasner, G. (1983). *Smalltalk-80: Bits of History, Words of Advice*. Reading, MA: Addison-Wesley.

Kulkarni, K. G., and Atkinson, M. P. (1986). "EFDM: Extended Functional Data Model." *The Computer Journal*, 29(1).

Kung, H. T. and Robinson, J. (1981). "On Optimistic Methods for Concurrency Control." *ACM TODS*, 6(2).

Kuper, G. M., and Vardi, M. Y. (1985). "On The Expressive Power Of The Logic Data Model," *Proceedings of the ACM SIGMOD*, (pp. 180–187). Austin, TX.

Kuper, G. M., and Vardi, M. Y. (1984). "A New Approach to Database Logic." *Proceedings of the ACM International Symposium on PODS*. April, Waterloo, Canada.

Leach, P. J., Stumpf, B., Hamilton, J. A., and Levine, P. H. (1982). "UIDS as Internal Names in a Distributed File System," *Proceedings of the First Symposium on Principles of Distributed Computing*. Ottawa, Canada.

Lecluse, C., and Richard, P. (1989). "The O2 Database Programming Language," *Proceedings of VLDB 1989*.

Lecluse, C., Richard, P., and Velez, F. (1988). "O2 and Object-Oriented Data Model," *Proceedings of ACM SIGMOD*. Chicago, IL.

Ledbetter, L., and Cox, B. (1985). "Software-IC's." *BYTE*, June.

Lenzerini, M. (1987). "Covering and Disjointness Constraints in Type Networks." *Proceedings of the 3rd IEEE International Conference on Data Engineering*. Los Angeles.

Lieberman, H. (1986). "Using Prototypical Objects to Implement Shared Behavior in Object-Oriented Systems," *Proceedings of OOPSLA-86*. September, Portland, OR.

Lieberman, H. (1981). "A Preview of Act 1." MIT AI Lab Memo No. 625.

Lieberman, H., and Hewitt, C. (1983). "A Real-Time Garbage Collector Based on the Lifetimes of Objects." *Communications of the ACM*, 26(6).

Lippman, S.B. (1989). *C++ Primer*. Reading, MA: Addison-Wesley.

Liskov, B., and Guttag, J. (1986). "Abstraction and Specification in Program Development." Cambridge, MA: The MIT Press.

Liskov, B. H., and Zilles, S. M. (1975). "Specification Techniques for Data Abstractions." *IEEE Transactions on Software Engineering*, SE-1.

Liskov., B., Snyder, A., Atkinson, R., and Schaffert, C. (1977). "Abstraction Mechanisms in CLU." *Communications of the ACM*, 20(8).

Maier, D. (1983). *The Theory of Relational Databases*. Rockville, MD: Computer Science.

Maier, D., and Stein, J.C. (1990). "Development and Implementation of an Object-Oriented DBMS." In S. Zdonik and D. Maier (eds.), *Readings in Object-Oriented Database Systems*. San Mateo, CA: Morgan Kaufmann.

Maier, D., and Stein, J. (1986). "Indexing in an Object-Oriented DMBS," *Proceedings of 1986 International Workshop on Object-Oriented Database Systems*. Pacific Grove, CA.

Maier, D., Stein, J., Ottis, A., and Purdy, A. (1986). "Development of an Object-Oriented DBMS." *Proceedings of OOPSLA-86,* Portland, OR.

Manola, F., and Dayal, U. (1986). "PDM: An Object-Oriented Data Model," *Proceedings of 1986 International Workshop on Object-Oriented Database Systems*. Pacific Grove, CA.

McCarthy, J. (1960). "Recursive Functions of Symbolic Expressions and Their Computation by Machine, I." *Communications of the ACM*, 3.

McCarthy, J., et al. (1965). *LISP 1.5 Programmer's Manual*. Cambridge, MA: The MIT Press.

Melton, J., and Simon, A. R. (1993). *Understanding the New SQL: A Complete Guide*. San Mateo, CA: Morgan Kaufmann.

Meyer, B. (1988). *Object-Oriented Software Construction*. Englewood Cliffs, NJ: Prentice-Hall.

Minsky, M. (ed.) (1968). *Semantic Information Processing*. Cambridge MA: The MIT Press.

Moon, D. A. (1986). "Object-Oriented Programming with Flavors," *Proceedings of OOPSLA-86*. Portland, OR.

Moss, E. (1981). Nested Transactions: An Approach to Reliable Distributed Computing. Ph.D. Dissertation, Massachusetts Institute of Technology. Cambridge, MA.

Moss, E., and Wolf, A. (1988). "Toward Principles of Inheritance and Subtyping in Programming Languages." COINS Technical Report 88-95. University of Massachusetts.

Mullen, M. (1989). *Object-Oriented Program Design with Examples in C++*. Reading, MA: Addison-Wesley.

Mylopoulos, J., Bernstein, P. A., and Wong, H. K. T. (1980). "A Language Facility for Designing Database-Intensive Applications." *ACM Transactions on Database Systems, 5(2)*.

Naure, P. (ed.) (1960). "Report on the Algorithmic Language ALGOL 60." *Communications of the ACM*, May.

Nahouraii, E., and Petry F. (eds.) (1991). *Object-Oriented Databases*. Los Alamitos, CA: IEEE Computer Society.

Nodine, M. H., Ramoswamy, S., and Zdonik, S. (1992). "A Cooperative Transaction Model for Design Databases." In A. K. Elmagarmid (ed.), *Database Transaction Models for Advanced Applications*. San Mateo, CA: Morgan Kaufmann.

Object Design (1992a). *ObjectStore User Guide*. Burlington, MA: Object Design.

Object Design (1992b) *ObjectStore Reference Manual*. Burlington, MA: Object Design.

Object Design (1992c). *ObjectStore Administration and Development Tools*. Burlington, MA: Object Design.

Objectivity (1990a). *Objectivity/DB Documentation Set: Volume I*. Menlo Park, CA: Objectivity.

Objectivity (1990b). *Objectivity/DB Documentation Set: Volume II*. Menlo Park, CA: Objectivity.

O'Brien (1985). "Trellis Object-Oriented Environment Language Tutorial." DEC Eastern Research Lab Report. DEC-TR-373, November.

Ontologic (1991). *ONTOS Object Database Documentation Set*. Burlington, MA: Ontologic.

Ontologic (1989). *Client Library Reference*. Billerica, MA: Ontologic.

Ontologic (1988). *Vbase, Integrated Object Database Manual*. Billerica, MA: Ontologic.

Ozsoyoglu, M. Z., and Ozsoyoglu, G. (1983). "An Extension of Relational Algebra for Summary Tables," *Proceedings of the 2nd International Conference on Statistical Database Management*, (pp. 202–211). Los Angeles.

Papadimitriou, C. H. (1979). "The Serializability of Concurrent Database Updates." *Journal of the ACM*, 26, 631–653.

Parnas, D. L. (1972). "On the Criteria to be Used in Decomposing Systems into Modules." *Communications of the ACM*, 12, December.

Parsaye, K., Chignell M., Khoshafian, S., and Wong H. (1989). *Intelligent Databases*. New York: Wiley.

Pedersen, C. H. (1989). "Extending Ordinary Inheritance Schemes to Include Gerneralization," *Proceedings of OOPSLA, 1989*.

Peterson, G. (1987). *Object-Oriented Computing Volumes I and II*. Washington, DC: IEEE Society.

Pooley, R. J. (1989). *An Introduction to Programming in SIMULA*. Blackwell Scientific.

Popek, P., et al. (1981). "LOCUS: A Network Transparent, High-Reliability Distributed System," *Proceedings of the Eighth Symposium On Operating Systems Principles*, December.

Quillian, M. R. (1968). "Semantic Memory." In M. Minsky (ed.), *Semantic Information Processing*. Cambridge, MA: The MIT Press.

Randell, B., and Russell, L. (1964). *ALGOL 60 Implementation*. New York: Academic.

Reiner, D., Brodie, M., Brown, G., et al. (eds.) (1985). "The Database Design and Evaluation Workbench (DDEW) Project At CCA." *Database Engineering* 7(4).

Rentsch, T. (1982). "Object-Oriented Programming." *SIGPLAN Notices*, September.

Richardson, J. E., Carey, M. J., and Schuh, D. T. (1989). "The Design of the E Programming Language." Computer Sciences Tech. Report #824. University of Wisconsin, Madison, WI.

Risch, T., Reboh, R., Hart, P., and Duda, R. A. (1988). "Functional approach to Intergrating Database and Expert Systems." *Communications of the ACM*, 31, 1424–1437.

Roth, M., Korth, H., and Siberschatz, A. (1984). "Theory of Non-First-Normal-Form Relational Databases." TR-84-36. Department of Computer Science, University of Texas at Austin. Austin, TX.

Roussopoulos, N., Faloutsos, C., and Sellis, T. (1988). "An Efficient Pictorial Database System for PSQL." *IEEE Transactions on Software Engineering*, SE-14(5).

Salton, G. (1989). *Automatic Text Processing*. Reading, MA: Addison-Wesley.

Salton, G., and McGill, M. J. (1983). *An Introduction to Modern Information Retrieval*. New York: McGraw-Hill.

Saltzer, J. H. (1978). "Naming and Binding of Objects." In Goos and Harman (eds.) *Lecture Notes in Computer Science*. Berlin: Springer-Verlag.

Schaffert, C., Cooper, T., Bullis, B., Kilian, M., and Wilpolt, C. (1986). "An Introduction to Trellis/Owl." *OOPSLA-86 Proceedings*, (pp. 9–16).

Schek, H. J., and Scholl, M. H. (1986). "The Relational Model with Relational Valued Attributes." *Information Systems*, 11(2).

Schmucker, K. J. (1986). *Object-Oriented Programming for the Macintosh*, Hasbrouck Heights, NJ: Hayden.

Schriver, B., and Wegner, P. (eds.) (1987). *Research Directions in Object-Oriented Programming*. Cambridge, MA: The MIT Press.

Seidewitz, E. (1987). "Object-Oriented Programming in Smalltalk and Ada," *Proceedings of 1987 OOPSLA*. October.

Selinger, P. G., Astrahan, M. M., Chamberlin, D. D., Lorie, R. A., and Price, T. G. (1970). "Access Path Selection in Relational Database Management System," *Proceedings of ACM/SIGMOD*. June.

Servio, (1990a). *Programming In OPAL,* Version 2.0. Servio Logic Development Corporation.

Servio, (1990b). *OPAL Kernel Classes,* Version 2.0. Servio Logic Development Corporation.

Servio, (1990c). *Topaz OPAL Programming Environment,* Version 2.0. Servio Logic Development Corporation.

Servio, (1990d). *GemStone C Interface,* Version 2.0. Servio Logic Development Corporation.

Servio, (1990e). *GemStone C++ Interface,* Version 2.0. Servio Logic Development Corporation.

Shalaer, S., and Mellor, S. (1990). *Object-Oriented Systems Analysis.* Englewood Cliffs, NJ: Prentice-Hall.

Shaw, G., and Zdonik, S. (1989). "A Query Algebra for Object-Oriented Databases." TR-CS-89-19. Dept. of Computer Science, Brown University, Providence, RI. Also in *Proceedings of DBPL.* June, 1989, Salishan Lodge, OR.

Shibayama, E., and Yonezawa, A. (1987). "Distributed Computing in ABCL/1." In A. Yonezawa and M. Tokoro (eds.), *Object-Oriented Concurrent Programming.* Cambridge, MA: The MIT Press.

Shipman, J. (1981). "The Functional Data Model and the Data Language DAPLEX." *ACM Transactions on Database Systems,* 6(1).

Shoshani, A. (1982). "Statistical Databases: Characteristics, Problems and Some Solutions," *Proceedings of the 8th International Conference on VLB,* Mexico City.

Shriver, B., and Wegner, P. (1987). *Research Directions in Object-Oriented Programming,* Cambridge, MA: The MIT Press.

Skarra, A. H., Zdonik, S. B., and Reiss, S. P. (1991). "ObServer: An Object Server for an Object-Oriented Database System." In K. R. Dittrich, U. Dayal, and A. P. Buchmann (eds.), *On Object-Oriented Database Systems.* Springer-Verlag.

Smith, J. M., and Smith, D. C. P. (1977). "Database Abstractions: Aggregations and Generalizations." *ACM Transactions on Database Systems,* 2(2), 105–133.

Smith, K. E., and Zdonik, S. B. (1987). "Intermedia: A Case Study of the Differences Between Relational and Object-Oriented Database Systems," *Proceedings of OOPSLA '87,* Orlando, FL.

Snyder, A. (1986a). "Encapsulation and Inheritance in Object-Oriented Programming Languages." *Proceedings of OOPSLA '86,* Portland, OR.

Snyder, A. (1986b). "CommonObjects: An Overview." *ACM SIGPLAN Notices,* 21(10), 19–28.

Snyder, A. (1985). "Object-Oriented Programming for CommonLisp." Hewlett-Packard Technical Report ATC-85-1.

Stadish, T. A. (1980). *Data Structure Techniques.* Reading, MA: Addison-Wesley.

Stamos, J. W. (1982). "A Large Object-Oriented Virtual Memory: Grouping Strategies, Measurements, and Performance." Xerox Technical Report, SCG-82-2. Xerox, Palo Alto Research Center, Palo Alto, CA.

Stefik, M., and Bobrow, D. G. (1986). "Object-Oriented Programming: Themes and Variations." *AI Magazine*, 6(4).

Stein, L. A. (1987). "Delegation is Inheritance," *Proceedings of OOPSLA-87.*

Stein, L. A., Lieberman, H., and Ungar, D. (1989). "A Shared View of Sharing: The Treaty of Orlando." In W. Kim and F. H. Lochovsky (eds.), *Object-Oriented Concepts, Databases and Applications.* New York: ACM.

Stemple, D., Sheard, T., and Bunker, R. (1990). "Abstract Data Types in Databases: Specification, Manipulation, and Access." In S. T. Zdonik and D. Maier (eds.), *Readings in Object-Oriented Databases.* San Mateo, CA: Morgan Kaufmann.

Stonebraker, M., and Rowe, L. (1986). "The Design of POSTGRES." Proceedings of SIGMOD-86.

Stonebraker, M. (1986). "Triggers and Inference in Database Systems." In M. L. Brodie and J. Mylopoulos (eds.), *On Knowledge Base Management Systems.* New York: Springer-Verlag.

Stonebraker, M., Rowe, L., Lindsay, B., Gray, J., and Carey, M. (1990a). "Third-Generation Data Base System Manifesto." Memorandum No. UCB/ELR. M90/23, April. The Committee for Advanced DBMS Function, University of California, Berkeley, CA.

Stonebraker, M., Rowe, L., and Hiohama, M. (1990b). "The Implementation of POSTGRES." *IEEE Transactions on Knowledge and Data Engineering,* 2(1).

Stonebraker, M., Wong, E., Kreps, P., and Held, G. (1976). "The Design and Implementation of INGRES." *ACM Transactions on Database Systems,* 1.

Straube, D. D., and Ozsu, M. T. (1990). "Queries and Query Processing in Object-Oriented Database Systems." *ACM Transactions on Information Systems,* 8(4).

Stroustrup, B. (1989). *C++ Reference Manual.* Murray Hill, NJ: AT&T Bell Laboratories.

Stroustrup, B. (1986). *The C++ Programming Language.* Reading, MA: Addison-Wesley.

Symbolics, (1988). *Statice.* Cambridge, MA: Symbolics.

Tanaka, M., and Ichikawa, T. (1988). "A Visual User Interface for Map Information Retrieval Based on Semantic Significance." *IEEE Transactions on Software Engineering,* SE-14, 666–671.

Tanenbaum, A. (1976). "A Tutorial on ALGOL 68." *Computing Surveys,* 8(2).

Teorey, T. J. (1990). *Database Modeling and Design: The Entity-Relationship Approach.* San Mateo, CA: Morgan Kaufmann.

Thatte, S.M. (1991). "Persistent Memory: A Storage System for Object-Oriented Databases." In K. R. Dittrich, U. Dayal, and A. P. Buchmann (eds.), *On Object-Oriented Database Systems.* Springer-Verlag.

Thaweethai, L. (1990). *A Concurrency Control Subsystem for An Object Oriented Database System.* M.Sc. Thesis, San Francisco State University, San Francisco.

Thomas, S. (1982). *A Non-First-Normal-Form Relational Database Model.* Ph.D. Dissertation, Vanderbilt University.

Touretzky, D. S. (1984). *A Gentle Introduction to Symbolic Computation*. New York: Harper & Row.

Tsur, S., and Zaniolo, C. (1986). "LDL: A Logic Based Data Language." *Proceedings of VLDB '86.*

Ullman, J. D. (1988). *Principles of Database and Knowledge-Base Systems*. Rockville, MD: Computer Science.

Ullman, J. D. (1987). "Database Theory—Past and Future," *Proceedings of 6th PODS,* San Diego, CA.

Ullman, J. (1980). *Principles of Relational Database Systems*. New York: Computer Science.

Ungar, D. M. (1987). *The Design and Evaluation of High Performance Smalltalk Systems*. Cambridge, MA: The MIT Press.

Ungar, D. M., and Patterson, D. A. (1983). " Berkeley Smalltalk: Who Knows Where the Time Goes?" In G. Krasner (ed.), *Smalltalk-80: Bits of History, Words of Advice*. Reading, MA: Addison-Wesley.

Unisys (1987a). *Info Exec Semantic Information Management (SIM) Programming Guide*. Unisys Corporation.

Unisys (1987b). *Info Exec Semantic Information Management (SIM) Technical Overview*. Unisys Corporation.

Valduriez, P., Khoshafian, S., and Copeland, G. (1986). "Implementation Techniques of Complex Objects," *Proceedings of VLDB,* Kyoto, Japan.

VERSANT (1991a). *VERSANT Language Interfaces Manual, Version 1.6*. Menlo Park, CA: Versant Object Technology.

VERSANT (1991b). *VERSANT System Reference Manual, Version 1.6*. Menlo Park, CA: Versant Object Technology.

Wegner, P. (1987). "Dimensions of Object-Oriented Language Design," *Proceedings of OOPSLA-87,* Orlando, FL.

Weiskamp, K., and Flaming, B. (1990). *The Complete C++ Primer*. San Diego, CA: Academic.

Wirfs-Brock, R. B., Wilkerson, B., and Wiener, L. (1990). *Designing Object-Oriented Software*. Englewood Cliffs, NJ: Prentice Hall.

Wilson, P. R. (1988). "Opportunistic Garbage Collection." *SIGPLAN Notices,* 23(12).

Wrigley, E. A. (ed.) (1973). *Identifying People in the Past*. London: Edward Arnold.

Wulf, W. A., London, R. L., and Shaw, M. (1976). "An Introduction to the Construction and Verification of Alphard Programs." *IEEE Transactions on Software Engineering,* SE-2.

X/Open and OMG. (1992). The Common Object Request Broker: Architecture and Specification. OMG Document Number 91.12.1, Revision 1.1.

Yokote, Y., and Tokoro, M. (1987). "Concurrent Programming in Concurrent Smalltalk." In A. Yonezawa and M. Tokoro (eds.), *Object-Oriented Concurrent Programming*. Cambridge, MA: The MIT Press.

Yonezawa, A. et al. (1987). "Modeling and Programming in an Object-Oriented Concurrent Language ABCL/1." In A. Yonezawa and M. Tokoro (Eds.), *Object-Oriented Concurrent Programming*. Cambridge, MA: The MIT Press.

Zaniolo, C. (1983). "The Database Language GEM," *Proceedings of the ACM SIGMOD Conference*, San Jose, CA.

Zdonik, S. (1984). "Object Management System Concepts," *Proceedings of the Conference on Office Information Systems, ACM/SIGOA*, Toronto, Canada.

Zdonik, S., and Maier, D. (eds.) (1990). *Readings in Object-Oriented Database Systems*. San Mateo, CA: Morgan Kaufmann.

Zdonik, S., and Wegner (1986). "Language and Methodology for Object-Oriented Database Environments," *Proceedings of the Nineteenth Annual Hawaii International Conference on System Sciences*.

INDEX

ABCL/1, 12
Abort Transaction construct, 244, 246
Abstract classes, 154
Abstract data typing, 2, 5, 10, 65–66, 323
Abstract data types, 14, 15–16, 42–58, 203–204
  advantages of, 58
  classes, 51–52
  constraints, 56–58
  containers and class extensions, 52–54
  data types and, 44–51
  defined, 45
  in Intelligent SQL, 193–194
  overloading and dynamic binding, 54–56
Abstract entity types, 145–146
Accessor method, 168, 215, 329
ACID test for transactions, 243, 245–250, 254, 279, 313, 330

atomicity, 243, 244, 245–246, 251, 330
consistency, 243, 246–247, 330
durability, 243, 250, 330
isolation, 243, 247–250, 330
Act 1, 12
Activation, 12
Ada, 9, 10, 14, 26, 30, 223, 322
Advanced Program to Program Communications (APPC), 288
Aggregation node type, 146
Algol, 9, 10
Alphard, 10
Alternatives, 275
Alto, 11
Amber, 176
ANSI/ISO standard, 190
ANSI/PARC architecture standard, 111–112
Application developers, 8
Application programming interface (API), 303